Praise for Toby Thompson

Positively Main Street

"A first-rate novelistic account of Thompson's own psyche as he uncovers the Dylan few people know. A new look at young Dylan, done with kindness, enthusiasm, and superb language."
William Kennedy
Look magazine

"Essential reading. Thompson, unprecedentedly, managed to interview not only Echo Helstrom, almost certainly the 'Girl of the North Country,' but Dylan's mother and brother, his uncle, his friends."
Michael Gray
Bob Dylan Encyclopedia

"Toby Thompson was there first."
Greil Marcus

Saloon

"I had a wonderful time with this book, reading it in two sittings. I found the writing strong, clear, occasionally electric. In some odd way it seems a sociological masterpiece. For the first time the American drinker has his Michelin, and for myself it would be unthinkable to start another journey without it."
Jim Harrison

"Toby Thompson found the place to study the countr~ got it down."

"This book is a good place to get a ~ ~igan

The '60s Report

"A stunning book. Insightful, lovingly crafted."

Tim O'Brien

"Toby Thompson's writing represents the best of 'The New Journalism.'"

Terence Winch

Riding the Rough String

"Toby Thompson is a writer and journalist of the old school, a standup guy who knows music and literature and walks the walk and understands the human heart...."

James Lee Burke

"Toby Thompson knows Montana's bars, books, bridges, and backcountry. I'll read anything he writes."

Tim Cahill

"...Toby Thompson played it smart and went west. His sharp eye and interviewer's ear caught every nuance. *Riding the Rough String* sets it all down with verve and assurance."

William Hjortsberg

Metroliner

"...first-rate collection, impressively diverse and vastly enjoyable. Toby Thompson is blessed with that rare journalistic talent for painting epic pictures with small, unforgettable details."

Carl Hiaasen

"'Ratfishing in Manhattan' is fabulous ... a piece of poetry that stands as a conceit of New York itself. Thompson is ... an intrepid tripper in the Merry Prankster sense, and an Urban Thoreau."

Tom Wolfe

"...graceful and entertaining ... to say nothing of the energetic reporting."

Tom Brokaw

FIRED ON

Targeting Western American Art

Toby Thompson

Bangtail
Press

Montana
2020

FIRED ON

ISBN-13: 978-0-9623789-8-0

Manufactured in the United States of America

Cover Image: "Fired On" by Frederic Remington, Oil on Canvas, 1907

The author and publisher would like to thank the following publications in which versions of these pieces originally appeared: "David Lynch: Alien," *Esquire*; "Twilight of the Drive-In," *American Film* and *Big Sky Journal*; "Streamside Vows," *The New York Times*; "Desolation Jack: Kerouac on the Brink," *Kerouac*, by Jen McKee; "Paul Kane and the Constant Sky," "Eastman's Westward Ho," "Thomas Moran and The Art of Progress," "Charles Schreyvogel: Defending the Stockade," "Frederic Remington: Fired On," "Otto Becker: Custer's Last Fight," "Images of Crockett," "Wyeth of the West," "Jo Mora: The Uruguayan Cowboy," "Bob Dylan: Gateways," and "Breaking the Prairie: Grant Wood As Uneasy Tiller," *Western Art & Architecture*; "Alexander Gardner: The Indian Shooter," "Isabel. F. Randall: A Lady's Ranch Life," "Ghost Signs of Montana," "Gene Autry: Public Cowboy Number 1," "Ed Lahey: Art As the Principle," "House Justified: Sam Peckinpah in Montana," "Tom Murphy: Back Country Mystic," "Blue Montana Waltz," "Bowen's Lament," "The Real Deadwood," "Elmore Leonard: A Westerner Complete," and "Jim Harrison: Livingston Suite," *Big Sky Journal*: "Glenn's: The Elaine's of Montana," *Montana Quarterly*; "Mariano Botas: Panorama," *Panorama*, by Mariano Botas: "New Atlas Saloon (with 'Atlas Axis,' by Ken McCullough)," *Reflections West*; "Bob Dylan: North Country Other, Christmas in His Heart," *The Bridge*. The remaining ten chapters were written for this book.

Published in the United States by

Bangtail Press
P. O. Box 11262
Bozeman, MT 59719
www.bangtailpress.com

To the memory of Alan Gowans, Robert Ennis,
Charles Carpenter, Douglas Day, and
Peter Taylor. Teachers.

Art ... being the fiend that it is
wraps me in a bundle
and sends me off
to the house of myself.
                                    T.C. Cannon

TABLE OF CONTENTS

TWENTY-FIRST

AUTHOR'S NOTE

This is an eclectic book, comprised of brief lives and random asides, saloon tributes and artist profiles, book and music notices. The earliest was written in 1983, the latest in 2020. Most were published in Montana's *Western Art & Architecture* magazine or in *Big Sky Journal*. Others were published as far afield as Manhattan's *Esquire*, Washington, DC's *American Film*, or in *The New York Times*. These pieces' length was dictated by editors, not by the author. Word count is the bugbear of contemporary journalism. In print, rarely does an essay run longer than 3,000 words. Most in this collection run from 1,200 to 1,800 words. Concision focuses both the author's and the reader's attention. Arguably, that's so.

The criterion for inclusion of these pieces has varied: a western artist is described as any painter, sculptor, author, actor or musician who was born or has worked west of the Mississippi; that boundary has been stretched to include the art of such mavericks as Bob Dylan, Xenia Cage, Sam Peckinpah, Jack Kerouac (a decent painter) and David Lynch (an excellent one). Each was born or lived west of the Mississippi, but works or worked primarily in Los Angeles or New York.

What comprises western art is more difficult to say. Characteristics are an affinity in the work for nature, landscape,

1

the portrayal of exotic animals, military operations, a nonspecific spirituality, individualism, cowboy life, and the depiction (adoring or damning) of Native Americans—on the plains, in lodges, in peace or at war. Psychologically, a bruised individualism characterizes the western artist. But that might be said of any creator. Western artists were explorers—in George Catlin's, Paul Kane's and Seth Eastman's cases, quite literally. Others, to tweak Bob Dylan's phrase, are emotional expeditionaries. A desire to work alone and a certain compulsivity are traits. Again, these are universal peculiarities. Some western artists studied formally and romanticize the artists' life. As David Lynch has said, "In the Art Life you don't get married and you don't have families and you have studios and models and you drink a lot of coffee and you smoke cigarettes and you work mostly at night. Your place smells like oil paint and you think beneath the surface things and you live a fantastic life of ideas."

I have known several of the included artists personally. Lynch, Russell Chatham, Margot Kidder, Xenia Cage, Jim Harrison, Mariano Botas, Tom Russell, Amber Jean, Tom Murphy, Cathryn Reitler, A.D. Maddox, and Peter Bowen have been acquaintances or friends. I have immersed myself deeply in the work of others. To each I owe a debt. As Picasso said, "Art washes away from the soul the dust of everyday life." Mine has been wiped clean.

This book's title, *Fired On*, is taken from that of a 1907 oil by Frederic Remington. In it, a night patrol of cavalry is ambushed by an invisible foe, the troopers' horses turning and rearing at the shots. It is a dark work. I have stood before it, on the second floor of the Smithsonian American Art Museum, more times than I can count. Its meaning is opaque. It was painted decades after the frontier had closed. Perhaps the troopers' adversaries were Remington's critics, unconscious "others," or his advancing years. And perhaps his cavalry were artists, often if not always bushwhacked under fire.

It seems a fitting title.

NINETEENTH

PROLOGUE:
THE THORN IN CATLIN'S ROSE

In early 1872, a grizzly-bearded man, seventy-six years old and often dressed in buckskin trousers, western boots, a military-style vest, a leather coat and a cap made from the skin and head of an otter, haunted the corridors of the Smithsonian Institution. He was George Catlin, a guest of its secretary, Joseph Henry, and the legendary artist, author, explorer, ethnologist, showman, inventor, entrepreneur and painter of over 500 portraits of Native Americans—the collection of which he'd dubbed his Indian Gallery. Henry was showing Catlin's work, and from kindness had offered sustenance and lodging to the ailing painter, which Catlin quickly accepted. He proved a difficult guest. Though lingering near the Henry family's residence in the Smithsonian's Castle, and working in a rose-windowed, third-floor chamber in its main tower, he complained bitterly, disliking Washington and calling the Smithsonian "this horrible place."[1]

He had first attempted to sell his collection to the institution at its founding in 1846. His price then had been $65,000.

---

1   Smithsonian American Art Museum: Brian W. Dippie, Therese Thau Heyman, Christopher Mulvey, Joan Carpenter Troccoli, *George Catlin and His Indian Gallery* (Boston, W.W. Norton & Company, 2002), 266.

Congress withheld its approval to fund the purchase. Forced, in 1852, to relinquish ownership of most of his Gallery to assuage creditors (he'd spent time in an English debtor's prison), he now, in 1872, demanded Henry authorize purchase of the remaining paintings, provide a stove in his Smithsonian exhibition space, and a skylighted room in which to work. The north-facing, rose window in the studio he'd been given provided insufficient light, he argued. He was unhappy in the capital, brooding, ill, and foul-tempered, though at that moment his Indian collection was Congress's top candidate for purchase as a record of the lives of what many considered a vanishing race.

One reason Henry coddled his guest was that the Smithsonian had suffered a fire in 1865 which destroyed several galleries, as well as the painter Charles Bird King's Indian portraits and an exhibit of comparable paintings by John Mix Stanley. Both collections had been under consideration for purchase by the government. After the fire, as Therese Thau Heymann, writes in her essay, "George Catlin and the Smithsonian," Henry "immediately understood the change of status for Catlin: suddenly his existing work became the sole remaining resource of its kind."[2]

Catlin knew Henry was ambivalent about the quality of his paintings. The secretary considered them "as pictures in an anthropological point of view." Having "little value as works of art, they ought [to be regarded] as faithful representations of the features, manners and customs of the Indian Tribes."[3]

Frustrated by Henry's slowness in authorization of a purchase for the Smithsonian, Catlin stewed in his rose-windowed suite. He had professional enemies—the ethnologist, Henry Rowe Schoolcraft[4] had been an early one—who questioned

---

2   Ibid, 266.

3   Ibid, 264.

4   Author of the government-commissioned, six volume, *Historical and Statistical Information Respecting the History, Condition, and Prospects of the Indian Tribes of the United States*, published between 1851 and 1857.

the quality and authenticity of his work, particularly that depicting O-kee-pa, the Mandan initiation ceremony. But no critic questioned his authority.

Catlin's history with Native Americans was deep. Born in 1796 at Wilkes-Barre, Pennsylvania, his mother and grandmother had been captured by Natives in the Wyoming Valley Massacre of 1778, then released. Through his childhood, Catlin's mother had entertained him with tales of Indian life and of the frontier. His interest in nature seems to have derived from her; he wished to paint it. But his father was more practical in suggesting a vocation and urged him to study law, which Catlin did. Quitting that after several years, he tried a career in art, painting portrait miniatures in Philadelphia and New York. He attended the Pennsylvania Academy of the Fine Arts where he met the painters Charles Sully, John Neagle, Rembrandt Peale, and Charles Willson Peale. But their influence was marginal compared to that of a delegation of Natives he met in Philadelphia, an experience which changed his life. Their feathers, skins, jewelry, and war paint astonished him. "The history and customs of such people preserved by pictorial illustration and themes worthy of the lifetime of one man," he wrote, "and nothing short of my life shall prevent me from visiting their country and from being their historian."[5]

Catlin (with the exception of Titian Ramsay Peale) may have been the first serious artist to paint Indians west of the Mississippi; his earliest trip to the frontier, from St. Louis to Fort Crawford, with Captain William Clark, was in 1830. He made four subsequent trips, the longest being some 2,000 miles up the Missouri to its confluence with the Yellowstone at Fort Union. Not satisfied with exploring North America,

---

Schoolcraft had been government superintendent of Indian affairs in northern Michigan in 1822. He initially asked Catlin to illustrate his work, but Catlin refused. His second choice was Seth Eastman, who accepted. Schoolcraft died in 1864.

5   George Catlin, *My Life Among the Indians*: (Lulu.com,1909) Kindle edition.

he spent years painting Central and South American tribes, and toured Europe with his Indian Gallery in a western extravaganza that included costumed Natives, their weapons, artifacts, and two grizzly bears. *Catlin's Indian Gallery* as theater predated *Buffalo Bill's Wild West* by decades.

In Washington, he remained odd-man-out. He was known as an eccentric who had written a book titled *Shut Your Mouth—And Save Your Life*, which argued that open-mouthed breathing was the cause of civilization's ills[6], and a compulsive, possibly manic, sketcher, painter, and repainter of his works.[7] Since 1829, he had petitioned the government for its patronage, first to underwrite his Missouri River explorations, writing to the outgoing secretary of war that his ambition was "Historical painting" and that he wished "appointment to some little Agency among the Savage Indians, up the Missouri River ... where, among the naked Savage I could select and study from the finest models in Nature, unmasked, and moving in all their grace and beauty."[8]

Catlin, like Seth Eastman, Paul Kane, Karl Bodmer, Alfred Jacob Miller, George Caleb Bingham and numerous artists, saw Natives as members of a race whose customs and dress must be documented before they rubbed too fiercely against the advances of westward expansionism, and disappeared. The culture's decline, Catlin believed, might be seen most clearly at the margins between civilization and frontier, where conditions deteriorated to "the most deplorable vice and darkness," he wrote, a border across which the artist's journey takes him "through the most pitiable misery and wretchedness of savage degradation ... until he gradually rises again

---

6   He wrote, "There is no person in society but who will find ... improvement in health and enjoyment..." from keeping his or her mouth shut." George Catlin, *Keep Your Mouth Shut*, eighth edition (Trubner & Co., London, 1882), 86.

7   In Brussels during the 1860s, he copied his lost Indian Gallery, largely from memory. This would become what he called his Cartoon Collection.

8   Smithsonian, *George Catlin and His Indian Gallery*, 32.

into the proud and heroic elegance of savage society, in a state of pure and original nature, beyond the reach of civilized contamination."[9]

This was idolization of the indigene as noble savage—an 18th century notion that many intellectuals adhered to. Soon this idea would conflict with the legacy of Andrew Jackson's Indian Removal Act, and with the expansionist ethic of Manifest Destiny. Colonial America was moving westward and its artists would record that journey.

If the Indian, in Romantics' eyes, was the uncorrupted other, the western artist was inherently corrupt—not in morals, necessarily, but in character. He was broken in the places where all artists were broken. Loved too little or too much as a child, praised erratically, socially bereft as an adult, narcissistically grandiose, yet a loner by nature. N.C. Wyeth, Frederic Remington, Charlie Russell, Paul Kane, Thomas Moran, Albert Bierstadt, and in film, Sam Peckinpah, fit this paradigm. So did many others. Their love for the West was real, though their observations would change that which they loved. That change would be reflected in portrayals of settlers, animals, frontier folk, and always the Native American.

Many artists like Catlin bragged of their independence yet sought patronage. Many wished congressional funding or commissions; Seth Eastman, Emanuel Leutze, John Gast, and others were among those who sought public or private support. Patronage would bring fame and recognition, but nothing like that which Catlin desired. In Europe, understanding theatricality and the value of publicity, he became an impresario—the artist as showman. In performance he dressed as a Native, wore red face, war-whooped, chanted and danced. In 1843 he hired nine Ojibwe and, later, fourteen Iowa, to perform with him in London, painted their portraits and put all in his show. The number of portraits for the 1848 extravaganza was 555. He displayed his collection for Queen Victoria at Windsor Castle. He took the Gallery and his "Ioways"

---

9   Ibid, 28.

to Paris in 1845, where all met King Louis Philippe of France.

The French loved Indians, and still do (*Buffalo Bill's Wild West* show plays today at Disneyland Paris). But the English had been first to embrace the concept of a noble savage. Earliest to use the phrase was John Dryden, in his 17th century play, *The Conquest of Granada*. To 18th century Sentimentalists, the indigene became "nature's gentleman," an honorific that Charles Dickens lampooned in his 1853 essay, "The Noble Savage." There, Dickens skewered Catlin and his *Indian Gallery*, writing that the painter with "his Ojibbeway Indians" was "an energetic, earnest man, who had lived among more tribes of Indians than I need reckon up here ... With his party of Indians squatting and spitting on the table before him, or dancing their miserable jigs after their own dreary manner, he called, in all good faith, upon his civilized audience to take notice of their symmetry and grace, their perfect limbs, and the exquisite expression of their pantomime ... they were wretched creatures, very low in the scale and very poorly formed; and as men and women possessing any power of truthful dramatic expression by means of action, they were no better than the chorus at an Italian Opera in England." He added that, "I have not the least belief in the Noble Savage. I consider him a prodigious nuisance and an enormous superstition. ... I call him a savage, and I call a savage as something highly desirable to be civilized off the face of the earth."[10]

Catlin's affection for England waned proportionately to this insult.

With debtor's prison behind him, family members dead in Europe or deserted in America, schemes to create a "Museum of Mankind" on a ship that might be "a floating museum,"

---

10   The *Illustrated London News* disagreed with Dickens. It reported on the Iowa Indians: "The appearance of the party in their romantic costume, and armed with tomahawks and other warlike weapons, is very picturesque.... Their features, generally speaking, are regular, and do not betray a savage or ferocious disposition; they have fine aquiline noses, and the contour of their faces is anything but repulsive; their chests are broad and manly; their carriage erect, and in their general mien and behaviour more resembling civilized tribes than a rude and savage horde."

that would "visit the seaport towns of all countries"[11] abandoned, numerous books published and the inability to sell his Gallery omnipresent, Catlin sat in the Smithsonian nearly as imprisoned as he'd been in London. His Indian portraits, though awkwardly executed, were brilliant in their portrayal of character. Each was different from the next. That of Black Hawk differed from that of Big Sail. That of The Surrounder differed from that of Four Bears. Everyone praised these paintings' originality as well as Catlin's ambition, early on, to become an American, rather than a quasi-European artist. How could the superintendent demur? More irritating than Henry's hesitation to push harder in recommending the Gallery's purchase might have been Catlin's residency in the Castle. Designed by James Renwick in1846 and completed in 1855, it was a mishmash of 12th century English styles, from Norman to Gothic to Romanesque. It was fashioned of red sandstone and was a dark-blood mausoleum of medieval spires, buttresses, turrets, towers, a campanile, and two rose windows. Catlin there was a Prisoner of Zenda, awaiting patronage or pardon.

What were his transgressions? That he praised Natives, having spent years living with and painting them; that he revered their culture, having spent his life celebrating it; that his inclinations toward self-promotion and showmanship were ahead of his time—predating even those of Buffalo Bill Cody? That his love of Native and frontier costumery forecast that of a youth culture 100 years hence?

The National Mall that Catlin saw through his third-story, rose window was a vast expanse that in 1872 was little more than pasture, but by the late 1960s was a landscaped greensward that would be crowded with young people protesting the Vietnam war, arrayed in every sort of Native finery—from buckskins to war paint to flowered headdresses. The Bob Hope "Honor America Day" of July 4, 1970, pitted antiwar citizens against right-wingers on Hope's stage in an

---

11   Smithsonian, *George Catlin and His Indian Gallery*, 76,

unforgettable manner. As this author wrote in his 1979 book, *The '60s Report*, there had been police "lobbing tear gas into the crowd ... demonstrators heaving bottles, screaming ... so chaotic Bob Hope shot it four times before he got a take." This was "theater, televised theater, but it was likewise war, for real heads were broken ... Actors soaked in blood, fondling sheep guts, wandered through the crowd. Non-actors fell into the Reflecting Pool emitting scarlet flumes, or spat teeth at curbstones ... Running at or from police—waves of blue descending, clubs raised, holsters unsnapped—one had no doubt he was ... in the heart of spectacle."[12] The May Day demonstrations of 1971 likewise were celebrations of street theater. Freaks, hippies, Vietnam vets and Gold Star mothers, many costumed in Indian finery or frontier rusticity, railed against the establishment. They raged against government as Catlin did; but their protests were theatricality on a scale he only might have imagined.

One could argue he helped create it.[13] Though his Indian Gallery finally was donated to the Smithsonian in 1879 by Mrs. Joseph Harrison (whose husband obtained it in 1852 as collateral for Catlin's debts), its influence already was felt.[14] And would be for the next century. The Gallery's detail of Native dress, ornaments, and weaponry would be referred to by many directors of plays, films, and television shows, as they are among the finest ever rendered. They would be seen not just in museums, but in countless reproductions—Currier & Ives' prints among the earliest. The best portraits—such as that of the Blackfeet chief, Buffalo Bull's Back Fat, or that of the Otoe chief, The Surrounder—were not merely descriptive, but narrative, telling a story of their subjects' lives. In the

---

12   Toby Thomspon, *The '60s Report:* (New York: Rawson, Wade Publishers, Inc., 1979) 165.

13   Was he the first hippie?

14   Much of the Indian Gallery hangs in the Smithsonian American Art Museum. There are more of his paintings on permanent display there than those of any other artist. There are 629 in the Smithsonian's collection.

Natives' faces one saw pride, hardship, resignation, sadness, joy, pain—the gamut of earthly emotions.

And Catlin's paintings were distinctly American. He'd separated himself from the European tradition as surely as he'd separated himself from the civilized East. Which in his estimation was epitomized by Washington—the seat of a government that had failed to support him, and whose limited patronage via its national museum infuriated him.

The Indian Gallery screamed independence from tradition, but perhaps its loudest and angriest portrait was one titled *Wi-Jun-Jon, Pigeon's Egg Head (The Light) Going to and Returning from Washington*. Catlin painted it between 1837 and 1839, and it depicts the Assiniboine warrior in a before-and-after tableau. At its left, Pigeon's Egg Head arrives in the capital, dressed in feathered and buckskinned regalia. At its right, he returns to his tribe dressed in an army general's suit with whiskey bottles in his pockets, wearing a top hat and carrying an umbrella and a Chinese fan. These had been presented by the government during his eighteen-month-stay in the East. Pigeon's Egg Head's primary indignity, Catlin felt, was "a pair of water-proof boots, with high heels, which made him 'step like a yoked hog.'"[15]

As Joan Carpenter Troccoli later wrote, "Catlin's message—civilization destroys Indian culture—doesn't get much clearer than this."[16]

Catlin would not be so fortunate as Pigeon Egg's Head to return to the West. Stone deaf, crippled, and suffering from heart and kidney disease, he remained in Washington nearly until the end. Finally, Joseph Henry urged him to go to New Jersey, where the painter had family. With his abandoned daughters near, he died on December 23, 1872, in his room at the D'Arcy Hotel, Jersey City. As his biographer, Benita Eisler wrote, "According to Elizabeth, the eldest, her father spent his last days sitting upright, stoic as an Indian, his face averted

---

15   Smithsonian, *George Catlin and His Indian Gallery*, 202.
16   Ibid, 202.

from those offering comfort and sympathy. His only sign of suffering came in the anguished question: 'What will become of my gallery?'"[17]

Catlin's family buried him, not on Indian scaffolding in the Dakotas, but at Green-Wood Cemetery in Brooklyn, near his wife, Clara, and his son, George. His grave, once marked by a plain stone, is imprecisely located.[18] But his paintings grace the museums of the nation he longed to represent.[19]

As, he wrote in 1870, having copied his lost paintings for posterity, and returning to America, "Now I am George Catlin again."[20]

---

17   Benita Eisler, *The Red Man's Bones: George Catlin, Artist and Showman.* (New York: W. W. Norton & Company, 2013). Kindle Edition, 404.

18   As Eisler notes, "Catlin's grave was once marked: On July 26, 2012, a bronze statue by the American sculptor John Coleman was unveiled in Green-Wood Cemetery, near Catlin's simple gravestone of 1961. Coleman's sculpture is an 'interpretive' representation of 'The Greeter,' the name given to Black Moccasin. Known to both Lewis and Clark, as well as to George Catlin, this long-lived Hidatsa chief was chosen to symbolize the historical span of Indian-white friendship that coexisted with the legacy of suffering and violence." Ibid. 442.

19   In October, 2019, *Picturing the American Buffalo: George Catlin and Modern Native American Artists*, opened at the Smithsonian American Art Museum for a six-month-long run. Thirty-six of Catlin's paintings were displayed.

20   Marjorie Catlin Roehm, ed., *The Letters of George Catlin and His Family: A Chronicle of the American West* (Berkeley: University Of California Press, 1966), 371.

PAUL KANE AND THE
CONSTANT SKY

He was a rugged expeditionary, a man who in 1845 trekked alone through much of the Canadian outback, then from 1846 to 1848 traveled with Hudson's Bay traders through the Northwest Territories. Yet he was a perceptive artist who made hundreds of sketches on those trips, and once home transformed them into stunningly colorful oils. He'd been a boy in Toronto when that city was a rural outpost called York, yet he was a connoisseur of European art who turned his studies of Indian chiefs into portraits evoking Rembrandt's or Velasquéz's. He was a realist who transformed his observations of native life into Romantic narratives for both aesthetic and monetary gain. He was the Irish-born Paul Kane, recognized in his time as the patriarch of Canadian painting, yet remaining one of its more controversial practitioners.

The controversy is this: "If we're looking at a Paul Kane sketch," the Royal Ontario Museum's Kenneth Lister has said, "and we look at a Paul Kane oil painting, can we assume that what we're looking at [in the latter] is what he actually saw?"

It's the old debate between realistic and romanticized depictions, one which raged in the 19th century about the work of painters as diverse as George Catlin and Alfred Bierstadt. ROM owns the largest collection of Paul Kane's sketches and paintings, the befores-and-afters of which now can be compared. Lister, author of *Paul Kane, The Artist: Wilderness to Studio*, is expert in Kane's art—and an anthropologist, archaeologist, and explorer who has searched by kayak and car for the painter's 19th century sketching sites. "It is amazing to sit or stand on the rock that Kane sat on to make this particular sketch," he's said. His passion is characteristic of that felt by many Kane aficionados, for the artist lived a fearlessly intrepid life.

Born in Ireland in 1810, he immigrated as a boy to Toronto where his father, a former Royal Horse Artilleryman, sold liquor. Kane's talent surfaced first in portraiture, then in sign and furniture painting. Though entranced by Indian life around Little York, he soon left Canada, spending five years touring America's Midwest as an itinerant portrait painter, eventually voyaging down the Mississippi to New Orleans. In 1841 he booked passage to Europe and spent the next two years visiting museums in Genoa, Florence, Venice, and Rome, and copying the work of masters. He hiked south from Rome to Naples, then trekked north through the Great Saint Bernard Pass to Switzerland, traveling to Paris and eventually London. There he heard the American artist George Catlin lecture, a circumstance that would lend direction to his life.

Catlin, between 1830 and 1836, had made five trips to Indian country, and in 1842 was lecturing on Native American life and exhibiting his *Indian Gallery* paintings in London. Kane attended and may have met Catlin. He was enormously impressed by the painter's directive to "salvage" native culture from European civilization. And by the sheer adventurousness of his treks.

Canada's Northwest was largely unexplored; it was a deep wilderness. Kane would return to the States and spend the next two years acquiring funds for an expedition there. His goal was to field sketch Indians and their culture for ethnographic purposes, but also to make studies for future oil paintings. The "noble savage" concept was in vogue, its main idea being that primitives lived in prelapsarian bliss, and that their life-style should be emulated. This was a Romantic notion, and as the ROM's Arlene Gehmacher writes in her monograph, *Paul Kane, Life & Work*, "In embracing his own 'salvage' project, Kane was very much in line with the Victorian imperialist belief that North American Aboriginal peoples were all but certain to vanish, threatened by settler contact and encroachment."

In June of 1845, Kane set out, trekking and boating west above the Great Lakes, sketching Natives in Saugeen territory, before being convinced by a Hudson's Bay officer of the folly of continuing alone. In November Kane returned to Toronto, planning both to acquire permission from Hudson's Bay to explore its territory, and to have its assistance.

"This was before Canada became a nation," Lister says. "The Hudson's Bay Company essentially owned the northwest." As Gehmacher writes, "Beginning in late May 1846, [Kane] traveled by canoe, York boat, horse, and on foot across prairies, the subarctic, and mountains, with fur-trade brigades or with hired local guides." He sketched under the most hostile of circumstances. For more than two years he followed Hudson's Bay routes, "venturing as far north as Fort Assiniboine and as far south as Fort Vancouver in the Oregon Territory, exploring that vicinity and northward on Vancouver Island." He made life studies of Cree, Métis, Chinook, Ojibwa, Blackfoot and other First Peoples—sketches that upon returning to Toronto he spent seven years transforming to oils. "The sketches were his ticket into the studio," Lister says. "He knew exactly what he was doing."

Kane wrote in his memoir, *Wanderings of an Artist Among the Indians of North America*, that his goal had been "to sketch pictures of the principal chiefs, and their original costumes, to illustrate their manners and customs, and to represent the scenery of an almost unknown country." He would take liberties with the accuracy of these paintings, however. *Flat Head Woman and Child*, is case in point. The painting purportedly shows a Cowlitz woman with a slanted forehead (fashionable in this tribe), holding an infant which lies upon a flattening board. "It was with some difficulty," Kane wrote, "that I persuaded her to sit, as she seemed apprehensive that it would be injurious to her." In fact, the studio oil was rendered from two watercolor sketches, one depicting a Songhees woman, and the other a Cowlitz baby. This conflation infuriates ethnographers, and appears to negate Kane's own pledges to accuracy. A second oil depicts Mount St. Helens erupting on a night during Kane's visit. "I had a fine view of Mount St. Helens throwing up a long column of dark smoke," Kane wrote. In fact the volcano had erupted several years previously. Other oils, *Assiniboine Hunting Buffalo* and *The Man That Always Rides*, show Indians mounted on improbable white Arabians—a trope favored by European painters, from Eugene Delacroix to Théodore Gêricault.

Kane was European in style and temperament, a trait abhorred by some academics. "Clearly Paul Kane's work cannot be understood on a formal or biographical level without completely obscuring its part in an imperialist and racist discourse," Heather Dawkins has written. Lister counters in an email, "[Dawkins] is reading [*Wanderings*] in a different century and is unaware, or ignored, his field notes that show no comments that could be considered racist. Any racist comments surely came from the narrative formula of the time (through a ghost writer), not his personal perspective." Gehmacher takes further issue: "Kane would not have seen his use of aesthetic conventions [in his paintings] as contradicting his pursuit of accuracy. For Kane, truth was not necessarily objective verisimilitude, but the transcendence of the particular in order to evoke a more profound essence of his subject."

In other words, he was working as an artist.

The studio oils reflect this commitment. He'd assess what a sketch depicted, then trust his subconscious to reshape it. As Gehmacher notes, "Many of the oils embody conventions of Romantic painting: the tableau-like, staged compositions; the dramatic, moody skies; the diffuse, murky tonalities; the spectacular light effects ... the sublime or picturesque views; and the idealization of the individuals who were his subjects."

Such idealization is most apparent in his portraits of Native Americans. The "noble savage" cliché was that their closeness to nature provided a more perfect lifestyle. But Kane, in his memoir, is unsparing in his criticism of what he describes as Indians' occasional brutality and skimpy hygiene. None of this appears in his portraits; violence is portrayed as heroic, and uncleanliness as oneness with nature. Kane's portrait of the half-Cree, half-British woman, *Cunnawa-bum*, shows a Métis girl of striking beauty holding a swan's-wing fan in what Kane described as "a most coquettish manner." Cunnawa-bum's European features permit Kane to idealize them for his Canadian viewers, and as Gehmacher writes, she "becomes a sort of cover girl for Kane's life project." In his portrait of Cree chief, Kee-akee-ka-saa-ka-wow, *The Man That Gives the War Whoop*, the half-nude subject in Kane's watercolor sketch bristles with gravitas, while in the later oil Kane Anglicizes his physiognomy and warms him in colorful buckskins. Even Kane's photographic portrait of himself, hair tousled and chest clad in a fringed and beaded shirt, suggests the European gone native.

Idealization was marketable, and picturesque renditions of First Peoples and their landscapes sold. *The Constant Sky*, a portrait of mother and child in an Arcadian setting, suggests to the well-heeled viewer that primitive people and unspoiled nature go hand-in-hand. And his riverscape, *The Cackabacka Falls*, which Kane may have sketched with a camera lucida, evokes, for the knowledgeable, the Hudson River school's fealty to the Sublime.

In 1851, Kane's patron, George W. Allan, paid him $20,000 for 100 paintings that took him five years, in his Toronto studio, to complete. These oils would constitute the bulk of Kane's output. Even then he was a celebrated painter. But it is his role as an ethnographer which distinguishes him. As

Gehmacher writes, "It is the subject matter of his work that has guaranteed his place in Canada's art history."

The adventurer spent the remainder of his life quietly in Toronto, but what he saw and experienced during his years of exploration may have haunted him. He's described by Allan's daughter, Maude Cassels, as having been "melancholy," and "disgruntled and despondent." Though wealthy, his eyesight was failing, he'd taken a bad fall, and 90 percent of his work was in a private collection, unavailable for public view. On February 20, 1871 he died of "a liver complaint," a euphemism for undiagnosed maladies—in his case, possibly syphilis contracted among the voyageurs, or alcoholism.

His stature as the father of Canadian art is not disputed. "As a studio painter Kane was an artist first and an ethnographer second," Lister writes. "He made grand on canvas what he recorded accurately in his field sketches." And, "No other artist in Canada's history has provided us with both the wilderness notes and the studio record to the degree that Kane has. No other artist has granted us a detailed ethnographic and environmental record of a moment in Canada's past, and then using that record, developed a series of paintings that invites us to understand the nature of the artist's response to the philosophical character of the country." The resurrection of his reputation began in 1925, with the republication of his 1859 memoir. J. Russell Harper's book, *Paul Kane's Frontier*, was published in 1971, the centenary of Kane's death, followed by several shows of his work. In 2002, his 1845 painting, *Scene in the Northwest: Portrait of John Henry Lefroy*, sold at Sotheby's Toronto for $5,062,500, and is timeless. It depicts a beautifully dressed gentleman in the snowy outback, flanked by sled dogs, an aide, and a native woman. Though in their company, Lefroy—like Kane in the wilderness—stands alone.

—*Western Art & Architecture*, 2017

EASTMAN'S WESTWARD HO

He was a man of contradictions: a career soldier and an artist, an occupier of Indians' land, a conqueror and a celebrant of their lives. He was a military cartographer who painted some of the most delicate watercolors of the early 19th century. He was a soldier at a fort deep in Sioux territory, yet an affectionate chronicler of his enemy's traditions. He was a New England aristocrat and West Point graduate who admired the culture of Native Americans so much that, as a young lieutenant he wed a Sioux woman and had a daughter with her. He was a northerner who cherished people of color, yet took for his second wife a southerner who wrote *Aunt Phillis's Cabin*, the most widely read, pro-slavery creed of the pre-Civil War era. He was Bvt. Brig. Gen. Seth Eastman (1808-1875), an artist praised during his life, but whose reputation would be eclipsed by that of George Catlin, Karl Bodmer, Edward Curtis, and others.

"His are not the sort of grand paintings you would pull up in an American art survey course," says Felicia Wivchar, curatorial assistant for the House Collection of Fine Art and Artifacts at the U.S. Capitol. "But they're done with a certain degree of skill."

Wivchar—a slight brunette who, in her thirties, is arguably

the preeminent Eastman scholar—has led me from the ground floor of the House, beneath the Capitol's Rotunda, where tourists have filed past in ranks, through a tunnel beneath Independence Avenue to Congress's Longworth Building and a hearing room once reserved for the House Committee on Indian Affairs.

"In 1867," she says, "Eastman was commissioned to make nine paintings for the committee's chamber, which was where people were sitting and deciding on policy toward Native Americans." The paintings would be "a visual representation of these cultures," she adds. "The impetus behind wanting to document them was the belief that these cultures would be fading into obscurity."

Eastman was expert on Native American ways, having served in 1829 at Fort Crawford, near Prairie du Chien, Wisconsin, then from 1830-32 and again from 1841-48 at Fort Snelling, on the Mississippi River near present-day Minneapolis. Fort Snelling was much the frontier, and it was the army's northwestern-most post, and surrounded by Indian encampments. The Dakota Sioux were friendly; the flow of pioneer settlement was but a dribble. Eastman fathered a daughter by his Indian consort, Stands Like a Spirit, during his first tour, and began sketching in watercolor first landscapes, then every facet of Dakota and Chippewa life.

By 1841, when Eastman returned to Fort Snelling, he was married to the Virginia-born Mary Henderson Eastman, who there would research and write her book, *Dahcotah or, Life and Legends of the Sioux* (with twenty-one illustrations by Capt. Eastman). The upper Mississippi had become popular with tourists; Minnesota would acquire territorial status in 1849 and pioneer settlement already had increased. By 1846, while commandant of the post, Eastman had completed some 400 drawings and paintings. As visiting artist Charles Lanham wrote, his portfolio was "the most valuable in the country, not even excepting that of George Catlin." He dubbed Eastman a "soldier-artist of the frontier," one who had committed to "the study of the Indian character, and the portraying upon canvas of their manners and customs."

"He did not fall into the trap of romanticizing the Indian," author W. Duncan MacMillan has written. He "set out to preserve a visual record of Indian life, which was then undergoing rapid change."

An element of change was the growing resentment of Indians toward settlers throughout the Midwest, and especially near Fort Snelling. Andrew Jackson's Indian Removal Act had been implemented, and unfair or broken treaties were common. In 1861 the War of the Outbreak occurred in Minnesota, during which settlements were attacked and five whites killed by Santee Sioux. Three-hundred-and-three Indians were convicted and thirty-nine hung in the largest mass execution in U.S. history. Soon after, the Dakota were relocated and plains warfare began.

It was during this period that Eastman painted the nine House canvasses—his record of a more peaceful era.

A near Edenic passivity is evident in these oils. Their titles well describe their subjects: *Rice Gathers, Feeding the Dead, The Indian Council, Indian Woman Dressing a Deer Skin, Buffalo Chase, Indian Mode of Traveling, Spearing Fish in Winter, Dog Dance of the Dakotas* and *Death Whoop*. With the exception the latter, which portrays a scalping, they are what in Flemish painting might be called domestics. As Sarah E. Boehme, of the Buffalo Bill Historical Center, noted in *Seth Eastman: A Portfolio of North American Indians*, they "form a cycle" and are "depictions of the manners and customs of the Dakota as Eastman knew them from the 1840s."

And they are unique to the U.S. Capitol. As Wivchar has written in a *Federal History* essay, "To a modern viewer, Eastman's sympathetic and naturalistic approach appears to contrast fundamentally with that of the other Capitol artworks that extolled white supremacy and Christianization of American Indians."

Oddly, from a soldier's hand, the paintings eschew

warfare as subject for ritual and work. *Rice Gathers*, for instance, shows Chippewa women in a marsh, batting rice grains into a canoe—the figures classically grouped in an amber light. *Indian Mode of Traveling* shows a family on foot and on horseback, dragging a travois. *Spearing Fish in Winter* depicts a group of Dakotas fishing through ice in a composition that mimics Dutch sketches of communal skating. *Dog Dance of the Dakotas* shows braves stepping canine-like around a pole from which hang strips of dog liver they're devouring. The Indians labor in buckskins or simple coats. Little beadwork is displayed; there are few feathers and no war paint. With the exception of *Death Whoop*, calm is pervasive.

That painting first appeared to illustrate Mary Eastman's *The American Aboriginal Portfolio* (1853), then in Henry Rowe Schoolcraft's six-volume *Historical and Statistical Information Respecting the History, Conditions and Prospects of the Indian Tribes of the United States (1857)*, for which Capt. Eastman provided 275 drawings and watercolors. It shows an Indian scalping what appears to be a white settler, the brave raising his trophy in a scene which Mary Eastman described thus: "[The Indian's] blood-stained knife he grasps in one hand while high in the other he holds the crimson and still warm scalp ... Right joyfully falls upon his ear the return of his death-whoop; it is the triumph for his victory, and the death-song for his foe."

Responding to Native American concerns, the 1867 version of *Death Whoop* was removed from the committee room first in 1987, returned in 1995, then removed again in 2007.

Here in that room I ask Wivchar which of eight surviving Eastmans she prefers. She steps toward *Feeding the Dead*. "I really like this Indian burial. It's a lovely landscape, the subject matter is a balance of quiet empathy, as well as a clear illustration of a cultural custom. It captures what seems to have been the point of this group of paintings."

The canvas shows two Indians before a coffined figure lying on a raised platform. "It's nicely balanced," Wivchar says, "between showing the domestic or cultural activity and giving you a view of what this upper Mississippi environment looked like. It shows the person putting food up on top of the burial scaffold ... the soul took a certain number of days hanging around with the body after death. So you had to bring food to the grave every day. The painting's nice and quiet. I think it probably gives a better idea of what Native American life might have been like than a buffalo hunt, or a ceremonial dance."

One is struck by the affection for Indian culture in these paintings, if not affection for the Indians themselves. Eastman was soldierly reticent in his correspondence and remarks; one wonders if the subjects in his art weren't the objects of his purest love. "I was looking at an obituary from his hometown newspaper in Maine," Wivchar recalls, "and it was saying that as a youth 'he was remarkable for nothing more than his diffidence and adherence to rules.' He had a military personality, it seemed. When you read his letters he's always straightforward, not expressing any feelings."

After completing the Committee on Indian Affairs assignment, Eastman took one final commission: to paint, for the House Committee on Military Affairs, images of seventeen forts that had held prominence in settling the West or in winning the Civil War. "In those paintings," Wivchar says "the underlying message was supposed to be about union. The Civil War is over and here is the grand reach of the United States military. It goes from New Mexico to Maine. And from Fort Jefferson, off the Keys, to northern Minnesota."

We have viewed these oils, which hang in dark corridors beneath the Capitol Rotunda. Eastman's forts are set in tranquil land or waterscapes, rendered with Hudson Valley School detail and a Rembrandt-ish light. A riverscape set on the barricades of West Point, with cadets at ease, and one courting a sweetheart, is particularly lovely. Eastman considered this his masterpiece. Despite the academy's rigors, he'd been content there—first as a student, and later as an instructor of topographical drawing. In a separate hallway we've viewed Eastman's portrait of Fort Snelling, the scene of his finest watercolors and, living near the Sioux, arguably his greatest happiness. The fort hangs above the Mississippi, with its bankside tipis and prairie, like a wilderness Parthenon.

On August 31, 1875, in Washington, Eastman—long in failing health, and a painter whom art critic Patricia Condon Johnson, over a century later, would call, "Arguably the foremost pictorial historian of the American Indian" —collapsed at his easel and died.

—Western Art & Architecture, 2016

THOMAS MORAN AND THE ART OF PROGRESS

When I tire of Washington's political machinations, I walk eight blocks from Capitol Hill to the Smithsonian American Art Museum—a Greek Revival temple high above the Mall—where hang two portraits of *The Grand Canyon of the Yellowstone*, each so vast as to transport one instantly to Wyoming. They are by Thomas Moran, an artist whose talent, more than any other's, was responsible for Congress declaring Yellowstone our first National Park in 1872. The more impressive canvas, 84 inches x 144 1/4 inches, was shown that year and sold to Congress for $10,000, then a gargantuan sum. A second larger view, painted from 1893 to 1901, flanks it, as does Moran's 84 3/8 inches x 144 3/4 inch, *The Chasm of the Colorado*, painted from 1873 to 1874. These are the only paintings in the small, Moran gallery, and to stand encircled by them is to be flooded by the water and space they depict.

I am a Washingtonian, a journalist who has covered this city, but I am also a wanderer who, since 1959, has summered and often wintered in Montana, not far from Yellowstone Park. On a recent Sunday, pining for the West, I entered American Art and rode to its second-floor galleries. To my left was George Catlin's Indian Gallery, ahead were Alfred Wertheimer's photographs of the young Elvis, but to my right was an explosion of light I knew to be the vibrancy of Moran's unique canvasses. Confronting their colors—rust red, yellow, rose pink, mauve—was like emerging from a darkened theater to the high desert at noon. A docent stood beside the space's circular stool, covered by a worn bison skin, or robe. I squinted against the paintings' brightness and watched as two children spotted the robe, then headed for it.

The docent was patient as they rubbed and tugged its matted hair. She explained that the bison had been essential to Plains Indians' survival, and that they had wasted not a part of it. She took from her cart a small hide parcel she called a Bison Box. "This was the Indians' shopping mall," she said. From it she withdrew horns, sinew, teeth, soap made from bison fat and even the bison's bladder, used as a canteen. The children cringed, but the docent explained that the bison had provided everything the Indians needed.

Except landscape, I thought. Those paintings before me, passionately orchestrated renderings of waterfalls, cliffs and gorges, were not exaggerated but real. And quite necessary. The effect of Romantic Sublimity (Wagnerian rapture) they were thought to instill was for me, perhaps Moran, and certainly Native Americans, not an abstract theory but an accurate depiction of one's emotions in the wilderness. One *became* enraptured. I stepped forward and was smitten by a 3-D vision of canyonland, a painterly light show evoking wilderness's splendidly erotic ambiguities: "a sort of delightful horror," as Immanuel Kant categorized the Sublime, "a sort of tranquility tinged with terror."

On another day, in a journalistic funk, I'd left the White House and its daily press briefing, and walked two blocks to the Corcoran Gallery. There, in a far alcove of its American Art wing, hung Alfred Bierstadt's epic *The Last of the Buffalo*, a 74 1/4 inches x 119 1/4 inches painting completed in 1888 that dwarfs even Frederick Church's 42 ½ x 90 ½ inch

Niagara and the canvasses that surrounded it.[21] Like Moran's 1872 *Yellowstone*, Bierstadt's is a painting that, in its time, was considered political. Where *Yellowstone* was seen as a broadside for westward expansionism, and a postcard both preserving wilderness and luring settlers to adjoining regions, *Last Buffalo* was viewed as a plea for conservation and a lament for the frontier's salad days. In its foreground it depicts a Native hunter as a picador engaged in a Wild West showdown with a furious bison. Before them are skulls and carcasses spread against the plains fronting the Wind River peaks. For me it's the landscape, a Turneresque depiction of ocher grassland and snowtipped mountains, that holds the power.

Minutes before I'd been listening to commentary on trade imbalances, but now I was immersed in the "picture show" unreality of a carnival-like tour de force that for me was exquisitely real. Like Moran's *Grand Canyon*, It was meant to provoke sentimentality, yearning. (Cynically speaking, landscape was "the dreamwork of imperialism," in W.J.T. Mitchell's phrase.) Though both artists had toured the West, Moran painted *Grand Canyon* from sketches in Newark, New Jersey, and Bierstadt his *Last Buffalo* in New York City. I stood here in Washington and felt their longing. Or as Bill Clinton might have said, their "pain."

Early in Clinton's administration, when the president was still jogging, I spent an afternoon at the National Gallery then drove my little sports car at a clip, past the rear gate of the White House. Black SUVs appeared, a runner darted out, and I hit the brakes, skidding. Before me was Clinton, his hands raised protectively, his great frame draped in sweats and his face ashen. I waved. He waved back. I was enveloped by Secret Service, and as they sent the president along I couldn't help picturing the Corcoran's *Last Buffalo* and wondering if Bill weren't hurrying to see it.

---

21   Both *The Last of the Buffalo* and *Niagara* hang today in The National Gallery, Washington, DC.

As a boy it was my luck to have a grandmother and great aunt who made certain I visited the icons of our nation's capital. These included the Washington Monument, the Lincoln Memorial, the National Archives' Declaration of Independence, the Library of Congress, the Capitol with Congress in session, and the Smithsonian. I don't recall whether I saw Moran's *Grand Canyon*, but in art books I studied Thomas Cole's 1836 *The Course of Empire* and Emanuel Gottlieb Leutze's 1862 *Westward the Course of Empire Takes Its Way*: the first cautionary, the second championing empire's limitless possibilities. That the latter would be hung in American Art, once the Patent Office dotted with myriad inventions that sought to ease America's struggle to fulfill its Manifest Destiny, was not lost on me. I might have seen John Gast's *American Progress*, an 1872 painting that critic Alan C. Braddock considers "an allegory of technological conquest." In it, a goddess figure soars across the plains, in one hand a book of knowledge, in the other telegraph wires. "Progress was God," the governor of Colorado would write in 1873.

My great aunt worked at Patent, as had Walt Whitman, during the Civil War. He nursed wounded soldiers, bivouacked in its halls, and wrote, "It was a strange, solemn sight, the glass [invention] cases, the beds, the forms lying there ... then the amputation, the blue face, the groan, the glassy eye of the dying." Whitman was employed briefly at The Bureau of Indian Affairs, housed at the museum, but was dismissed when *Leaves of Grass* was deemed by his superiors "an indecent book."

Art was not held sacrosanct by government, though it might exploit it. This paradox was conspicuous on the museum's first floor. Removed from Moran's, Bierstadt's, and Church's ecstatic celebrations of landscape, stood a folk assemblage titled *The Throne of the Third Heaven of the Nations' Millennial General Assembly*. It had been made by a Government Services Administration janitor of African heritage, named James Hampton, who dubbed himself "Director,

Special Projects for the State of Eternity." His was the premier piece of Washington art and it was junk; I don't mean that pejoratively. Constructed of found objects such as light bulbs, jelly glasses, old tables, and armchairs wrapped in silver and gold foil and collected in alleys not far from the Capitol, it was inspired by the Book of Revelations, predictive of apocalypse, critical of bureaucracy and magnificent. Often I contemplated its mysteries. "Fear Not," was written above its throne. In the garage where Hampton had constructed it hung a quote from Proverbs: "Where there is no vision, the people perish." Hampton was a visionary who claimed to have seen the Virgin Mary hovering above the Capitol, pointing him toward his goal. Which was to build God's throne from the detritus of empire. To me, back in the Moran gallery, Hampton's Virgin seemed a phantom not far in substance from Gast's muse in his *Vision of Progress*, shepherding the pioneers west.

My progress from a fourth-generation Washingtonian to a spiritual Westerner had been encouraged not just by the escapism of Roy Rogers comics, Hopalong Cassidy TV, and summers in Montana, but by the psychedelically mind-altering paintings at hand. Even today their colors staggered. Destiny (call it progress) in my dotage may be to follow the path they've suggested. On this gray afternoon in the capital, Moran's canvasses, drawing me in, pointed the way.

—*Western Art & Architecture*, 2011

CHARLES SCHREYVOGEL:
DEFENDING THE STOCKADE

He had a city boy's fascination with the West. And though he'd often visited, and was influenced by explorer artists such as George Catlin and Thomas Moran, he painted not on the dry prairie or desert plain but on the flat roof of Hoboken brownstone. He'd seen Montana, but his Rockies were not the Big Horns or Absarokas but the bluffs of New Jersey's Palisades. And though he'd befriended military, the costumed trooper before him was not a veteran but a teenage athlete from Hoboken's Stevens Institute. The gangs he recollected were less those of Jesse James or Butch Cassidy than the Bowery Boys of Manhattan. His name was Charles Schreyvogel (1861-1912), the son of a German immigrant from the Lower East Side, and an artist who came to rival Frederic Remington in reputation if not in output.

At Remington's death in 1909, the popular *Leslie's Weekly* called Schreyvogel "America's greatest living interpreter of the Old West. It added, "He is more than a historian ... he is giving us an invaluable record of those parlous days of the western frontier, when a handful of brave men blazed the path for civilization and extended the boundaries of empire for a growing nation." A Metropolitan Museum curator would note that, "Schreyvogel helped to engineer the concept of the cowboy and the cavalryman as icons of American masculinity." He championed soldiers of the Indian Wars and painted his Natives judiciously. But his legacy would not be without controversy. He and other artists of his period would be criticized by Stanford historian Alex Nemerov for having demonstrated anti-immigrant, even racist tendencies. Anglo-Saxon founders were "native" Americans, and Indians were heathens at the gate—represented at New York's Ellis Island by a 19th century influx of European aliens. Nemerov would argue in an essay titled "Doing the 'Old America'," in the 1991 collection, *The West as America: Reinterpreting Images of the Frontier,* that "the iconography of cowboys and Indians that arose so vigorously around the turn of the century is best understood in relation to the urban, industrial culture in which this iconography was produced."

Schreyvogel was nothing if not urban. And New York, according to Nemerov, was under siege by immigrants. Schreyvogel's father had owned a candy store near Avenue B, and though the family was first-generation German-American, they fled the Lower East Side because of the overflow of tough Irish and Italian hooligans from the gang-ridden Five Points. The Schreyvogels were decidedly middle class; a neighbor later described Charles as "A gentleman, full of old-world courtesies." To escape the gangster hordes, his father, during the 1870s, moved his family to then-rural Hoboken, which had a polite German population and a small-town charm. Charles roamed its fields and scrambled up its cliffs, quickly seeing New Jersey as a surrogate for the West. It was as if he anticipated Saul Steinberg's 1976 *New Yorker* cover, *View of the World from Ninth Avenue,* suggesting the frontier began at the Hudson.

He'd worked as a goldsmith's and a lithographer's apprentice, and had studied with the painter Karl von Marr in Germany. But his fiercest teachers would be the western novelists, cowboy filmmakers and Wild West impresarios of the day. He met Buffalo Bill in New York and spent hours sketching the horses, cowboy and Indian performers of his show. As had Theodore Roosevelt, Schreyvogel first visited the West's dry climate for his health— as antidote to his asthma and depression—and secondarily to draw. In 1903, he returned from five months spent sketching Indians and troopers around Colorado's Ute Reservation, "his face dark as old leather," writes James D. Horan in his book, *The Life and Art of Charles Schreyvogel*, "and his health improved." He carried his sketches to the Hoboken rooftop and began painting.

Success did not come quickly, but in 1900, when a canvas titled *My Bunkie* (depicting a trooper rescuing an unhorsed bunkmate from an Indian onslaught) won the Thomas B. Clarke Prize at the National Academy of Design in New York, he caught the eye of critics and fellow painters—including Frederic Remington who recognized Schreyvogel as a competitor. Remington may also have disliked Schreyvogel for his immigrant heritage. As the artist fumed, "Jews–Injuns–Chinamen–Italians–Huns, the rubbish of the earth I hate." The anger he would unleash toward Schreyvogel—a "Hun," as Germans were called—would be unprecedented in American artistic feuds.

Schreyvogel had traveled West between 1893 through the early 1900s, and "Custer fascinated him," Horan writes, particularly his campaign of 1868-1869 against the Southwestern Plains tribes. Etched in Schreyvogel's mind was the story of Custer's order that Santana, the Kiowa, and the other chiefs surrender and return to [Oklahoma's] Fort Cobb." It had been a dramatic standoff. During the winter of 1902, Schreyvogel began painting it.

Custer's Demand was completed in 1903. It showed Custer, accompanied by officers, on a winter plain entreating his Indian counterparts to leave the field. Horan writes, "Schreyvogel, as always, had first done extensive research to make sure that the scene was historically correct: horses, the costumes of the men—red and white—and their equipment, even to the thickness of the stirrup leathers." The painting was shown at

New York's Knoedler Galleries and was "an immediate success." Schreyvogel told his wife, Lulu, "I think it is the best thing I have ever done."

Then the New York *Herald* reproduced the painting accompanied by a four-column interview with its creator and a photograph of him in a derby, painting on the Hoboken rooftop. Remington was incensed. He wrote to the *Herald*, "While I do not want to interfere with Mr. Schreyvogel's hallucinations, I do object to his half baked stuff being considered seriously as history." He disputed the size of Custer's horse, the color of his trousers, the stirrup cups employed, and other of the painting's details.

As both men were icons of western painting, "The controversy produced a national stir." Custer's widow and an officer present attested to the canvas's accuracy, and even President Roosevelt (a former rancher and a symbol of the new West) chimed in. He told Schreyvogel, "What a fool my friend Remington made of himself, in his newspaper attack, he made a perfect jack of himself, to try to bring such small things out, and he was wrong anyway."

It's unclear as to why Remington resented Schreyvogel. Remington was at the height of his fame; Schreyvogel was just attaining his. Remington admitted to a friend that "I despise Schreyvogel." Remington had wanted to paint Custer, and as Horan writes, "It was obvious that Remington was seething with jealously that he had a rival in the field." And, "Schreyvogel, painting on a roof—of all places in Hoboken—may have been an affront to [his] view of a true westerner."

Schreyvogel never criticized his accuser. He said simply, "He is the greatest of us all."

Urbanity was Schreyvogel's lot, and it worked in his favor. His canvasses, largely of military personnel, were dramatic without being romantic. And their frantic activity—troopers pursuing Indians, Indians being slain by troopers—anticipated the frenzy of the new century's comic books, western films and TV shows. As Horan writes, "The viewer could almost hear the thunder of the horses, the wild, shrilling cries of the warriors, the crack of the Winchesters, the thud of saber steel on bone, and the scream of wounded horses." A majority of these paintings reinforced the belief that Indians were violent savages whose extermination, or removal, was crucial to the Manifest Destiny.

A siege posture in Schreyvogel's canvasses supports Nemerov's thesis that his "last stand" pictures were unconscious allegories of immigrant intrusion. *Defending the Stockade* (circa 1905) is case in point. It shows a bevy of wounded troopers, besieged by Indians, hurrying "to close the fort's gates to the enemy," Nemerov writes. He argues this may represent "an Anglo-Saxon race in a world 'overrun' with immigrants ... If Schreyvogel made 'closing the door' his central theme, he did so because the terms he possessed for representing the West emerged from a culture in which the idea of closing the door, of enacting anti-immigration legislation, was important."

Well, perhaps. Schreyvogel himself was of immigrant stock, and he venerated the Indians he met on his trips, complaining that they were treated miserably. "The conditions on the reservations never failed to appall him," Horan writes. "He spent hours describing to Lulu the poverty of the tribes," and how the Indian Bureau had failed them. His daughter remembered that, "he would sound very bitter when he talked about the terrible conditions on the reservations. Particularly the children. He would give them every penny he had...."

His sympathy for Indians was emphasized in a 1901 canvas titled *How Kola*. It shows a mounted trooper vaulting toward a fallen Indian, then holding fire when the Indian shouts "How kola," or "stop friend." The scene was based on an incident from an 1870s, hand-to-hand skirmish with the Sioux. A trooper had been saved by an Indian from freezing to death in a blizzard, and when later he recognized that Indian in combat, his life was spared. With *My Bunkie*, it became one of Schreyvogel's most popular paintings.

His family bought a Catskills farm in 1905, and spent their final summers there. Schreyvogel's paintings acquired a ruminative tone, his impasto thick and his subject matter rural. He never ceased painting the West, however, with his signature motifs: "The vivid, remote, startling blue sky," Horan writes, "the stark yellow light of the plains, the crystal clear air, the brown barren earth, the rearing nervous horses ready to plunge from the canvas, and the fighting men, white and red." Schreyvogel lamented that "the last of the frontier was gone," and in Hoboken, painting on his rooftop studio, Horan adds, "he daily turned his back on one of the most striking views in the world, New York's rising skyline, to face the somber, rocky face of the lower Palisades."

Schreyvogel died before them—a victim of septicemia—in January, 1912.

He left perhaps 100 paintings, numerous sketches and a few bronzes. His rival, Remington, had left some 2,500 works. Yet recently a Schreyvogel oil, *Dispatch Bearers*, sold at Christie's for $245,000, and in 2015 a watercolor, *Mountain Man*, sold at Sotheby's for $6,250. A bronze, *The Last Drop*, in 2007 sold there for $108,000. The National Cowboy and Western Heritage Museum in Oklahoma City, the Sid Richardson Museum in Fort Worth, and the Gilcrease Museum in Tulsa hold the majority of his paintings. What Walt Whitman said of Thomas Eakins seems a fitting epitaph for Schreyvogel. And it's a sentence Remington might have muttered of his adversary: "He is not a painter, he is a force."

—*Western Art & Architecture*, 2017

FREDERIC REMINGTON: FIRED ON

Out of the darkness, comes danger—the fear—as a patrol is fired upon. Its enemy is unseen, the gunshots unheard by the viewer as horses rear and riders flinch, drawing pistols and stiffening against saddles as bullets pock the river's surface or explode on rocks before it. A horse, ashen with moonlight, seems paralyzed as it leans back, away from its assailants, away from danger and into the fear.

Fired On, at the Smithsonian American Art Museum, is one of Frederic Remington's celebrated nocturnes—brooding meditations on darkness and light—and was the most commented upon in his 1907 Manhattan show, the second of three fine arts exhibits that introduced the new Remington: one who had turned his back on magazine illustration and made every effort to become a respected painter. Critics were generous in their praise and in the lyricism of their descriptions: "In such a low tone that it is almost monochrome in black and white," the *Brooklyn Eagle* wrote, "a white horse in the foreground shows the only big light ... and in the gloom beyond the other horse are plunging about in terror." While extraordinary, *Fired On* is representative of the seventy-odd night scenes Remington concentrated upon in the last years of his life. "In these he has made a great stride forward," the *New York Daily Tribune* wrote, "Study of the moonlight appears to have reacted upon the very grain of his art ... *Fired On* [is] one of the most truly dramatic compositions he has ever put to his credit ... it would be difficult to congratulate Mr. Remington too warmly." These and other reviews delighted Remington. In his diary he wrote that his show was "a triumph ... I have landed among the painters and well up too."

If *Fired On*'s subject is fear, or knee-jerk panic, it's one familiar to a connoisseur of Remington's late work. "Filled with uncertainty and threatened violence," The National Gallery's Nancy Anderson has written, "they reflect Remington's personal disquiet as well as that of a newly modern world." Abstract art was de rigeur, and there may have been fear in tackling fine art. But there certainly was fear unleashed in the nocturnes from his childhood and his months in Cuba covering the Spanish-American War.

Remington's father had been a Civil War hero, and as Peggy and Harold Samuels write in *Frederick Remington, A Biography*, the colonel "had not believed in Remington's early talent." And, "Remington felt that he had not been a dutiful son to this normally gentle bur martially fierce man...." The solution was combat. When Theodore Roosevelt gathered his Rough Riders for that "splendid little war" of 1898, Remington was keen to experience "the greatest thing which men are called on to do." Since he knew Roosevelt from illustrating his writings, and from their shared experiences out West, he accompanied him on the adventure Remington hoped would make him "a heroic war correspondent" for William Randolph Hearst's *New York Journal*. The suffering and random carnage he found in combat sickened him. "I didn't get over Santiago for a year," he wrote. Added to its terrors had been the unpredictability of jungle warfare, its guerrilla fighters as the unseen enemy and projecting an "unknown" that haunted him the remainder of his days.

That fear was captured vividly in 1898's painting, *Scream of Shrapnel at San Juan Hill, Cuba*: Troopers fall helter skelter looking in contrary directions for the source of the danger. It is a tableau of confusion and panic. Anderson notes that "He had wanted, he wrote, "the roar of battle." Instead, he found the unnerving "scream of shrapnel" coming from an unknown direction...." And screams of the wounded.

His nocturnes were an attempt to join the ranks of American painters such as Homer, Ryder and Hassam. But while their nocturnes were peaceful or at their darkest contemplative, Remington's were startling—meant to startle, as their subjects have been startled. In *A Taint on the Wind*, a lantern-lit stage coach hurtles down a silvery road as its horses flare from the presence of an unseen danger. In *Shotgun Hospitality*, a cowboy, seated against his wagon with a shotgun across his lap, rubs his chin as three robed Indians emerge from the darkness, their intentions unclear. In *Moonlight, Wolf*, the solitary predator stands as if himself surprised, eyes shining yellow in reflection of the stars in a field of gray-green and black, or as if considering the viewer as prey. Anderson notes, "Remington's wolf is a killer. They eyes that engage the viewer are those of death."

Remington was not healthy—he was gluttonously alcoholic—and death may have preoccupied him. It may have done so since boyhood. He was an only child, whose father had been at war the first years of his life, and who wished West Point and a military career for his son. Instead, Remington attended Yale art school, playing football for the team, but dropped out in 1879, at age eighteen, to nurse his tuberculous father—who died at forty-six. "The loss was greater," Peggy and Harold Samuels write, "because it was before Remington had developed a separate life." He had sketched soldiers and cowboys from an early age, and in 1881, inheritance in hand, he visited Montana, admiring the unfenced prairies, hunting grizzlies, apprising the last of the cavalry-Indian conflagrations, and sketching. He sold his first illustration to *Harper's* and, after stints in Kansas as a sheep rancher, hardware merchant and saloon keeper, returned to New York to study at the Art Students League and launch his career as an illustrator.

Cuba would change that. Home, in a 1908 backyard fire he would burn the sketches he considered illustrations, the work of "a black and white man," having turned his full attention the examination of color and light. But in '98, having produced his sketches for Hearst, he took a recuperative vacation to Montana and Wyoming. Despite a realization that the West he'd known as a boy had vanished, the trip inspired him. He revisited cowboys and Indians as subjects, but sketched them in nocturnes, experimenting with star, fire, and moonlight, in a manner that was startlingly innovational.

He had seen an exhibit by Charles Rollo Peters during the fall of 1899, which contained sixteen views of California missions by moonlight. These paintings were in the contemporary mode—that of Whistler, George Bellows, and the photographer Alfred Stieglitz, whose work celebrated an illuminated darkness, particularly that of cities, which recently had become electrified. Remington's reexamination of the West—its frontier days passed—incorporated the startle responses of flash photography into *plein air* scenes, using fire, star and moonlight instead. Illumination in combat represented danger, as it had in the old West. One ventured into moonlight or built a fire at one's peril. Something was "out there," in critic William C. Sharpe's phrase, and if it saw you it could get you.

It also lurked inside. Sharpe writes, "For what's 'out there' is in here—the modern artist looking into himself." Such self-reflection was *au courant*. Remington's nocturnes were envisioned, Sharpe adds, "at the time when Joseph Conrad in *Heart of Darkness* (1899) and Sigmund Freud in *The Interpretation of Dreams* (1900) began their own explorations of inner darkness." Remington moved closer to a metaphorical and painterly Impressionism.

Mortality haunted him. At forty-eight, he was ill with gastric distress and at 300 pounds, grossly overweight. Surgery in December of 1909 for a burst appendix was complicated by his obesity. He died of peritonitis a short time later. Premonitions had been rife in his work. As an observer wrote of his last New York show, 'in all of Remington pictures the shadow of death seems not far away.'"

Nowhere is it better portrayed than in the previous year's *Fired On*. Approach it in the Smithsonian Museum of American Art. Horses flare and rear at an unseen danger; men flinch and draw weapons, and one almost can hear their cries. The same holds true for *A Taint on the Wind*, at the Sid Richardson Collection in Forth Worth, Texas. Remington's hurtling coach is as imperiled by its own force of energy as by its invisible assailant. Both seem impossible to stop.

He had been happy that *Fired On* was purchased on 1908 for $1,000, then donated to the National Museum. At that point it represented the finest of his nocturnes. Money did not preoccupy Remington—he was wealthy from his sales of paintings, illustrations, and sculptures—but one can imagine what he might have thought in 2012 when Sotheby's sold *A Halt in the Wilderness*, an earlier nocturne, for $2,770,500— the tenth highest auction price for a Remington, including sculpture.

Several shows recently have featured Remington's nocturnes. "Treasures from the Frederic Remington Museum" was exhibited at the Museum of the Big Bend, in Texas, from September through December, 2013. The National Gallery of Art mounted "The Western Frontier," from March 28th to August 24th, 2014. The Sid Richardson Museum has permanently displayed five Remington nocturnes in a single room. And a comprehensive catalogue of Remington's work by Peter Hassrick, formerly of the Buffalo Bill Museum in Cody, was published by the University of Oklahoma Press in spring, 2014.

Meanwhile, *Fired On* hangs on a far wall of the American Art Museum's second floor, darkly sentient and stealthy, as if to bushwhack the unwary viewer.

—*Western Art & Architecture*, 2013

ALEXANDER GARDNER:
THE INDIAN SHOOTER

He was longhaired, full bearded, and seemed a veteran of the 1960s. He'd been a champion of socialist causes, a chronicler of war yet an advocate for peace, a witness to the execution of presidential assassins and a restless patriot, an artist discarding old forms for experimentation with new technology, a counterculture journalist and commune founder, a champion of Native Americans as first citizens, and a proponent of life insurance as a kind of social welfare. Yet Alexander Gardner's decade of greatest productivity was the 1860s—a full century before such values became fashionable.

During the fall of 2018, an exhibit of his Indian photographs appeared at Big Horn, Wyoming's Brinton Museum, in celebration of the 150th anniversary of the Fort Laramie Peace Talks. They were twenty-seven of some sixty-odd pictures Gardner made on the occasion, in 1868, of those talks—between a federally appointed commission of generals, politicians and Plains Indian leaders. They remain gripping images of Native chieftains, U.S. dignitaries, and the Wyoming landscape in which they stand. Above all, they show the mastery Gardner had acquired from decades of practicing portrait photography.

Born in Scotland in 1821, he apprenticed first as a jeweler

but became intrigued by journalism and the new craft of photography. Daguerre had developed his process only in 1837. Philosophically, Gardner was influenced by the writings of Robert Owen, a Welsh socialist and communard; from Owen's example, Gardner and his friends bought land in Iowa for a cooperative, but the first settlers' contraction of tuberculosis prevented Gardner from living there. He returned to Scotland, founded a radically democratic journal, *The Glasgow Sentinel,* and took up photography. At London's Great Exhibition of 1851, he saw the work of the American photographer, Mathew Brady, and by 1856 had become an assistant at Brady's gallery in New York, where he photographed military officers, politicians, and social luminaries. By 1858, he and his younger brother James were selected to run Brady's Washington, DC gallery.

Lincoln had been elected president, and Brady photographed him at the White House and in the field at least seven times. War was declared in 1861 and Gardner—ever open to adventure—secured an honorary captaincy to serve as photographer to U.S. General George B. McClellan. (Gardner may have been America's first combat photographer.) He became so trusted in Washington that after Lincoln's assassination he'd be the only person invited to photograph the conspirators' hanging. Gardner was familiar with bodies, having photographed the corpses of soldiers at Antietam and Gettysburg. Those battlefield images horrified viewers when shown—Gardner's intended effect. As he wrote in *Gardner's Photographic Sketchbook of the War,* "Such a picture conveys a useful moral: it shows the blank horror and morality of war, in opposition to its pageantry. Here are the dreadful details! Let them aid in preventing such another calamity from falling upon the nation."

As a socialist, Gardner saw both Yankee and Rebel conscripts as pawns in a game of the privileged. The original pawns were America's displaced Natives, squeezed to mid-board by the populations of both coasts. Natives were increasingly threatened by the transcontinental railroad, which crossed their hunting grounds and dispersed bison. Gardner photographed Native delegations in Washington (he was photographer for the Office of Indian Affairs), and in the Brinton Museum show there were striking prints of Natives posing at the White House, and in regalia during more formal, studio sessions.

But he had not traveled to Indian country.

He would do so from 1867 to 1868, as survey photographer for the Union Pacific Railway (later the Kansas Pacific), becoming one of the first photographers of the American West. He worked in a small, horse-drawn darkroom that is visible in several of his shots. His images of the Southwest would be presented in an 1868 book, *Across the Continent on the Kansas Pacific Railroad*. There are staggering images of rail cars atop bridges and against the vastness of the Kansas prairie. In Arizona and New Mexico, he photographed Natives on the plains and in their pueblos. But it wasn't until he visited Fort Laramie to make the photographs that would comprise *Scenes In the Indian Country* that he produced his finest work.

Of the twenty-seven prints included in the Brinton Museum show, the most dramatic were of Native American chiefs, with names such as Man Afraid of His Horses, Fire Thunder, Shot in the Jaw, Packs His Drum, Whistling Elk, and Pipe. The chiefs appear regal yet defeated in their everyday garb, while the generals Alfred H. Terry, William T. Sherman, William S. Harney, Christopher T. Augur, and others look imperious in dark uniforms or business suits—especially so in a shot of the group seated beneath a tent fly, with Natives slumped before them. These are not journalistic photographs; they are carefully posed. In one, of the six generals and an Arapaho woman, Terry and Augur stand angled toward the group, Harney braces at attention facing the camera, Sherman and civilian committee-member John B. Sanborn flank the tiny Arapaho, and the civilian Samuel E. Tappan stands at ease. Theirs is a posture of both indifference and intimidation. In a photograph titled "Deaf and Dumb Indian," a tall Native in a Confederate overcoat with a strand of silver conchos over his shoulder, an insignia-decorated hat, and a musket leans against a brindle mare, as her white colt stands beside her. Gardner posed the shot two different ways—one with the colt facing left, and the other facing right; and one with the Indian hatted, then hatless. Even in landscape shots, such as "Bluff on the Platte, Black Hills in Distance," "Bluffs on the Laramie River Near Fort Laramie," and "Chimney Rock on Plains Between Cheyenne and Fort Laramie," Gardner situates figures across the portrait's frame, suggesting both scale and human insignificance. Most effectively, Gardener foreshadows the Indians' capitulation in portraits of their burial sites—solitary trees, near Fort Laramie, with bodies lashed to their branches. They are prairie crucifixes.

As critic Keith F. Davis suggests in *Alexander Gardner: The Western Photographs, 1867-1868*, a tension existed in Gardner's work between portraiture and landscape. "His years in the portrait studio gave him a sophisticated sense of lighting, composition, and pose," Davis writes. "His experience on the battlefields of Antietam and Gettysburg underscored the power of blunt facts. His work in the American West hovers between these two aesthetic poles, a potent blend of deliberation and contingency, of art and information."

The peace talks that Gardener memorialized closed with modest success. A treaty was signed on April 29, then augmented on May 25. Eventually it was broken. As Brinton Museum curator of exhibitions, Barbara McNab writes, "Unfortunately, conflicts over hunting rights and ownership of land were to continue well into the next two decades. The discovery of gold in the Black Hills in 1874 had much to do with the unraveling of the treaty."

But Gardner's photographs stand as both a monument to the talks, and as art. Primarily they stand as art. As Davis writes, "Gardner's photographs seamlessly meld art and history." This is true of both his Civil War photos and those of the West. "Our cultural memory of these places and events is shaped powerfully by the fact that these remarkable photographs were made by him."

—*Big Sky Journal,* 2018

OTTO BECKER:
CUSTER'S LAST FIGHT

During the summer of 1972, I was embarked upon a four-year search for the Great American Bar, a trip that took my Volkswagen Beetle 30,000 miles across this nation's roughest roads and myself into its oldest, most colorful dives. That quest resulted in a book, *Saloon*, which would be published with cork-popping effervescence in 1976. One afternoon I visited the Idaho Hotel bar, in the ghost town of Silver City, an emporium reached after a two-hour drive up twenty-five miles of mountain road that was a spike strip of stone and shale, and which deposited me before the 1863 structure, parched and crabby. I entered the hotel and in its once-elegant saloon found ten customers (the town's population) arguing neither politics nor baseball, but whether the Seventh Cavalry's uniforms were accurately depicted in the lithograph that hung before them.

It was Otto Becker's *Custer's Last Fight*, an 1896 print distributed by Anheuser-Busch to scores of bars across America, seen repeatedly by me in my travels, and touted, by mid-twentieth-century, as the piece of art viewed by more Americans than any other. "If not the best liked of all American pictures," noted Professor Robert Taft, who published his "Pictorial History of the American West" in the *Kansas Historical Quarterly* in 1946, "it doubtless has been the most extensively examined and discussed of any."

Inspired by an 1885 painting of the battle of the Little Big-horn by Cassilly Adams, the lithograph was splendid in its violence, dubious in its historical accuracy, and, in its portrayal of a golden-haired George Armstrong Custer, Romantic to a fault. Yet as my experience affirmed, its presence in saloons across the U.S. caused a ceaseless spate of chatter. It had been created before television yet provided comparable entertainment as promotion for Anheuser-Busch beers. This was the Pleistocene of subliminal advertising. Art such as *Custer's Last Fight* created in the drinker a trance-like reverie easily infiltrated by the sponsor's product. Patrons stood hypnotized by the lithograph's gruesome battle scene, glanced at its Anheuser-Busch logo, and ordered a Bud.

Depictions of the 1876 massacre of Seventh Cavalry troops, at a time when the flamboyant Civil War hero, Custer, may have been planning to run for president—and when Indians were considered not just America's enemies but bloodthirsty heathens—already had captivated viewers. No less a critic than Walt Whitman characterized John Mulvany's popular 1881 painting, *Custer's Last Rally*, thus: "Swarms upon swarms of savage Sioux, in their war bonnets, frantic, driving through the background, through the smoke, like a hurricane of demons ... deadly, heroic to the uttermost; nothing in the books like it, nothing in Homer, nothing in Shakespeare ... I could look on such a work at brief intervals all my life without tiring."

He and many Americans would, as Mulvany's 20 feet x 11 feet *Rally*, containing forty-odd figures, toured this country and undoubtedly Europe, as a kind of Wild West Show on canvas. Its impact was huge. William Merritt Chase admired Mulvany's painting to a degree that he traveled to Europe to study with his teachers. Frederic Remington saw *Custer's Last Rally* and was inspired to sketch his version of the subject. Another artist who undoubtedly saw Mulvany's work was Cassilly Adams.

He was a Civil War veteran, like Custer, but descended from the John Adams family of Boston. He had been trained in painting, and by the late 1870s was employed in St. Louis as an artist and engraver. Members of that city's Art Club commissioned him to recreate the battle scene "for exhibition purposes," Robert Taft wrote, "stimulated no doubt by the success of the Mulvany picture." Adams' rendition was large: (9 feet, 6 inches x 16 feet, 5 inches), and included end panels that portrayed Custer "as a small boy in his father's shop playing with toy soldiers," the second showing "Custer dead on the field of battle." Adams' son recalled that figures "were posed by Sioux Indians in their war paint and also by cavalrymen in the costumes of the period." There was little attempt at historical accuracy, as no army participant had lived to verify it. The painting was finished about 1885, and toured widely. It did not realize a profit, however, and was sold to a St. Louis saloon, where it hung for years. Anheuser-Busch obtained it after the saloon keeper's death, and a Milwaukee artist, Otto Becker, was hired to make a chromolithograph of it, which would be copyrighted in 1896.

We depend upon Professor Taft—a Kansas University chemist as well as a historian—for details of the artist's life. Becker was German by birth, had studied at Dresden's Royal Academy of Fine Arts, and so far as an interpretation of Custer's death went, was independent of mind. His daughter, Blanche Becker, told Taft that her father had painted for the Milwaukee Lithographic and Engraving Company, specializing in western scenes, "after the manner of Remington." Becker understood the art of advertising. He must have been struck by Custer's plight, though, for his interpretation of the battle, "Taken from [Adams'] Sketches," the original lithograph noted, is more classically framed and far more dramatic than its predecessors. As Taft wrote, "It is indeed a picture that tells a powerful, if melodramatic and horrendous, tale ... Troopers are being brained, scalped, stripped; white men, Indians, and horses are dying by the dozens; Custer with flowing red tie and long ringlets is about to deal a terrible saber blow to an advancing Indian who in turn is shot by a dying trooper; and hundreds of Indians are pictured or suggested in the background. A careful survey of the lithograph is enough to give a sensitive soul a nightmare for a week."

Yet the print's subtler message was cautionary, as Custer's hubris was an issue. By dividing his regiment and not waiting for reinforcement, he had insured defeat in a skirmish thought unloseable. "Custer was a fool who rode to his death," Sitting Bull said. Insults like his inspired endless commentary before Becker's print—and at times fisticuffs.

In its celebration of war, the print was meant to incite passions, chief among them rage at the killing of a white hero by Sioux, Northern Cheyenne and Arapaho warriors: racial "others." In two years, America would invade Cuba, then the Philippines and Europe; during WWII armed forces would enter the Pacific theater, decimating Japan. Thousands of *Custer's Last Fight* prints had been shipped by the Defense Department to U.S. service folk.

The lithograph's main purpose was not jingoistic, it was to sell beer. And that it did. It stands as one of Anheuser-Busch's most successful ad vehicles. By 1946, the company had produced over 150,000 copies of the lithograph; it is still producing it. A 1933 letter from Becker to his daughter states, "I painted *Custer's Last Stand* in 1895. The original painting is still in my possession, but unfortunately I was forced to cut it into pieces so that a number of artists could work on it ... making the color plates." Becker died in Milwaukee in 1945, at age 92. His painting hangs at Anheuser-Busch headquarters, in St. Louis. Cassilly Adams' canvas, upon which it had been based, was presented to the Seventh Cavalry at Fort Riley sometime between 1888 and 1896. It was lost in various moves, restored by the WPA and rehung at Fort Bliss by 1938, then destroyed by fire in 1946.

Copies of the lithograph still exist in taverns ("Keep this picture under fly-netting in the summer time and it will remain bright for many years," Anheuser-Busch advised), and I recently purchased a 36 inch x 27 inch print from the Custer Battlefield Museum. Spread across my desk, it is a vivid reminder of my travels. Its colors are Technicolor bright, and while not so classically rendered as Mulvany's *Custer's Last Rally*, it is more grippingly dramatic in its rendition of Custer, shown in buckskins and holding both saber and a pistol wielded as a club. The horror of the battle is plain, with Indians tearing scalps from troopers' skulls, and stabbing them where they lie. Mutilation would follow. Taft, who hung a copy near his University of Kansas laboratory, wrote: "The reaction of those who have never seen the picture before is always interesting to observe. Incredulous first glances are always followed by study of all the gory details. 'Holy H. Smoke! Was it as bad as that?'"

It was the battle that had been horrific, and the lithograph—no gorier than war paintings in museums round the world—makes no claim to high art. The 1890 massacre of Lakota Sioux at Wounded Knee, by a Seventh Cavalry troop near Pine Ridge, South Dakota, had been, in part, payback for Little Bighorn, and one Saturday, during 1985's Crow Fair, I entered a saloon in Hardin, Montana, near the battlefield, that was crowded with Native Americans. To the back bar's left was Becker's print, defaced with pen and pencil, and bearing colorful epithets. I wore my blond hair Custer-long, and this was a frightening place. I did not linger, but I did ask the bartender why he kept the painting. "So we don't forget," he said. At the American Legion down Center Avenue a friend's band was playing, and when I entered the packed room I saw we were the lone Anglos. What the hell, I thought, and invited a girl to dance. Thereafter I was asked by Native women to jitterbug at least fifty times, and no one disapproved.

Custer's Last Fight was not on display.

—*Western Art & Architecture*, 2012

IMAGES OF CROCKETT

At nine years old I wore a coonskin cap, fringed jacket, faux-leather britches and carried a muzzle-loading rifle. That flintlock was a broomstick fitted with cabinet latches, but the coonskin cap was real, ordered from a supply house that shipped to kids 5,000 a day. I hummed "The Ballad of Davy Crockett" and could have been that boy standing in the 1955 *Your Hit Parade* skit, being sketched by a fifth-grade art class, as the glamorous Gisèle McKenzie trilled the song. It would sell 10 million copies and stay on the charts for 13 weeks.

I was not that boy, though my uncle, William A. Nichols, wrote the skit. I might have been present in the NBC studios at Rockefeller Center when it was aired. I don't recall, but it was at NBC that my personal relationship with Crockett began. My uncle, a writer for television's *Your Hit Parade*—the live revue that dramatized each week's hits with musical skits—was driven mad by "The Ballad of Davy Crockett." It was his job to create a new sketch each week to dramatize Fess Parker's rendition of the song. The first sketch was easy: a vocalist with a group of school children before the Alamo, where Crockett died, singing a history lesson. But where to from there? There were skits with BB-gun-flintlocks and with stuffed bears—one of which, the song claimed, Crockett killed "when he was only three." After 12 weeks, my uncle cried, "Not another sketch!"

I was reminded of this when I stumbled upon Chester Harding's 1834 painting of Crockett in a side room of Washington's National Portrait Gallery. Most of us remember the Canebrake Congressman from Walt Disney's glorification of him as a buckskin-and-coonskin-cap wearing frontiersman in the television mini-series and subsequent film of 1955. But in the Portrait Gallery's Victorian corridors, flanked by busts of presidents and politicians, hangs an image of Crockett as a modest well-groomed fellow, dressed in a dark suit, tan vest, white shirt and black tie—in contrast to popular portrayals of him as a bumpkin, "half-horse, half-alligator," and "a little touched with snapping-turtle."

The formality of Chester Harding's canvas should have been no surprise. Harding (1792-1866) earned his reputation making notables' portraits—he was the Richard Avedon of his day—and his paintings of Daniel Boone are the most accurate images of what was America's first white frontier hero. Davy Crockett was its second, a congressman from Tennessee when Harding painted him, and in Boston to support the anti-Jacksonian Whigs. As the AMAA's website states, "The image agrees with a contemporary description: 'Colonel Crockett is an uncommonly fine looking man. His face has an exceedingly amiable expression and his features are prominent and striking. He wears his hair which is black, (with a light shade of brown) parted down the centre of his forehead, combed back from his temples, and ending in a slight curl at the neck not unlike the simple manner of many of the clergy.'"

Crockett's story has been a staple of schlock, not high art, for nearly two centuries. Plays and books about him (not the least, his autobiography) were popular throughout his life, and remain so. He may have been America's first media celebrity. Paul Andrew Hutton, in *Texas Monthly*, has written that Crockett was "perhaps the first American to make a living portraying his own fanciful image." As early as 1831, a tongue-in-cheek drama about his life, *The Lion of the West*, introduced the cliché of Crockett's coonskin cap, and ran for years. After his death, a second play, *Davy Crockett; or, Be Sure You're Right, Then Go Ahead*, ran from 1872 to 1896 in the U.S. and England. Some twenty films about Crockett have been made, the most recent being 2004's *The Alamo*, a revisionist epic starring Billy Bob Thornton. Everyone from Fess Parker to John Wayne and Johnny Cash has played him. EBay groans under the weight of Crockett memorabilia. Even the U.S. military has not been immune to sentimentality. In 1956, a tactical nuclear recoilless gun, "The Davy Crockett," was named for him. And deployed.

This does not surprise, as historically the frontiersman, not the cowboy or Indian, was the first romanticized figure of the American West. His fighting prowess was said to be legendary. Lord Byron spent a few verses of his epic, "Don Juan," praising Daniel Boone, and James Fenimore Cooper's Leatherstocking Tales made the fictional, gun-toting frontiersman, Natty Bumppo, an American hero—concomitantly with Crockett's election, in 1827, to congress.

As a boy, I embraced Crockett's legend. My generation (the first subjected to Saturday morning TV) had been conditioned to idealize the frontiersman, and Crockett's legend, ingeniously marketed by Disney through fashion, captivated all of us. Stores were deluged with perhaps the first flood of non-political commemorative art: lunch boxes, thermoses, cocoa cups, plates and saucers, game boards, paintings and posters, T-shirts, ladies underwear and most famously a 45 rpm disc: "The Ballad of Davy Crockett." We loved this schlock, and decades later, when I met the great-great-great-great granddaughter of Crockett, I was enormously impressed. Crockett had been her schoolmates' hero, and she admitted that sharing the same last name as Davy had been difficult: "They wondered why I didn't wear a coonskin cap."

As fifties kids, we were children of the post-WWII migration to a leafy and often wooded suburbia which, in contrast to the inner city, felt like a frontier. Disney capitalized on this displacement, even as artists like Harding and John Gadsby Chapman, during the 19th century, had employed images of Crockett and Boone to help legitimize Manifest Destiny and America's westward expansion. After Crockett's death, when paintings such as Robert Jenkins Onderdonk's *The Fall of the Alamo* appeared, Crockett's image became politicized. It remains so today. "Remember the Alamo" is a rallying cry for anti-immigration activists, who associate Crockett's resistance to Santa Anna's troops with President Trump's opposition to Mexican workers crossing the southern border. As Hutton writes in his introduction to *A Narrative of the Life of Davy Crockett*, by Himself: "Crockett quickly emerged as a symbol of the dawning 'Age of the Common Man'" and "represented to many the triumph of pure democracy and a complete rejection of the European values of social class and aristocracy."

Recently at the National Portrait Gallery, I appraised Harding's portrait of Crockett—a Jacksonian Democrat and two-term Tennessee congressman—and considered today's political climate. His was a time when congressmen did not fear opposing their party's mandates (Crockett became an energetic anti-Jacksonian over the Indian Removal Act) when it least suited their careers. Having lost the election of 1834, he said, "I bark at no man's bid. I will never come and go, and fetch and carry, at the whistle of the great man in the White House no matter who he is." Then he added: "I told the people of my district that I would serve them as faithfully as I had done; but if not ... you may all go to hell, and I will go to Texas.'"

He died there in a manner befitting a folk hero, and paintings of his combat at the Alamo are as common as those of him as youthful frontiersman. *Davy Crockett's Almanack*, suffused with tall tales and rough woodcuts, was published between 1835 and 1856. And books about his life have not ceased appearing. As William Henry Huddle, of the Texas

State Library Archives has written, "So maybe Davy Crockett escaped from the Alamo after all. He's still up in the misty heights of the topmost Rocky Mountains cavorting with Death Hug [his pipe-smoking bear], Mississip [his pet bison], and all his other critters." His legend is secure, as is the art depicting him—both fine and popular—that survives.

My uncle, struggling in the afterlife to write yet another Crockett sketch for *Your Hit Parade,* might feel justified.

—*Western Art & Architecture,* 2013

WYETH OF THE WEST

It is not a man's world, so much, as a boy's: the *Treasure Island* frontispiece say, its illustration bulging with enlarged feet and arms of musket-bearing pirates that "jump out at you and grab your neck," as N.C. Wyeth's son, Andrew would observe. It is the bushwhacking archers of *Robin Hood* or the impossibly muscular Indians of *The Last of the Mohicans*, illustrations of a sort that N.C.'s grandson Jamie, would categorize as "electrifying," with "a bravado" and "the intense colors—all done before television." Perhaps more than these novels' texts, N.C.'s illustrations fling us back in time—to medieval and eighteenth-century England, to the pirate-infested Caribbean, to King Arthur's court—transporting readers from the torpor or terror of childhood to lands where adventure is paramount, heroism possible, and romance a state worth preserving. And though N.C.'s work illustrating historical fiction is what we best remember him for, his career did not begin there. It began in the wild West of the American present.

He was the first son of a troubled mother, "hysterical" and "nervous," in the day's parlance, who at age eight and in a fit of jealousy may have drowned her infant brother in the Charles River. Hattie Wyeth would so cling to her first son that when N.C. left his Needham, Massachusetts home at age twenty for the Howard Pyle Academy, in Wilmington, Delaware, she memorialized the approximate date, October 19, 1902, and never let him forget it. A midlife painting by N.C.—*My Mother*—suggests her sorrow at his departure and the stooped-shoulder resolve of the figure leaving. Hattie would spend decades infantilizing N.C. In 1906, at his engagement to his future wife, she showed him a recently framed baby picture and said, as David Michaelis in *N.C. Wyeth: A Biography* reports, "I felt I must get you back in that form."

Bronco Buster, a 1902 sketch for *The Saturday Evening Post*, was N.C.'s first cover work. And its exuberance set him apart from the apprentices at Pyle's studios in both Wilmington and Chadds Ford, Pennsylvania. It would be the first of the Western illustrations he published throughout his life. It is alive with the exhilaration of escape.

He fled to the American West, as had Frederic Remington, Edward Curtis, Thomas Moran, and Theodore Roosevelt, in part to solidify his manhood. "Wyeth wanted his art to be 'virile,'" says Christine Podmaniczky, Curator of the N.C. Wyeth Collections for the Brandywine River Museum, and editor of his *Catalogue Raisonné*. "What better subject than 'the great West?'" During two trips, one in 1904, the other in 1906—Wyeth herded cattle, delivered mail via pony express, and rejoiced in his freedom from maternal bonds. The trips produced work that was stunningly original. As Podmaniczky says, "Wyeth's energy is palpable, the action amazing, and the color gorgeous."

His paintings were ecstatic. And youthfully consistent: the frenzies of 1905's *Cutting Out* or *Rounding Up* are not far removed from the comic enthusiasms of *The Wild, Spectacular Race for Dinner*. His colors are vivid: bright blues, reds and blinding whites against the chestnut hides of cattle or horses. Even the grim stoicism of the dust-blown freighter, in 1907's *The Ore Wagon*, is overwhelmed by a joyous rush forward. Paintings from N.C.'s 1906 trip to Colorado, for an *Outing*

Magazine story, "How They Opened the Snow Road," are "alternately subtle and intense," says Podmaniczky. "Wyeth captured so well the look of the icy temperatures, the snow and the winter sky. The painterliness with which he creates these scenes is so accomplished."

The pictures were grounded in observation—Wyeth had been there. Stylistically they did much to separate him from the medievalism of his teacher, Howard Pyle, the premier illustrator of his day, a champion of the old and decrier of the new. And it helped gird him against the constant attentions of his mother, who wished them to be "children together," as Michaelis reports, she his "one and only," and he her "shining light."

Wyeth's frontier mentor had been Frederic Remington. N.C. believed "the great West ... has never been painted except by [him]," but "he has only pictured the brutal and gory side of it ..." Remington's palette often was dark—his most accomplished paintings were nocturnes—but Wyeth, with bright colors and sublime liveliness, celebrated its jubilant side. Expressing his joy in the company of men, and the distance felt from Hattie—and from his new fiancé, Carolyn Bockius.

That lightness and energy proved popular with magazines. From the first Wyeth's success there was the envy of his contemporaries. The earliest of his Western illustrations were for *Scribner's*, *McClure's*, *Outing* and *The Saturday Evening Post*. He did advertising work for Cream of Wheat, Coca Cola and other companies. Editors commissioned paintings that by the time of his death numbered several thousand. Hollywood directors plagiarized his sketches, but not without flattering him. N.C. wrote of the 1920 adaptation of *The Last of the Mohicans,* that the director "very obviously followed my pictures with marked fidelity ... At times I felt as though some of my pictures had suddenly come to life." *Mohicans* had been a Scribner's Classic, and Wyeth would illustrate numerous others for that house, including *The Deer Slayer, Kidnapped.*

Robinson Crusoe, The Mysterious Island, and *Westward Ho!* Despite his commercial success, he held the illustrator's singular dissatisfaction with the trade: "If only someday I can be called a painter!"

Ironically he had the fortune to be working in the golden age of American illustration, the early twentieth century. That was an era before photography's dominance, when modern printing more accurately reproduced a painting's color and when almost every book, story or article required one. Wyeth wrote, in a 1912 *New York Times* essay titled, "A Suggestion and Comment on Illustrating Fiction," that "The illustrator must first feel the power of a story in all its rhythm and swing ... You have to register in your mind how it works ... you must single out the color of the story." The illustrator must also encourage a suspension of disbelief, creating a meditative space where the reader's and buyer's subconscious is captivated by the product. "[A picture] is in short a form of advertisement." Such dreamlike commercialism required negotiating the territory between romance and reality, fantasy and fact.

That tight-rope walk was a feat Wyeth struggled to maintain. His western illustrations celebrated the romance of a vanishing frontier, yet moved him toward realism and reality—away from the fantasy life he'd cultivated to bear the dominance his mother. That he resented this work's demands is both curious and understandable. "The artistic powers of an illustrator spring from the same source as do the powers of the painter," he wrote, "but the profound difference lies in the fact that the illustrator submits his inspiration to a definite end; the painter carries his into infinitude."

Hattie Wyeth died on August 11, 1925. She had been hospitalized for depression, but had returned to her Needham, Massachusetts home. N.C. was not present at her demise. Afterward, in sadness, he scrawled, "How little I have expressed the *true me,* and how much there is of *me* to express." Their relationship had been crippling. And the enmeshment he'd known—that compulsive caring and drive to be cared for—would be transferred to his surviving family. As Michaelis writes, "Emotional stability eluded him. He would be dependent on others to maintain equilibrium all his life."

His western art grew brighter after Hattie's death, and its subjects less frenzied. In 1937's *Cowboy Watering His Horse* (an ad for Coca Cola), the rider hunkers Buddha-like beside his mount as it drinks from a stream. The cowboy's shirt is alfalfa green and the Rockies loom white as the Himalayas. In 1935's *Seeking the New Home*, a pioneer woman stoops beside a Conestoga wagon to fix a meal for her children with the contentment of a mother serving dinner in a New England saltbox.

In Hattie's absence, Wyeth's paintings of the East—though their colors were striking— grew darker and more meditative. Nineteen-forty-one's *The War Letter* is predictably bleak, and 1935's *April Rain*, while light blue-gray in tone and spring-like, shows a farmer hunched in contemplation or melancholy as he tends his herd. These must have been satisfying to N.C. as art. Yet he'd said as early as 1912, that he was "sick" of illustration. "I want to start over, I want to wipe the slate clean of everything but my family."

He added, "There has been in my cosmos two factions warring ever since I can remember." He meant his inclination to, in his view, produce "bad" rather than "good" art, and his wish to create the latter. A compromise had been reached: when illustrating, he tried to make the resultant paintings count. In magazines they would be reproduced, at best, in a 10 x 14 inch format. But as Jamie says, "For some reason [he] did these huge things"—42 x 32 inches, and sometimes 52 x 34 inches. As Michaelis posits that "Wyeth had used his clashing selves to give popular literary forms a graphic concreteness they had not had before." Already he had "succeeded in making westerns, folktales, historical romances, and stories of adventure and exploration his own emotional property."

The public, and some critics, found his private work less compelling. In his middle years the Pennsylvania landscapes and Maine seascapes became dreamlike, even hallucinatory—after the style of Thomas Hart Benton. Michaelis argues that Wyeth, in his personal work, was unable to confront the feelings of rage and entrapment seething from his relationship with his mother. Yet others feel that N.C.'s Chadds Ford and New England paintings represent the best of his mature efforts. "Ultimately, of course," Podmaniczky says, "Wyeth realized that he loved Pennsylvania and New England too much to devote his life and art to the West."

It was in Chadds Ford that he would conclude that life. Though working diligently, he'd entered a deep relationship with his daughter-in-law, Caroline Pyle Wyeth (Howard Pyle's niece), that some, including family members, believed was not foolishly romantic, but sexual. On the morning of October 19, 1945, his car was struck on railroad tracks near the Wyeth farm by a locomotive that flung the station wagon and its passengers, N.C. and Caroline's four-year-old son, Newell, 143 feet forward, killing them both. Some thought the accident had been suicide. Others believed that Newell had been N.C.'s child. Everyone knew the painter had been gravely depressed. And he was a son who would have remembered that October 19, 1902 was the date his mother always said was the day he'd left her for Pyle. That last morning he had been painting *First Farmer of the Land*, a portrait of George Washington—himself no meek explorer of the frontier. The West could not have been far from N.C.'s mind.

Its vigor would remain with the Wyeths, who in their art and colorfully individualistic lives have remained genteel outlaws. Andrew eschewed painting the West, but Jamie, in 1965's *Draft Age*, embraced its spirit if not its fact. "I have to think that Jamie Wyeth's work is closest to N. C.'s," Podmaniczky says. "NCW and Jamie both love the tactile qualities—the malleability—and possibilities of oil paint. As far as *Draft Age* goes, I think it's one of Jamie's finest paintings."

In that work, the artist—celebrated for his portraits of JFK, Andy Warhol, Rudolph Nureyev, and others, painted a teen-aged Chadds Ford neighbor in a zippered motorcycle jacket, black gloves and wraparound shades, above a Brando-esque sneer. It is so western that the black jacket might have been a cowboy's duster, the tapered glasses a cocked Stetson. It would not be until 1969 that Peter Fonda's and Dennis Hopper's film *Easy Rider* hitched motorcycle outlawry to the bronco busting ethos of a lost frontier. For years *Draft Age* hung in the Chadds Ford Inn, not far from where N.C. Wyeth had died. It seemed Jamie had crafted the painting not just to remind viewers of their status and mindset in 1965, but to celebrate his grandfather's sojourns in Colorado and New Mexico, the legacy those trips produced, and his family's debt to the American West.

—*Western Art & Architecture*, 2015

CHARLES MARION RUSSELL:
THE STORYTELLER

His trademark was the death's head, a horned bison-skull positioned near his signature in nearly every painting he made. Yet he was a humorist with a mannered rusticity that made even Will Rogers laugh. He named his Lake McDonald cabin Bull Head Lodge, as that title referenced not just his signature buffalo skull but the death of the West he loved. He was a legitimate cowboy, having wrangled and herded in Montana from 1880 until 1893. Despite his artistic proficiency, he was self-taught, the sketches he made for friends during the 1880s becoming the oils he sold for tens of thousands of dollars by the 1920s. After his death in 1926, a Montana wilderness would be named for him, a statue of his likeness would be placed in the United States capitol, and his twenty-five-foot-wide painting, *Lewis and Clark Meeting Indians at Ross' Hole*, would hang in the chamber of Montana's House of Representatives. An elegy to him would be composed by the songwriter, Ian Tyson.[22] He was Charlie Russell, "the Cowboy Artist," more famous than any painter would be in the West, and a significant figure in American art. Yet despite his talent, he was a multifaceted, complicated man.

Born at St. Louis in 1864 to wealthy parents, he was a

---

22   Ian Tyson, "The Gift": *All the Good Uns*: (Vanguard, 1996).

private-school boy with every advantage. He was a cotillion prancer, a reluctant Episcopalian, and the youthful master of a 100-acre estate called Oak Hill. He was also a scamp, a truant, and a rapscallion. His passion was for making art and reading the dime novels of his day—especially those that romanticized the West. Yet he had a learning disability (dysgraphia) that made writing difficult and school a torment. According to his biographer John Taliaferro,[23] Russell's "early teachers treated him like a dunce; they whipped him and made him sit in the corner."[24] He played hooky and was the prankster extraordinaire. Despairing of his obstinacy, while recognizing his artistic gifts, his parents shipped him East to military school, behind the promise that within six months he might realize his dream of going west. He lasted ninety days in New Jersey; before his sixteenth birthday (March 19, 1889) he was en route to Montana.

Russell's adventurousness was in St. Louis citizens' genes. Near the confluence of the Missouri and Mississippi Rivers, St. Louis was the Cape Canaveral, the Kennedy Space Center of its era. Steam vessels propelled explorers 2,000 miles upriver to Fort Union on the Yellowstone, then west on the Missouri to Fort Benton. Some of those explorers were artist-adventurers: George Catlin, Charles Schreyvogel, John Mix Stanley, Karl Bodmer, and George Caleb Bingham among them.

Russell did not book steamboat passage to Montana. He took the train. By 1880, rail service ran northwest from St. Louis to Omaha, from there to Ogden, Utah, and from there to Red Rock, Montana. A stagecoach carried Russell the final 150 miles to Helena.[25] His partner in this adventure was Willis L.W. "Pike" Miller, an acquaintance of the family and

---

23   I quote various passages from Taliaferro's magnificent work in this essay. John is a diligent biographer, a half-year Montanan, a friend, and— with his wife, the painter Malou Flato—a member of the Livingston artistic community I explore in this book's epilogue.

24   John Taliaferro, *Charles M. Russell: The Life and Legend of America's Cowboy Artist* : (Norman, OK: University of Oklahoma Press, 2003), 22.

25   Ibid, 31.

a porter at a St. Louis hotel. Miller owned a small Montana sheep ranch in the Judith Basin, and it was there he and Russell were headed.

Young Charlie made an odd looking cowboy; his patrimony showed. He was "blond as a Swede,"[26] his nephew remembered; he had blue eyes, a wide face and a stocky build. A 1905 self-portrait, *When I Was A Kid,* shows Russell mounted in buckskins, cradling a rifle and leading a packhorse. The hair is long, the face is that of a young Marlon Brando.[27]

In the Judith Basin he acquired a rusticity that hid the politeness of his raising. He spoke and wrote in the argot of an unlettered cowboy—with irregularities of punctuation, spelling, and syntax that were bolstered by his dysgraphia. He was an early adherent of redneck chic. Its speech was the hip argot of the day, a coded language that let cognoscenti know he was in on the joke. Mark Twain was celebrated for it, as would be Ernest Hemingway—with his pidgin Indian slang—fifty years later. And Russell was a storyteller. Of this Will Rogers wrote, in the introduction to Charlie's 1927 book, *Trails Plowed Under,* "I always did say that you could tell a story better than any man that ever lived. If I could a got you to quit that crazy painting idea, and took up something worth while like joke telling, why I would a set you out there on the stage at the tail end of an old chuck wagon...."[28]

Russell paid his dues behind Montana chuck wagons, as a night wrangler, herder, sketcher, and raconteur. His pencil sketching of Western situations began immediately, but his use of bright tones arrived later. His shadowy graphite/watercolor, *A Dream of Burlington* (1880), shows young Russell, in fringed trousers, cowboy bandanna and hat, dozing

---

26   Ibid, 17.

27   It is the face he would paint on countless Indians, cowpunchers, outlaws, sheriffs and dudes. Except for the faces of women, particularly Native women, the expressions of his subjects were wooden.

28   Charles M. Russell, *Trails Plowed Under:* (Benediction Classics, Oxford, 2010), 2.

in a log hut while dreaming of the military school he'd abandoned. *Breaking Camp* (ca. 1885) features a bevy of cowhands aboard bucking and prancing broncs before a morning roundup. And *Caught in the Act* (1888) shows an Indian family found poaching a steer by cowhands.

Within months, Russell parted ways with Pike Miller. The two couldn't get along. Soon Charlie would meet Jake Hoover, a mountain man whose cabin and livestock Russell would tend for two years. In Hoover's Pig Eye Basin, Charlie claimed to have worked as a "meat-skinner, packer, and camp-tender."[29] But he mostly house-sat, sketching on a variety of objects. This employment of ready-at-hand materials was a habit he employed for decades. What might be his most famous sketch, *Waiting for A Chinook* (1887) was painted on the bottom of a small box.

Taliaferro notes that "with Hoover, Charlie began to lose some of his rich-kid cockiness." He "acquired the subtle etiquette of camp life ... Chief among these lessons was the law of self-effacement."[30] His friend, John Barrows, recalled that "We lived in an era of story telling ... There was one inflexible rule: the narrator could tell of his misadventures, but was not allowed to tell of his exploits. He could tell about the heroism of others, but was careful to avoid bragging."[31]

His talent at sketching bolstered his charm. A third friend noted, "At night [Russell] would come in, flop on his belly, and paint a water color in the very sight of all assembled." He was good at courting the ladies, too. "The visiting girls were titillated by his frontier dress and mannerisms, but his roughness came with references, and his impecuniousness was immediately recognized as an affectation by anyone who knew his lineage."[32] A rancher friend, returning East, asked what he might need from civilization. Russell said, "I need paints and

---

29   Taliaferro, 40.

30   Ibid, 42.

31   Ibid, 42.

32   Ibid, 43.

brushes and paper for my sketches."[33] She sent them.

From being Hoover's chore boy, and through the goodness of Horace Brewster, "boss of the Judith roundup,"[34] Charlie found his first real work as a cowhand.[35] For Brewster he moved cattle and horses across the unfenced prairie; bison, elk, wolves, and other wildlife were plentiful. Russell enjoyed hunting, but his passion was for painting. And sculpture. Even as a boy he'd carried beeswax that at idle moments he'd fashion into a horse, a bear, or Romantically a knight in armor. He was self-taught but had seen fine art in St. Louis—most notably that of Carl Wimar, the German painter whose renderings of the West included narrative canvasses such as *Attack on an Emigrant Train, The Abduction of Boone's Daughter by The Indians, The Captive Charger*, and *Indians Crossing the Upper Missouri*. Wimar painted landscapes as well as buffalo hunts. A National Portrait Gallery profile of him states, "His canvases tended to perpetuate mythic ideas about the West and the Native Americans who lived there, yet he was one of the earliest painters to devote himself exclusively to this subject." Wimar's murals decorated the St. Louis Courthouse and were owned by the better families. "I have always liked his work,"[36] Charlie said. "I wish I could paint like he did."[37]

The talent Russell possessed, outweighing that of his contemporaries, was an enormous gift for visual narrative and what pejoratively might be dubbed "illustration." Russell

---

33 Ibid, 43.

34 Ibid, 50.

35 As critic Joan Carpenter Troccoli has observed, "Cowboys have always enjoyed an elevated position in American popular culture, a status due in part to their rebellion against the strictures of polite society, but in real life they were occupants of a lowly rank in the class structure, poorly paid seasonal workers with short careers and utterly insecure prospects for retirement." Joan Carpenter Troccoli (Editor), *The Masterworks of Charles M. Russell: A Retrospective of Paintings and Sculpture:* (University of Oklahoma Press, 2009), 48.

36 Russell cared little for modern art. "Charlie dismissed Impressionism as 'smeary.'" Taliaferro, 181.

37 Ibid, 27.

told the humorist, Irvin S. Cobb, "I make pictures for regular men,"[38] and claimed in his introduction to *Trails Plowed Under*, "I am an illustrator."[39] To a New York editor in 1921 he said, "I have always liked to tell stories with the brush so have tried in a way to keep memories' trails fresh."[40] And as critic, Brian W. Dippie, writes in *The Masterworks of Charles M. Russell*, "Russell's mature paintings favored anticipation over direct action and aftermath. They have been called 'predicament pictures,' with *predicament* defined as an unresolved incident, because they involve the viewer in the story by leaving its outcome uncertain."[41]

Russsell's painting *Meat's Not Meat Till It's in the Pan* (1915), is case in point. A hunter, on a snowy precipice, views a bighorn sheep he's shot, the carcass of which balances on a narrow ledge below. The hunter scratches his head, wondering how to retrieve his kill. In a cartoon titled *Sun Shine and Shadow*, two cowboys rest in the shade of a butte, as their horses bolt. One man says, "I wonder what's the matter with them fool hosses?" The other, seeing the shadow of a grizzly behind them says, "I ain't wonderin'! From looks them horses is wise." In numerous of Russell's bucking-bronc and camp-life scenarios, the situation is unresolved. The artist teases the viewer with the question, "What will happen next?"

That irresolution is heightened by the balletic contortions of his figures—whether a horse is twisting or falling, as in *A Bad One* (1920), *The Broken Rope* (1904), and *In without Knocking* (1909) ... or cowboys are thrown, as in *The Cinch Ring* (1909), *A Tight Dally and a Loose Latigo* (1920), and *Jerked Down* (1907). Critic Joan Carpenter Troccoli writes in *Masterworks* that "Russell's goal was to capture the movements peculiar to his subjects, which by orthodox artistic standards were ungainly, if not downright bizarre."[42] Like

---

38   Troccoli, 163.

39   Russell, 5.

40   Troccoli, 163.

41   Ibid, 166.

42   Ibid, 32.

Degas' ballerinas, Russell's "men and animals [are] arranged in poses ... that are physically impossible to hold."[43] We wait for them to fall, piquing our curiosity as to when. A good narrative, Charlie sensed, *was* unresolved incident.

"Storytelling is the primary goal of all these compositions,"[44] Taliaferro notes. And many of Russell's paintings involved stories of Indians. *The Buffalo Hunt* (1900) and *Salute to the Robe Trade* (1920) are examples. The stories suggested are dramatic and accurately depicted. Russell felt a deep kinship with Native Americans, having lived with and studied them his entire career. He painted hundreds of Indian portraits, showing them hunting bison, meeting travelers in a friendly manner, and fiercely fighting other tribes. Unlike Remington or Schreyvogel, he rarely painted them attacking whites. They stand dignified in his paintings, with every detail of their dress, weapons, and camp life exquisitely drawn.

Storytelling is a form of dissociation—one creates alternative worlds to escape past or present realities—and Russell, while an avid reader, never conquered his dysgraphia. It may have proved a blessing rather than a curse. In St. Louis it mattered if one appeared unlettered, but in Montana such a disability was unremarkable (and the sign language he spoke with Indians erased it). His condition bothered his future wife, Nancy, only insofar as it compromised her ambition and his productivity.

He met Nancy "Mamie" Mann, in Cascade, Montana, in 1895. Their meeting changed his life. She was a fatherless girl of seventeen who had been taken in by the Roberts family in Cascade, a small town twenty-six miles from Great Falls, and was working as a domestic. They met over dinner at the Roberts' table. Charlie was virtually homeless and drinking heavily. But the two hit it off. She would provide the stability Russell needed, and manage his career in a way that brought him international fame. And considerable fortune.

The couple set up housekeeping in Great Falls, oddly, for its

---

43   Ibid, 32.

44   Ibid, 58

reputation as "Electric City" made it the most contemporary of Montana's towns. The Russells would remain city dwellers the rest of their days (childless, in 1916 they would adopt a son, Jack Cooper Russell). They built a modest clapboard house, beside which Charlie designed a log workspace, reminiscent of his frontier digs. There he would create some of his most important work, which included the paintings *When the Land Belonged to God* (1914), *Lewis and Clark Meeting Indians at Ross' Hole* (1912), *The Camp Cook's Troubles* (1912), *The Lewis and Clark Expedition* (1918), and the sculptures *Smoking Up* (1904) and *A Bronc Twister* (1911).

Despite his dysgraphia, he had concentration. "When fully engrossed in his work, Charlie was a man who had left the here and now ... Nancy called Charlie's absorption 'the Great Silence' ... he preferred to work on two or three paintings at one time."[45] He'd finish for the day about noon, have lunch, then hit the saloons.

He did more than drink there. He socialized in a way that Nancy found difficult to explain to the more polite echelons of Great Falls society. He was celebrated and men bought him drinks. Charlie reciprocated and regaled them with stories. Though biographers differ as to whether Russell was an alcoholic (he quit drinking after an appendectomy in 1907), his pal John Barrows said that "Charlie was nearly spoiled by his addiction to drink ... And Charlie Holmes, a cowboy Russell knew in his drinking years, described him fondly as one of the foulest-mouthed men he ever knew."[46]

Russell had sold paintings to bars since his residence in the Judith Basin, but the art he made for Great Falls saloons was different. There his outlaw pictures were popular, but the hits were his Indian erotica. Especially the four he made for the Silver Dollar saloon. These pictures, in sequence, portrayed a cowboy at work, on horseback during a rainstorm, seated on a prostitute's bed, then grimacing from the discomfort of gonorrhea. *Just a Little Sunshine, Just a Little Rain, Just a*

---

45   Ibid, 132-133.
46   Ibid, 72.

Little Pleasure, Just a Little Pain was the series' title. Though racially insensitive and in contrast to his fine-art portraits, it was nothing compared to a peepshow he created for the Silver Dollar. For a coin the viewer entered a phone-booth size cabinet and was treated to the scene of a cowpoke sexing an Indian woman, their physical union explicitly revealed. The kicker, elsewhere in the painting, was that "the cowboy's faithful dog [was] proudly displaying his own arousal."[47] The watercolor is titled, *Joy of Life*.

Russell's vulgarities might have been an effort to further mask his breeding, or they may have been the result of his divided nature. A curious affectation for him was the Métis sash he wore as a belt or cummerbund. The Métis were mixed breed Natives—part Indian, part French—and were seen as outsiders by both nations. Charlie was part St. Louis, part Montana. The sash, as much as the bison skull, became his signature.

It was a theatrical touch, and in 1920 the Russells spent the first of six winters in or near Los Angeles. Charlie had met William S. Hart, the western film star, in Great Falls; Will Rogers already was a friend. Nancy rented a house in Pasadena, the tony enclave northeast of Los Angeles. Russell, taken by the movies' incomparable talent for relating pictorial narratives, spent considerable time on Hollywood sets. Hart admired the costumes in his paintings, and the director John Ford "freely admitted to borrowing from compositions by Russell (and Remington, too) throughout his career."[48] Movies held Charlie in high esteem."

With barbed wire, homesteading, and tourist incursion, Charlie's wild West had largely disappeared. But through Hollywood storytelling, a simulacrum thrived. Movies rode the wave of a cowboy renaissance that had begun with Theodore Roosevelt's odes to the strenuous life, published during the 1890s, and had much to do with a jingoistic reaction to the influx of southeastern European immigrants that was

---

47   Ibid, 124-125.
48   Ibid, 224.

crowding Eastern cities. As Troccoli writes, "Russell's idyllic realm exists in opposition to modern urban civilization. To Russell, the latter was the domain of the artificial, the hypocritical, the constrained, and every other component of the impersonal, profit-driven march of progress ... In focusing his art on nature, Russell gave voice to contemporary Americans' deep-seated misgivings about the consequences of urbanization and industrial development, which exploded in the decades after Russell's birth. His anxiety was hardly unique in his day. In the United States around 1900, it was not uncommon to reject modern technology and the city or to celebrate Indians as the first and only 'real' Americans. What made Russell unusual was his firsthand knowledge of those displaced by progress and his outspoken defense of them."[49]

Remington and Owen Wister (who published his novel *The Virginian* in 1902) were reactionaries and racists. Taliaferro writes that, during the 1890s and early 20th century, the new wave of immigrants were seen by their ilk as "'depraved dregs'" and "'alien breeds.'" And "Looking for a new hero, preferably a throwback, the nation settled on the cowboy ... The frontier was where America must turn to cure its effeteness and unify as a race." Roosevelt's thesis was that "If social Darwinism called for the survival of the fittest and if the West was the crucible of the New World, then the cowboy—the Anglo-Saxon cowboy—was the element that could not be ground down or amalgamated."[50]

Wister took it farther. In a piece for *Harper's Weekly*, titled "The Evolution of the Cow-Puncher," he asserted that "'the Anglo-Saxon bloodline is a master race ... [To] survive in the clean cattle country requires a spirit of adventure, courage, and self-sufficiency; you will not find many Poles or Huns or Russian Jews in the district.'"[51]

Hollywood, by inference or accident, reflected this notion. Charlie spent many days on movie sets, and while decidedly

---

49   Troccoli, 11.
50   Taliaferro, 97.
51   Ibid, 98.

not racist, he abhorred the civilized East[52] and gloried in films' resurrection of the unspoiled West. (Troccoli notes that, "The overall trajectory of Russell's work represents a retreat from a dynamic present portending a mechanized future to a primeval, sunset-gilded paradise of wild creatures and unspoiled landscapes.[53]) He wrote a friend that "to an old romance loving boy like me [movie making was] the best thing Iv seen in Calif. At least they were live men with living horses under them." And "I take back aney thing I ever said with my hat in my hand about moove [movie] cow boys. Thair good riders and hard to scare."[54]

Meanwhile Nancy was pressuring Russell to produce art. His fees had escalated—he would receive "$30,000 for the frieze, *History of the West*, painted for the oilman, Edward Doheny. But there was a cost to Russell. One friend said, "Nancy treated [Charlie] like a child ... she was forever correcting him or chiding him in front of others."[55] She had eyes for Los Angeles society, and though Charlie's rusticity was endearing to others, it troubled her. His professional reputation was solid, however. As Taliaferro writes, "After the death of Frederic Remington in 1909, Russell became America's leading western artist."[56] Of this Hollywood was aware.

Soon the Russells were hobnobbing with its biggest stars—Mary Pickford, Douglas Fairbanks, Charlie Chaplin, and the director, D.W. Griffith (*Birth of a Nation*). "We are both picture makers," Russell told Fairbanks.[57] There was talk of

---

52   He wrote, "Civilization is nature's worst enemy. All wild things vanish when she comes. Where great forests once lived, nothing now stands but burned stumps—a black shroud of death. The iron heel of civilization has stamped out nations of men, but it has never been able to wipe out pictures...." Troccoli, 100. And, "The Native peoples of the northern plains were Russell's ideal ... Russell summed up Indians' enviable concord with nature: 'their God was the sun / their Church was all out doors / their only book was nature / and they knew all its pages.'" Troccoli, 11.

53   Ibid, 10.

54   Taliaferro, 223.

55   Ibid, 200.

56   Ibid, 8.

57   Ibid, 229.

Charlie directing a film; nothing came of it.

Fame—though it threatened his productivity—did not diminish Charlie's love of wilderness. The Russells built a house in Pasadena, but spent summers at Bull Head Lodge, their Lake McDonald retreat in what would become Glacier National Park. There friends visited, and Nancy pressured Charlie to paint, even on vacation. A studio was adjacent to the cabin, but both structures became crowded with guests, distracting Russell from work. Nancy would admit later to having cracked the whip too hard on her husband: "I know now that I ruined the last years of Charlie's life," she said. "We had plenty, but I always wanted more and drove him to make more, keeping him from idling with the friends he enjoyed ... Life for me is torture and I made Charlie's life a torture."[58]

But Russell told a reporter in 1919, "I will say my wife has been an inspiration to me in my work. Without her I would probably have never attempted to soar or reach any height ... I still love and long for the old West, and everything that goes with it. But I would sacrifice it all for Mrs. Russell."[59]

Nancy's loyalty inspired him. It is estimated that in his lifetime Russell produced some 4,000 paintings, sketches, and sculptures.[60] And Nancy urged him to take his storytelling gifts to paper. In 1921, he published the collection, *Rawhide Rawlins Stories*, which he followed up with *More Rawhides*, and posthumously, *Trails Plowed Under*. While these illustrated pieces were pithy, they did not have the impact of his paintings, and it was well he saw them as corollaries to his principal work.

Over the years Charlie struggled with various maladies: sciatica, a goiter, a hernia, emphysema, and eventually heart disease. At the Mayo Clinic, to which he was admitted in 1926 for thyroid surgery, a physician predicted he had two years to live. Russell told a friend, "The old pump ain't working ... I am weak as a cat ... I have thrown my last leg over a

---

58   Ibid, 270.
59   Ibid, 118.
60   Ibid, 8.

saddle, the old pump is about to quit."[61] It did so on October 24, 1926, at his house in Great Falls. He had complained to Nancy of shortness of breath, and when his physician arrived, "he found Charlie sitting on the commode in the small bathroom at the top of the stairs. A froth of blood was on Charlie's lips, and as [his doctor] reached the landing, Charlie lunged forward into his arms."[62] The artist was dead at sixty-two.

Predictable tributes arrived, from Montana's governor, from William S. Hart, Will Rogers, and others. George Bird Grinnell wrote to Nancy, "I can think of no man who has filled so large a niche as he in the world of art, and one equally large in the field of history."[63]

On the day of his burial, two black horses drew a hearse through the streets of Great Falls toward Highland Cemetery. A riderless mount "that wore Charlie's saddle and bridle" was led behind. "As an added flourish, Charlie's Colt six-guns and holsters were strapped behind the cantle ... All schools, courtrooms, and city offices had closed for the afternoon, and thousands of solemn faces—children, old-timers, cowboys, Indians, merchants, smelter workers—lined the curbs."[64] A boulder is his headstone, with a plate that reads "C.M. Russell," in script, and his bull-head bison skull as a marker.

2020

Author and publisher gratefully acknowledge permission to reprint excerpts from John Taliaferro's Charles M. Russell: The Life and Legend of America's Cowboy Artist, *provided by University of Oklahoma Press, publisher of the paperback edition, copyright © 1996 by John Taliaferro.*

61   Ibid, 260.

62   Ibid, 260.

63   Ibid, 263.

64   Ibid, 264.

ISABEL F. RANDALL:
A LADY'S RANCH LIFE

Take the "lady" in Isabel F. Randall's 1887 memoir, *A Lady's Ranch Life in Montana* (University of Oklahoma Press, $19.95) seriously, for she does. In fact the drama of this little book—strikingly edited and introduced in a new edition by Richard L. Saunders—lies in young Isabel's relinquishment of her class-bound, English ways for democratization in the new world, or at least the grudging acceptance of classlessness in the name of survival.

Immigrating in 1884 to the Gallatin Valley, Randall at age twenty-four, is very much British gentry and the unlikeliest of ranch women. She detrains at Moreland (now Manhattan) with her husband Jem and two servants, whom she'll soon dispatch for their slovenliness. She's there, as a new bride, to raise horses, to graze livestock on the tax-free range, and to enjoy the sort of post-colonial high jinks for which upper-crust Britishers remain suckers. In the process, she gains a love for Montana, if not all its citizens, and learns self-reliance through danger, brutal ranch work and a kind of desperate housewifery.

A proto-feminist, Randall's delightful book consists of diary-like letters to her English kinfolk, and emulates the earlier and more successful "A Lady's Life in the Rocky Mountains," by Isabella Bird. But Randall's tongue is sharper, criticizing her neighbors for both their "filth" and class presumptions—"My first caller was the lady (they are all *ladies* out here) who supplies us with butter"—and marvels at those whom she considers functionaries wishing to be received as equals. She dubs them "natives." Such haughtiness is tempered by the need for interdependence on the frontier, and through hard experience, the young Isabel grows in independence—"I would not exchange my happy, free, busy healthy life out here, for the weariness and ennui that makes so many girls at home miserable"—and she opens her heart to the beauty of her surroundings. She writes captivatingly of Bozeman's toddlerhood, of sub-zero nights inside her cabin, frozen bridles, a dance at Three Forks, lush summer mornings, and long equestrian shooting trips. Saunders' introduction adds considerable insight to Randall's dilemma as an outsider, and reports that neighbors were not pleased at the publication of her book. She decamped permanently for England in 1890. Lampooning her retreat, one disgruntled neighbor (the "Rustic Artiste") versified in a Bozeman paper:

Now we see her at last as she enters the train
On the back of her ulster, a large grease stain
We will leave it the rest of the story to tell
While the "natives" extend her a long farewell.

—*Big Sky Journal*, 2005

TWENTIETH

THE URUGUAYAN COWBOY

He was the scion of distinguished European artists, yet a roughneck who proved himself as a cowboy on Texas cattle drives at the turn of the last century. As a young man he enrolled at the Art Students League of New York, apprenticing to the Beaux Arts painter, William Merritt Chase, yet later enjoyed a profitable career as a commercial illustrator. He was a Spanish-American from Uruguay who traveled the California coast sketching Roman Catholic missions, yet was an accomplished horseman who spent years in Arizona photographing, painting, and living with the Hopis. He was a historian of the American Southwest, yet a man who wrote children's books and scribbled cartoons his entire life. He was a sculptor of Remington-like bronzes and a travertine cenotaph honoring Carmel's Father, Junipero Serra. Yet he was a playful map maker whose images of national parks sold widely during the 1930s, and whose life would be celebrated in a song written by Mike Beck and Ian Tyson. His poster of cowboy life would adorn the cover of *Sweetheart of the Rodeo*, the Byrds' 1968 album of country-western ballads. He was Joseph Jacinto "Jo" Mora, widely known as a renaissance man of the West.

"To him, art was an entirely natural occupation," the

author Nigel Holmes has written, "whether it was drawing separated line work for a map, or painting a classical portrait in oils, or modeling a cowboy and his horse for a bronze statue."

Mora was born in Montevideo, Uruguay, in 1876, but his family had immigrated to America by 1880. His paternal grandfather was a sculptor in Catalonia and his father, Domingo Mora, would create architectural adornments for buildings as noteworthy as the Metropolitan Opera in New York City. Jo's older brother, F. Luis Mora, was a European-style, post-Impressionist painter who in 1904 would be elected as the first Hispanic member of the National Academy of Design. His portrait of Warren G. Harding hangs in the White House. But Jo was of a different stripe. By his early twenties, he was a successful cartoonist for *The Boston Herald*, and an illustrator of children's books. Unexpectedly he quit that life In 1903, and decamped for California.

Jo had heard his father's tales of Uruguayan gauchos growing up, and had seen Buffalo Bill's Wild West Show in New York City. Horace Greeley's advice to "Go West, young man," was in the air, and America's dime novels and magazines echoed that mandate. Mora's father held a keen interest in Native Americans; Jo had first met them in Mexico, where the Moras had fled to escape prejudice before and during the Spanish-American war. In that period, Jo worked as a cowhand driving cattle through Texas and Mexico. Frederic Remington saw Jo's work and told him, "Just keep doin' what you're doin', Son, you're doin' just fine." But by 1904, fascinated by the Hopi Indians' religious rituals and ways, Jo set out to join them. He would spend three years in their remote, desert outpost, sketching their colorful Kachina costumes and photographing their snake, buffalo, and other dances.

Stephen Mitchell, in his short biography of Jo, calls these years, from 1904-1906, "the most creative in Mora's professional career." The portable Kodak camera was new, and Jo took full advantage of its mobility. The photographs he took were mesmerizing. A retrospective of them appeared at the Smithsonian Institution in 1979. As Tyrone H. Stewart wrote in that exhibit's catalogue, his photographs and paintings "should eventually be recognized as one of the greatest visual contributions a non-Indian has produced on the Hopi culture." Mora was accepted by the Hopis so completely that he was welcomed into the tribe, undergoing an initiation ceremony that included flogging. "I received the Tunwap Flogging on my bare arms, thighs, and back," he wrote in his journal, "having first been acquainted with many tribal rituals and traditions." He was given the Hopi name, "Nalje."

He retreated to California's northern coast, where he married, in 1907. He set up a studio at Mountain View and, after Domingo's death in 1911, became riveted by sculpture—as if wishing to extend his father's and grandfather's legacy. "Domingo was as important a teacher to Jo as anyone else," says Peter Hiller, curator of the Jo Mora Trust Collection in Carmel and author of the biography, *The Life and Time of 'Jo Mora—Iconic Artist of the American West.* "Domingo was a classically trained sculptor." Jo would sculpt a number of cowboy-themed bronzes, as well as the bas-relief, Bret Harte Memorial at the Bohemian Club in San Francisco, the Miguel Cervantes Memorial, other relief panels and vast, multi-figured dioramas, such as "The Discovery of the San Francisco Bay by Portola," for the 1939-40 Golden Gate International Exposition. With 64 sculptures of humans and over 200 of animals, it was said to have been best-of-show at the event. He made a comparable diorama for the Will Rogers Memorial, in Claremore, Oklahoma. But a strikingly impressive piece was made in Carmel, at the Mission San Carlos Borromeo. It is the Father Junipero Serra Cenotaph. "He considered this his most important work," Hiller says.

Fashioned from bronze, travertine, and wood, it shows three priests praying over the body of Father Serra, which lies on a marble altar—materially suggestive of the cliffs and coastal bluffs nearby. The arrangement is classical, but the mood is California Spanish. In a photograph taken at the cenotaph's completion, Mora poses in a short jacket, wide sash, and snug trousers, like a Spanish grandee.

The cenotaph is also indicative of what may have been Mora's considerable interest in spirituality—as suggested by his work with the Hopis, and by his early travels along California's Mission Trail from Santa Ines to Encinada, Mexico. Hiller says that, "Primarily he saw the missions as historic buildings; he was more intrigued by the history of them than by religion." In his journals, Jo mentioned their striking appearance. On June 26, 1903, he wrote of San Juan Capistrano, "I wandered around and walked up to Mission. A beautiful old spot, with it's refreshing garden, and picturesque arches ...The sun had set, the colors had slowly faded out of things, and as I stood there in the twilight by the ruins of the once imposing structures ... I could not help but imagining myself back in the old mission days."

Mora's love of history was expressed not only in the two books he wrote about cowboy life, *Trail Dust and Saddle Leather* and *Californios*, but in the extraordinary poster-like maps he created during the Depression. They were illustrative, compositionally daring, and resembled Egyptian friezes in their pictorial format. These "cartes" portrayed subjects such as the evolution of the American Indian, scenes of life around Carmel-by-the-Sea, in Yellowstone Park, Yosemite, The Grand Canyon, the Monterey Peninsula, and other locations. The most famous poster, drawn in 1933, was titled "The American Cowboy (Salinas Rodeo)." It combined detailed illustrations of rodeo life and of cowboy history, from the Spanish-to-20th-century eras.

Mora considered himself very much an artist but also a horseman or "vaquero." He'd learned horsemanship on the vast, Donohue ranch near Solvang, California, and his knowledge of cattle drives, branding and roping, saddles and bits, and the minutiae of cowboy life—which he demonstrated in *Trail Dust* and *Californios* —is unparalleled. As Beck and

Tyson wrote in their song: *Jo Mora told the story / of the colors and the glory / In* The Californios *he rode / through the dapple green and gold … In old California.*"

He's recognized for his love of that state. The Monterey Museum of Art, which owns the largest collection of Mora's pieces, in 1998 mounted a retrospective of his work, and this past summer The Byrds performed in their *Sweetheart of the Rodeo* fiftieth anniversary tour, celebrating the historical importance of that album's release. Jo's poster was prominently displayed and seemed to speak both of his affection for the American West and of his dedication to popular, less-stylized arts. As Mora wrote in his preface to *Trail Dust*, "In presenting this book to the public, I assure you I had no high ambitions of the belles-lettres brand as my incentive." He would die on October 10, 1947, but in *Trail Dust*'s preface he'd added that, "I still have a long hitching rail under the pines within fifty feet of our garage entrance," and "I pray that good old Gabe when he takes down his saxophone, or whatever it is he uses these days, to give me the clarion call for that last inspection [he] will let me ease into the saddle with my boots on and jog to that rendezvous."

—*Western Art & Architecture*, 2019

BREAKING THE PRAIRIE:
GRANT WOOD AS UNEASY TILLER

The pitchfork is what one notices first, its tines sharp and unforgiving, its handle rigid in the farmer's grip. His eyes stare coolly, and his mouth is set in moral rectitude—or is it half-concealed levity? The woman by his side (his wife, his daughter?) looks askance as if to say, "Are the tines of this fork for skewering sinners or for making hay?" Behind them a Gothic window in a board-and-batten farmhouse overlooks the scene disapprovingly. Or does it endorse what in a certain light might be seen as a tableau of erotic frankness? We do not know. As with much of Grant Wood's painting, the effect is ambiguous.

He discovered the Iowa house portrayed in *American Gothic* 117 miles from Cedar Rapids, a city where he lived and worked for much of his life. He sketched it first on an envelope, then painted it on composition board. That oil won the Art Institute of Chicago's bronze medal for painting in 1930, and brought Wood fame, linking him to a corn-fed, regionalist tradition of Midwestern art that included works by Thomas Hart Benton and John Steuart Curry. The cornfed label was misapplied, a recent exhibit of his work at New York's Whitney Museum has suggested. For Wood was every bit the modernist. As Barbara Haskell wrote for the exhibit's catalogue, "Like Hopper, Wood portrayed the solitude and alienation of contemporary experience. By fusing meticulously observed reality with imagined memories of childhood, he crafted unsettling images of estrangement and apprehension that pictorially manifest the disquiet of modern life."

Wood's childhood had been troubled. Born on an Anamosa, Iowa farm in 1891, he was a chubby, unathletic boy whom his Quaker father, Maryville, disparaged for his dreaminess. Maryville died when Grant was ten, and his mother, Hattie, uprooted the family from its rural home to the relative urbanity of Cedar Rapids. Wood may have seen that move as an attempt by his mother to diminish his father's legacy. The effort failed. As Grant later noted, "To me, he was the most dignified and majestic of persons ... There was a certain mystery and loneliness about [him] that I sensed even as a child—a strange quality of detachment which no one would ever be able to understand."

As if in defense of his father's agrarianism, Wood later would compose a career-changing essay titled "Revolt Against the City." It railed against the cosmopolitan values of New York and Paris (where he had studied during the 1920s), and championed rural ones. "One of the most significant things in the art world today," he wrote, "is the increasing importance of real American art. I mean an art which really springs from American soil." The emphasis upon "real" versus "fake" in his communications has contemporary resonance. And, as Haskell observed, "The social and political climate in which Wood's art flourished bears certain striking similarities to America today, as national identity and the tension between urban and rural areas reemerge as polarizing issues in a country facing the consequences of globalization and the technological revolution. Yet ... its enduring power lies in its mesmerizing psychological dimension."

Wood believed art to be personal, and that good painters depicted on canvas their crucial life struggles. It was "the depth and intensity of an artist's experience that are the first importance," he wrote. Great art starts "by looking inside ourselves, selecting our most genuine emotions." He felt that "we're conditioned in the first twelve years of our lives ... everything we experience later is tied up with those twelve years."

Two paintings implying the conflict between his father's affection for the farm and his mother's for the city are *Spring Turning* (1936) and *Daughters of the American Revolution* (1932). Wood was familiar with Freudian psychology and, in the former canvas, Iowa's fields are inflated and rendered as part of the male anatomy. Conversely, in *Victorian Survival (1931)* and in *Daughters of Revolution*, women are portrayed as austere townsfolk, physically dry and without sensuality—though his portrait of his mother, *Woman with Plants* (1929), plays her remoteness as maternally nurturing.

Wood reputedly was homosexual; the Whitney catalogue makes much of his painterly allusions to gay desire. His oil, *Arthur Comes of Age* (1930), shows a plaintive young man posed before a distant body of water beside which nude boys romp. At the Iowa State Fair that work won a first in portraiture and a grand prize in painting—significant awards. Allusions to same-sex attraction would be hinted at in Wood's *Appraisal* (1931), where a farm woman holding a Plymouth Rock chicken gazes flirtatiously at a wealthier, more urbane female customer. But a more controversial work would be *Sultry Evening (1931)*, a painting and lithograph of a farmer rendered nude, while bathing from a horse trough. That lithograph was deemed pornographic by the U.S. Postal Service, which refused to mail it to customers. This action solidified Wood's antipathy to Victorianism, and puzzled him. "In my boyhood," he said, "no farms had tile and chromium bathrooms. After a long day in the dust of the fields, after the chores were done, we used to go down to the horse tank with a pail ... we would dip up pails full and drench ourselves." His subsequent allusions to same-sex attraction were not dampened.

Woods' best work speaks less to gay themes than to a celebration of agrarian life—and to a darkness at the heart of the American experience. After moving from Cedar Rapids to teach at the University of Iowa, in Iowa City, he drank heavily (a saloon keeper remembered Wood trading sketches for whiskey—up to two bottles a day), fought to keep academic employment, and would die at age fifty of pancreatic cancer. What he accomplished in various mediums (sculpture, painting, ceramics, stained glass, wrought iron, interior design) was not only the imagery of his best-known paintings, *American Gothic* and *The Midnight Ride of Paul Revere* (1931), but a unique take on the tortured side of American consciousness. Wood *was* tortured. As a populist he was denigrated for his middle-American values (critics during the 1930s considered them proto-fascist). And like the Midwestern writers, Sinclair Lewis and Hamlin Garland, he was vilified for his recognition of the hypocrisy of small town life, and for being unafraid to skewer it.

Wood's view of that life's white-picket-fenced and corn-fed simplicity, undergirded by repressiveness, is David Lynchian in tone. As with that filmmaker's best work—*Blue Velvet* or *Twin Peaks*—a malignancy lurks beneath Wood's perfect flower beds and lawns. A painting like *Spring in Town* (1941) is case in point. In its foreground, a shirtless man spades a garden as a woman hangs a quilt and a child bends a limb of a flowering dogwood. The house and church behind it are perfect, but the eye is drawn to the soil of the man's garden. In its turning, a darkness is unveiled, a gloom that clouds the pristine day.

Wood is not thought of as a Western painter, yet his canvasses express prairie wistfulness and a proclivity for dreaminess that overlie a thinly veiled melancholy. Emily Braun wrote in her Whitney essay, "Cryptic Corn: Magic Realism and the Art of Grant Wood," that his intentions may have been more surrealistic than precise: "Magic Realism, as its oxymoronic name suggests, evinces instability—not order or normalcy. Despite the style's polished surfaces and surfeit of detail, it signals its own lack of transparency, an ironic distance, and controlled ambiguity." Braun compares Wood's work to that of Henry Rousseau, and to Giorgio de Chirico's Italian metaphysical painting. She mentions the "snake plant, which appears in Wood's *Woman with Plants,*" as having derived perhaps from Giorgio Morandi's 1917 painting "of a weirdly obdurate *Cactus* ... did he know it was commonly referred to as 'mother-in-law's tongue?'" It again is seen, "creepily on the porch of *American Gothic.*"

That painting is the work by which Wood's legacy will be judged. As Peter Schjeldahl observed in his *New Yorker* review of the Whitney show, "*American Gothic* is, by a very wide margin, his most effective picture—though not his best, for which I nominate *Dinner for Threshers* (1934), a long, low, cutaway view of a farmhouse at harvest time....."

In *Threshers,* Wood retreats to his pre-adolescent fixations: the male figures are wraithlike, the women automatons. The painter, Barbara Haskell wrote, appears here and elsewhere to be "molding the eternal world into a portrait of his inner self [which] involved tapping into what Hopper called the 'intense, formless, inconsistent souvenirs of early youth.'"

At the end of his life, Wood—harried for his midland regionalism, dismissed by New York critics as irrelevant, vilified for what were seen as his reactionary aesthetics, weary from his battles in academia, and seriously ill—returned to his depictions of farm versus town. In 1941, *Spring in the Country* and *Spring in Town* existed only as drawings, but Wood hurriedly transformed them to the multi-colored oils that would be his last major works. Each was a testament to his parents' different lifestyles. From his hospital bed Wood pledged the greater loyalty to Maryville's, promising his sister that "In the year ahead, I'm going to do the best work of my life. My first painting will be a portrait of our father."

A month before Wood's death, Thomas Hart Benton visited him in the hospital and reported that "when he got well he was going to change his name, go where nobody knew him, and start all over again with a new style of painting." One can only speculate what that style might have been. In February, 1941, Wood died, his body traveling home—first to David Turner's mortuary in Cedar Rapids, behind which the artist had lived for 10 years with his mother, and then to Anamosa, where he lies next to Hattie in the family plot.

—*Western Art & Architecture*, 2019

GHOST SIGNS OF MONTANA

In 1940's Butte, a cabbie drops his fare before the Finlen Hotel's Park Street entrance, looks up and spots a four-story-tall sign in red, white, and green, hawking Wrigley's Spearmint gum. The image is of its package tilted rakishly, its spear angled skyward. The green background is an aqua sea, the white of the cellophane a tropical beach. His mouth begins to water. "The taste that lasts," the advertisement reads: "Buy it by the box." Beneath the green, painted over but visible, is an older ad—a ghost sign—for Elgin Watches. "It's time for ... " Contradictory emotions wash over him. Time for work, or time for gum? There's something about how that pack and its spear are angled. Maybe he'll snag a stick and chat up that girl at the hotel's candy stand.

Wall signs are among the oldest advertising media, and subliminal messages their fiercest tricks. And no Montana city has more signs than Butte—close to 100. Most employ letters without imagery, but the best—Bull Durham's in Walkerville, and Wrigley's uptown—employ both. For nothing creates dream space more quickly than a picture, and nothing sells like erotica. Coca-Cola's bottles are without exception angled provocatively, and cigar ads ... well. Ghost signs—ones that have faded, or that intrude upon others—have shown a new effectiveness, and cities such as Butte, Billings, and Missoula are working to preserve them. The organization, Mainstreet Uptown Butte, on their web page, calls ghost signs "an important part of our heritage ... if these signs can be preserved or restored, they should be." The National Trust for Historic Preservation has suggestions for their maintenance, and Butte has brought The Walldogs—"a national network of muralists and sign restoration specialists"—to the city for help in restoration. Technically such images are defined as "faded to the point of illegibility," Wm. Stage writes in *Ghost Signs: Brick Wall Signs in America*. They "become highlighted under certain conditions, such as the rosy glow of sunrise or sunset, or in the first minutes of rain." They are "the commercial archaeologists *pièce de resistance.*"

The also are good for tourism. Mainstreet Butte advises the visitor to allow "an hour or so of your time to walk or drive to see them and receive a message that was placed there more than a century ago." Former Butte preservation officer, Jim Jarvis, half-jokingly likens ghost signs to paintings of Renaissance masters. "Imagine some guy on a scaffold, painting one right on the side of a building, clinging there for days. Like Michelangelo in the Sistine Chapel." And not all signs are outside. "Often what would happen was that they would use the existing exterior wall of one building as the new interior wall of a new building. So if there were a ghost sign on that old exterior, it would end up on the interior of the new building. In the Acoma, one of those tricked out, loft apartments has this incredible ghost sign inside."

Butte has done what it can to retain its ghost signs, but they are protected "about as much as the buildings themselves are," Jarvis says. "Which is, again, that you are required to go through a review process. Some of the signs have faded to the point where they are truly illegible. There's nothing to see, it's just a weird smear of color. We encourage property owners to retain or leave alone the ones that are legible. And the ones that have truly faded to nothingness could be removed or painted over."

These are irredeemable spooky, their creators' identities lost to time. Stage compares them to painters "of the Ice Age ... Both worked at inscribing legends. The cave painters depicted highlights of the hunt, while wall dogs depicted symbols of commerce on the surfaces of urban monoliths."

The first ghost sign I recall being impressed by was the Rex Flour sign beside the Pony Bar in Pony, Montana. In the summer of 1972, Pony *was* a ghost town, with a handful of residents. One was the Pony Bar's owner, a woman named Bert Welch who, that August afternoon, startled me with her Packard's horn as I studied the sign's legend: "Use Rex Flour, Rex is King." The barmaid pointed at my VW and said, despite the fact that Pony was deserted, "You're in her place."

Signs such as Rex Flour and those in Butte survive because of their placement on walls—"northern exposure is best," Jarvis says—and because of the 19th and 20th centuries' use of lead paint. "Use at least one-third pure white lead," advised *Signs of the Times* magazine in 1906. This, mixed with linseed oil, turpentine, and dry pigments, then painted on smooth red brick, did the trick. Its toxicity poisoned walldogs, however, Many drank "to cut the lead." Their lives were nomadic. "They were a rugged lot," Stage writes, "in the tradition of cowboys, mariners, and Arctic explorers ... they embodied an eclectic mix of skills often associated with the draftsman, the chemist, the artist and even the acrobat."

A walldog who painted the Rex sign in Pony might have ridden down from Butte or traveled from as far east as St. Louis. Norman Rockwell was a walldog; he and other signers considered themselves artists. A veteran painter told Stage, "Some of them would go out West on a six-month circuit, and when they came to a town they would first paint the signs on the general store, the saloon and anything else." Half the week was dedicated to signs, the other half to "scenics—the little brooks, the mountains, commissioned portraits, too."

Rex Flour's sign might have made a bar patron feel like a

king, but most illustrated ads at the turn of the twentieth century were aimed at women. Pears soap may have had the first, but Freudian psychology was bursting its buttons (Sigmund's nephew was a PR man) and sultry pictorials such as that created for Woodbury soap ("A skin you love to touch") were selling with sex. Those that weren't used subliminal tricks to snare the subconscious. Beer bottles were tilted suggestively, cigars sported names like Cremo, and legends—such as that for Wilson liquor—read, "High Ball, That's All."

But back to Butte's Wrigley sign, at 83 East Park. Spearmint was launched in 1893 (Juicy Fruit slightly earlier), so the sign might have been painted as early as then. It's style and technique suggest later—*trompe l'oeil* was not prevalent in the 19th century—and the eroticism of its tilted package suggest 20th century psychology. Mainstreet Butte guesses its construction was between 1893 and 1913. I've always been fascinated by it, and only recently connected that fascination with two other signs—in Livingston.

On a sunny day last fall, I walked past ghost signs on the wall of a defunct cigar factory at 216 South 2nd Street, and paused. The ghosts—one for the Livingston Coal and Lumber Company the other for a cigar brand ("Every Puff a Pleasure") created a stereoscopic effect. The cigar being smoked was roundly phallic, the words coal and lumber suggesting heat and wood. I became aroused. I desired neither coal nor lumber, and I detested cigars. But I found myself remembering a girl I'd known forty summers previous who had lived in an apartment next door, at number 214. She'd had the first mid-body tattoo I'd seen, of a tiger, and she'd chewed gum. I was flooded with the memory of her kisses, of the sweet taste of Spearmint or Juicy Fruit—I couldn't recall which. So I hurried to TJ's Gas N Convenience and bought a pack of each.

I wasn't sold, but I was hooked.

—*Big Sky Journal*, 2017

GENE AUTRY: PUBLIC COWBOY NO. 1

There was no *noir* in Gene Autry's film or television persona. Neither Paladin nor Lash La Rue, he played a goody-two-shoes who, as Johnny Cash recalls in Holly George-Warren's meticulously researched biography of Autry, *Public Cowboy No. 1* (Oxford University Press, $28), seemed "a handsome man on a fine stallion, riding the bad trails of this land, righting wrongs, turning good for bad, smiling through with the assurance that justice will prevail."

His off-screen character was more complex, as George-Warren tells us. Autry was the hillbilly singer who, in the 1930s (much as Elvis would in the '50s) combined blues with ballads, and parlayed a successful singing career into a legendary one in films. He also was a philandering alcoholic whom friends had "to wire to the saddle to keep him aloft," but who, by his death in 1998, as owner of the California Angels, "was the only entertainer-turned-businessman listed in the *Forbes* 400."

Born in 1907 to second-generation, Texan parents, Autry "embraced the tools of the 20th century," George-Warren writes, becoming first a radio, then a recording star—one whose tenor would inspire vocalists as varied as Solomon Burke, Ringo Starr, and Aaron Neville. Beneath his mile-wide smile and snowy Stetson, he was a rascal, driven to accumulate both wealth and lovers, who could alternate a naughty blues like "High Steppin' Mama" with the tear jerker, "Silver Haired Daddy of Mine," and later the children's ballad, "Rudolph the Red-nosed Reindeer," one of the best selling Christmas songs ever. Yet he was a serious country-western singer who influenced the development of rock. James Taylor recalled in 2006, George-Warren notes, "that the inspiration behind his first hit, 'Sweet Baby James,' was to write a cowboy lullaby like the ones he'd heard Gene Autry sing in movies when he was a boy."

Those lullabies were soporifics to baby boomers jangled by the discordances of Hopalong Cassidy's and the Lone Ranger's characters, and indeed cold war uncertainties. Autry used his "softer look," a bit like Harry Truman's, to woo children as well as women. He was immensely popular. By career's end he'd recorded over 640 songs, but none of his ninety-three films, George-Warren reminds, "ever rose to the budgetary or artistic levels of a John Ford Western."

The details in her 406-page biography of Autry are staggering in depth ... and appropriately so, as Autry led an eventful life. She's excellent on the pop culture facets of his career. (Kris Kristofferson, Waylon Jennings, Willie Nelson and Cash were so bowled over by Autry's 1994 appearance at a Highwaymen recording date that they "turned into little kids" and warbled "Back in the Saddle Again.") But at times the sheer volume of whom Autry spoke to, and when, overshadows the personal. At book's end we're not certain we grasp the ambiguities of his character. Autry was a driven, complex artist who did much to shape our view of the world. George-Warren's book is terrifically well-researched, but her lack of a persuasive take on his troubled side disappoints.

—*Big Sky Journal*, 2008

NEW ATLAS SALOON

In my youth, I was restless enough to have spent four years on the road searching for the Great American Bar. I often visited thirty a day, learning in my travels that the mountain West—specifically Montana—held more saloons of that description than any other region.

This was my drill: I studied the exterior of a strange bar, its facade and structural demeanor, to decide whether I might find comfort there, or risk a step inside. I examined the bar's architecture and its poise within its geographical setting, and the whole was a place mat properly or improperly laid. One required form to frame or isolate chaos. A Great Bar and its architecture were not unlike that fine crystal sphere, a paperweight, if you will, or a child's toy in crib, that housed make-believe snowstorms. Snowstorms were the chaos; you wanted storms. But a glass ball was needed to contain them. And you wanted an interior adequately fixed to keep chaos in check. Front and back bars, antique furniture, dusty paintings and tattered pool tables were the primary artifacts of an interior landscape. They were like tiny log cabins, snow-covered sleighs and reindeer. You shook your glass ball as hard as the mood dictated. Or another something, faceless and edgy, shook it for you.

In late middle-age, I thought I was inured to the comfort

of saloons. But not long ago, on a snowy December evening, I stopped at the New Atlas in Columbus, Montana. It was a dark season of my life, heavy with loss and regret. As I approached the mahogany bar, I saw lights hanging from antlers of mounted deer and along the carved entablature of the mirrored back bar. A string band was completing its set. I glanced toward a figure beside me, but did not speak. The band finished, and its leader stepped between us. He called for a drink, nodded to each of us and began "Silent Night," a capella. We joined him without hesitation or irony, and sang heartily— three disheveled angels in a forgotten town on a frigid night, singing just to stay alive. At carol's end we embraced, shared a round, then hiked toward the blizzard, Christmas in our hearts.

ATLAS AXIS

the New Atlas Bar
Columbus, Montana

In the days before
interstate cappuccino
and llama ranch incursion
you'd stop here
before winding up
into westering hills
through a scrim of early snow.
It was your own
delirium tremens in waltz time.
Your conversation
was not so much
with the two-headed patrons
or the barkeep waxing at the tap
but with yourself
as you sat in buffalo coat
your cornucopia
of melancholy on the bar.

If you were sanguine
you'd last the night
and the old-timers
would put you on the clock—
if they suspected
a hidden agenda
you'd disappear into thinner air.
Times have changed now
but not the register—
the New Atlas
holding up the hills
with droll mahogany shoulders.[65]

—Ken McCullough

Reflections West
Yellowstone Public Radio, 2014

BOB DYLAN: NORTH COUNTRY OTHER, CHRISTMAS IN HIS HEART

During the 1950s, at an Episcopal boys' school in Washington, DC, we began singing Christmas hymns a bit after Thanksgiving. We convened, each morning, in a Gothic chapel with heavy overhead beams and leather kneeling pads to belt "Adeste Fideles," "The First Noel," "O' Little Town of Bethlehem," and "Hark the Herald Angels Sing" (each of which appears on Dylan's *Christmas in the Heart*), changing lyrics to "Hark the herald angels shout, three more weeks 'til we get out," and those of "We Three Kings" (which does not appear on *Heart*) to "We three kings of Orient are / tried to smoke a rubber cigar / It was loaded, it exploded / etc." Such kidding was mandatory after the sonorities of Thanksgiving hymns, such as "Glorious Things of Thee Are Spoken" and "Now Thank We All Our God." Christmas carols were featherweight in comparison; they begged to be satirized.

Outside, in Washington, was a skein of tail-finned, jingle-jangled Americana that adequately satirized itself. We worshiped in shadows of the National Cathedral, the last full-scale Gothic church built in America, and a 13th century throwback by anyone's standard. Yet cruising before it were Corvettes and Thunderbirds whose radios played rock at high volume and whose tires burned rubber, catapulting us toward orgies of teen hysteria masquerading as Christmas parties. They were society events, yet "Jingle Bell Rock" might be played as a lark, as might "Rockin' Around the Christmas Tree." Some gadabout might wear a Santa's hat above his dinner coat, reminding us Episcopalian lads that Christmas had been a pagan festival before it became Christian, and that wassail was king. We'd learned that in Sacred Studies.

This was Washington, during the Eisenhower era. Now picture Hibbing, Minnesota, a frontier mining town on a raw December evening, as Bobby Zimmerman, a seventeen-year-old Jewish rock 'n' roller, walks home from cleanup duties at Zimmerman's Furniture and Electric. It has been dark since 4:30 and is bone-shatteringly cold. Yet Howard Street, Hibbing's main drag, blazes with Christmas lights and silvery decorations—in store fronts, on lampposts and strung on wires across the snowy boulevard. ("Three angels," he will write, ten years later, "up above the street, each one playing a horn....") Crippa's Music features seasonal albums by Mario Lanza, Perry Como, Mel Torme, Al Martino, Frankie Laine, or Johnny Ray, in the window, on the turntable, or stuffed in bins. Though Jewish merchants own many stores on Howard Street, they (at shops like Feldman's, Sach's, Stone's, Hallock's, Herberger's, Stein and Shapiro Drugs) tout Christmas. Holiday treats are offered at the Edelsteins' theaters (owned by Bobby's uncle), as are discounts at Zimmerman's, and each is festively lighted. There are twenty churches in Hibbing, and one synagogue—converted from a Gothic-style, Lutheran structure by removing its steeple and adding a Star of David. A majority of the 300-odd Jews in Hibbing have families involved in trade. They are respected middle-class burghers in a polyglot, working class city of some 17,600 people. Orthodox to Conservative in practice, they are descendants of eastern European Jews who fled the pogroms. They are observant but flexible: as miners are paid on Fridays, and Saturday is the week's major shopping day, their stores remain open.

Bobby hikes past the Shell Station, where through its window, on a grimy wall, a buxom calendar girl (Bettie Page?), wearing an abbreviated Santa getup and gartered stockings, stops him in his tracks. Der Bingle is crooning "White Christmas" from the radio, as a pump jockey counts his tips. Bobby shrugs. The Hull-Rust mines are closed for the winter, and though times are lean, Iron Rangers remain optimistic. Bobby cuts right at Seventh Avenue, trudges by Blessed Sacrament Church, where the Zimmermans will attend Christmas Eve mass, as is their custom, singing traditional hymns, past Hibbing High where decorations have been hung and celebrations underway for weeks, to 2425 Seventh and home. He mutters something to his mother Beatty and little brother, David, then slips downstairs to flick on a Victrola. *Blue Christmas*. Elvis growls "Silent Night," "White Christmas," "I'll Be Home for Christmas," and the title song, this album's sole rocker. Bobby taps a foot, jiggles his knee, grabs a guitar, looks around and lights a cigarette.

Despite the schmaltz, everyone loves a Christmas lyric, particularly when sung by a popular artist. It's been noted that *Christmas in the Heart*, Dylan's first holiday album, is in the tradition of such releases, extending back at least to Tommy Dorsey's 1935 rendition of "Santa Claus is Coming to Town," and extending through this era's often eccentric offerings: James Brown's "Santa Claus, Go Straight to the Ghetto," Cheech and Chong's "Santa Claus and His Old Lady," Patti Smith's reading of "White Christmas," and Suge Knight's gangsta album, *Christmas on Death Row*. Despite the latter's omission, "Santa" seems the key word to repeat in a title. Gene Autry's 1947 hit, "Here Comes Santa Claus," is covered by Dylan on *Christmas in the Heart*, and two of the album's songs have Santa's name up front—including "Must Be Santa," for which Dylan made a rollicking video.

The business of Christmas *is* commerce, of course, and Santa—not that babe in a manger—is its poster boy. That's been true since 1863, when the German-American cartoonist,

Thomas Nast, began sketching fresh renditions of Santa—Father Christmas, Kris Kringle, Jack Frost—each year. From Nast's pen, Santa became Falstaffian in nature ... thus, his bloated face and sherry-red nose ... and a flagrant bestower of gifts. This had not always been so; there was the German tradition of coals-in-the-stocking for naughty children. But in America, the all-forgiving, capitalist democracy, sins were pardoned and Santa became its priest. During the 1920s, this new image was standardized by corporate advertisers (particularly Coca Cola's, whose colors were red and white), a metamorphosis not lost on Hibbing's merchants. For they were as red-white-and-blue as any of the 27 ethnic groups that worked Iron Range mines or contributed to Hibbing's prosperity through its minor industries.

Christmas in the Heart, with its pop and religious standards, its Mantovani-like arrangements and Lawrence Welkian chorus, is straight from the 1950s. There's not a song on it that would have been inappropriate for Hibbing's middle-of-the-road citizenry to applaud, or its radio station to have played. And though Bobby and David Zimmerman were bar mitzvaed Jews in a 99 percent Christian town, they probably sang them all. In a recent interview, promoting the album, Dylan has admitted as much. "I like all the religious Christmas albums," he told Bill Flanagan. "The ones in Latin. The songs I sang as a kid."

We know that he did not wear his Jewishness lightly. Echo Helstrom told me in 1968 that, soon after she met him, in 1957, she said, "Gee, *Zimmerman*, that's a funny name. Is it Jewish?" Bob "looked straight ahead with his face sort of funny," and did not answer. "Later," Echo added, "John Bucklen [his best friend] took me aside at school and said, 'Listen Echo, don't ever ask about Bob being Jewish again. He doesn't like to talk about it.'" Le Roi Hoikkala, Dylan's pal and drummer for the Golden Chords, told me, "Bob never talked about his family. But the Jews were looked up to in Hibbing. They were professionals, and they took care of people who had less." Robert Shelton, in his 1986 biography, *No Direction Home*, quotes a teacher at Hibbing High saying that there had been racial discrimination, and that "In Hibbing, the Finns hated the Bohemians and the Bohemians hated the Finns. Nearly everyone hated the Jews." Leona Rolfzen, the Zimmermans' neighbor and English-teacher B.J. Rolfzen's widow, told me that, in Dylan's era, "they wouldn't let Jews play golf at the country club," and that Dylan's father loved golf. "They were outsiders and I think that's why Beatty and I were friends—we'd just moved to Hibbing and felt like outsiders, too." I heard mild anti-Semitic remarks in Hibbing, while researching 1971's *Positively Main Street*. Dylan, in *Chronicles*, hints that he lost bands and gigs in restricted venues because of antisemitism.

Such sentiments were not always veiled. Dylan would have known that, in 1906, his great aunt, Ida Solemovitz, had been murdered in Superior, Minnesota, by a Christian lover devastated by Ida's refusal of marriage—on religious grounds. After shooting her, the lover shot himself. "In the newspaper," Dave Engel reports in his majestic, *Just Like Bob Zimmerman's Blues—Dylan in Minnesota*, that "the murder-suicide is called one of the most horrible tragedies to happen in Superior, the result of a hopeless love affair—a Scotchman and Christian falling in love with a *Jewess* whose parents consider a marriage to a non-Jew a virtual death."

Heartbroken over his sister's murder, Dylan's maternal grandfather, Ben Solemovich, would move to Hibbing and Anglicize his name. A change Bob eventually would imitate. The first person he informed of this was girlfriend, Echo Helstrom, the blondest, whitest Scandinavian in town. She told me in 1968: "Bob came over to my house after school one day and said he'd finally decided on his stage name ... it was 'Dylan,' after that poet, I think." She informed Shelton that, "I was surprised that Bob had anything to do with me because I had originally thought that Jewish people had *nothing* to do with other people ... I really sensed that Jewish people in

Hibbing felt they were different from others, but I know that Bob didn't want to be separated from anyone."

Overshadowed by Greil Marcus' brilliant essay on Hibbing High School, and its influence on Dylan, Marilyn J. Chiat's contribution to last year's, *Highway 61 Revisited—Bob Dylan's Road from Minnesota to the World*, may be the anthology's most provocative entry. It is titled, "Jewish Homes on the Range, 1890-1960." I sat on a panel with Chiat at the University of Minnesota's, 2007 Dylan symposium and—nervous about my presentation—paid insufficient attention to what she read. I did hear that, like myself, she had interviewed Beatty Zimmerman and despite Beatty's claim that she "didn't feel like an outcast," Chiat (who as director of the Project to Document Jewish Settlers in Minnesota) established that, during this period, there had been considerable antisemitism in the state, and particularly in Minneapolis, called by one author, "the anti-Semitic capital of the United States." There also was antisemitism in Hibbing. When news of *Christmas in the Heart*'s appearance surfaced, I dove for Chiat's essay.

Let me quote from it: "During the first decades of the past century, religion, class and ethnicity were all highly politicized on the Range and the source of division within Range life. The Protestant elite claimed that southern and eastern Europeans were 'black' (the term used by the elite); only 'true Americans (Yankees) and those of northern European descent were to be considered "white.' ... Protestants [called] in the Ku Klux Klan, which held cross burnings and parades to instill fear in the miners' hearts ... Coming primarily from eastern Europe, Jews could be considered 'black,' but their position firmly in the middle class placed them in the 'white' category." Chiat adds that, "they kept their leftist sympathies [about unionization] to themselves because of their status as retailers selling to both mining company interests and the workers ... as one merchant put it more bluntly, 'We kept our mouths shut.'"

Chiat writes, of the splendidly ornate Hibbing High, built from mining executives' largesse, that "The companies had a specific purpose: education was intended to acculturate the immigrants' children as a means of lessening their attachment to what were described as 'leftist' and 'subversive' ideas." This seems to contradict Greil Marcus' implication that HHS was raised as Hibbing's great symbol of "the mystery of democracy." Democracy may wish for acculturation, but in capitalism it is the ideal. And nothing heralded that in Hibbing more passionately than Christmas.

In the fifties and sixties, at Hibbing High, Christmas was celebrated with an intensity less partisan than inclusive. Dan Bergan, a 1964 classmate of David Zimmerman, and a writer, historian, and retired English Department Chair at the school, recalls that, "Fifty-to-sixty years ago the Christmas holiday had a much more ecumenical (in the Christian sense of the word) flavor ... everybody, regardless of religious or non-religious affiliation, seemed to accept or share in the general harmony or joy of the season ... the school had a band, a concert choir, an orchestra and all contributed to holiday concerts. When I was in school the final afternoon prior to Xmas vacation consisted of a concert put on by all of those music groups—from songs to choral arrangements to band numbers, etc. with all the music 'traditional' holiday fare from ... without worrying about hurting anybody's ethnicity." Bergan adds, "One great tradition that I fondly remember—and perhaps R.Z. would, too—is that the school's concert choir would stroll the halls in full concert uniform for a few days prior to the break, caroling and singing up and down those massive halls with all the attendant resonance. They would perform on one floor, then stroll to another, making their way up and down the staircases quiet as church mice between songs."

It is unlikely that Dylan was a member of those choral groups (there is no record of his participation, in either the '58 or '59 yearbooks), but David, involved heavily in the school's music program, undoubtedly was. He was active in Hibbing High's choir from tenth through twelfth grades, and served as student director of some eighty choir mates his senior year.

"Any activity engaged in by the choirs would have similarly engaged David," Bergan notes. And as Beatty told Chiat in her 1985 interview, the Zimmermans' "Christian neighbors would always be invited to their home for potato pancakes on Hanukkah, and in turn, the Zimmermans would attend midnight mass at the Catholic church on Christmas Eve." (David would marry a Roman Catholic classmate in 1968, a union of which his father disapproved.) Dylan heard Christian hymns and carols at Blessed Sacrament and, as noted, sang them. "I am a true believer," he admits in the Flanagan interview. Mrs. Zimmerman told me, in 1969, that "Bob has always been religious ... as a child, Bob attended *all* the churches around Hibbing; he was very interested in religions, and *all* religions, by no means just his own."

The musicians he idolized on record—Hank Williams, Johnny Cash, Little Richard—had roots in the evangelical movement he eventually would embrace, and their rock 'n' roll evolved from its hymns, mostly gospel. As Texas-born novelist, James Lee Burke, once told me: "Elvis, Jerry Lee Lewis, all of those guys came out of the same background, the Assembly of God church ... their lives were like vessels filled with all this great stuff: music and religion and cultural desperation and poverty."

Dylan has been playing Christian music—perhaps not realizing it—since he picked out his first Elvis tune on the guitar, pounded his first Jerry Lee or Little Richard boogie on the piano, or sang along with Hank's "I Saw the Light." So the only surprise to *Christmas in the Heart* is that it took so long for it to appear.

Rumors of a Dylan Christmas album have circulated since 1965, when Phil Spector was said to have produced one. Michael Gray reports, in *The Bob Dylan Encyclopedia*, that it was a hoax, perpetrated by editors at *New Musical Express*, "titled *Snow Over Interstate 80* ... (One of the tracks they claimed as included, 'Silent Night,' was later recorded by

110

Dylan at an *Infidels* session in New York on April 22, 1983; this has never circulated, but, unlike *Snow Over Interstate 80*, did exist.)" The post-Christmas song, "Three Angels," appeared on 1970's *New Morning*, and now we have *Christmas in the Heart*.

What to say that hasn't been said? It's the cheeriest of Dylan's albums. Gone is the nihilism of recent offerings, the cynicism about man and his endeavors. Found is joyfulness in the world as we see it. And despite its musical kitsch, it's rendered with no self-consciousness, no satirical edge (well, perhaps in the Bettie Page pinup). Jack Frost's production is without flaw (finally that pseudonym makes sense). And if there's a missed note on this album, I don't hear it. The chorus is precise, the arrangements considered, and Dylan's scabrous voice jubilant. This is singing by a man who loves Christmas. And isn't afraid to say so.

Not one song is composed by Dylan, yet the album mines the vein of multi-cultural American music he's produced for decades—a music of assimilation and acculturation. There is tension here between the sacred and secular, between faith and commerce. As it is in much of Dylan's work. But there's neither criticism nor pandering. Oddly, there's no African American music included, no gospel. Perhaps Dylan feels he's covered that. What we have is 1950s Hibbing, overwhelmingly white and Christian, middle American in taste, and vibrant. When asked if he were homesick at Christmas for his hometown, Dylan told Bill Flanagan: "Not really, I didn't think about it that much. I didn't bring the past with me when I came to New York. Nothing back there would play any part in where I was going." But one wonders. To wit: "Must Be Santa," the album's most energetic song, is a rip-roaring polka (sung in rounds) that might have been heard in the miners' bars of his youth.

Those who scrounge for secondary meaning in Dylan's work may be impressed by *Heart*'s message of acceptance, reconciliation, and peace. This may be Dylan's most political album since *The Times They Are A Changin'*. Whatever he and his family learned in Hibbing, about assimilation or acculturation, permeates *Heart*. That it appears in a season when America remains at war—one, in part, of religious intolerance—is significant. Its songs of peace suggest Christmas truces of the Civil and Great Wars, when presents allegedly were exchanged on battlefields, carols sung by enemies together, and music shared through barbed wire. Dylan croaks these Christmas classics like the old Jew in "Wicked Messenger," or Tevye in *Fiddler on the Roof*. He's a man who realizes that voices raised in Christmas cheer can tame the world's resentments and lift the soul.

—*The Bridge*, 2010

ED LAHEY: ART AS PRINCIPLE

One does not readily associate poetry with Butte, but its ghostlike lofts and haunted saloons have long fostered a bohemian art scene, and if Hollywood were to stage a Montana version of *Rent*, it might be filmed there. Sixty-nine-year-old Ed Lahey comes from an earlier Butte. His *Birds of a Feather: The Complete Poems* (Clark City Press, $25) evokes a city where the Berkeley Pit worked round the clock, and songs of its Irish, Cornish, or Finnish miners were never far from the ear: "I'm underground again / with Crazy Dan the Buzzy Wrecker, hand hooked up to a widow-maker/mind burned out by what I know of men," he writes, or, "Skimmet's daughter plays the piano, everyone applauds ... The plank barsill is loaded / with chunks of high grade ore ... The double-decker oil-drum stove glows with stolen company coal / fed lump by lump with laughter...."

Though Lahey worked Butte's mines as a youngster, he also studied poetry with Richard Hugo at the University of Montana and possesses a modern sensibility. Lahey's underground implies both the shafts honeycombing Butte's bedrock and the underground of the mind; of memory, myth, the unconscious. "I have a ghost town inside, vibrant memories of a life," he writes, and, "Deep in mined-out waste / carbide lamps illuminate mold, black damp in a caved-in raise / Shattered quartzite seams / crack inside the mountain/where quick men move (in calculated haste) / to fill pant-leg sample sacks / with gob and crumb." He might be describing the craft of a poet.

Lahey's good on miners' work and its tools, and to best comprehend these poems one's dictionary should include the terms "mucker," "whippletree," head frame," "bull gear," "Ingersoll," "horneblende," "spitter," and "moron's claw." His poems ring with the harmonies of modern verse, prosody dressed to blow free: "What does it matter, / sadness? Many must know it. / Many are alone. Some are alone / and don't know it. / I am alone. I know it." Even in his newer poems, he rarely strays from the lyric mania of Butte storytelling. Realizing he can't escape his forebears, he nevertheless tries: "I headed for the station/It was time to leave ... For me the town was dead ... The bus was right on time ... I was on my way to Missoula ... A new life, a place free of crumbling ... 'Live by water,' my mother said, / 'Sleep by a river.'"

Birds of a Feather is published in an elegant edition, designed by Russell Chatham, that includes the artist's heartfelt introduction. As Chatham writes of Lahey, "When the Idyll ends, as it always does, the forced return to civilization usually results in anger and chaos," but what matters finally is "relentless and honest perseverance, exemplified by forty years of writing and reading throughout the Northwest, guided by the unshakable conviction that Art is the Principle."

For anyone entranced by the voices of Montana, this book is not to be missed.

—*Big Sky Journal*, 2006

RUSSELL CHATHAM:
STAR PARTY '90

In June of 1990, critic Robert Hughes wrote in *The New Republic*, "There is much to suggest that in the 1980s New York not only lost its primacy as an art center, but also began to go the way of its predecessors ... the idea of the single art center is now disappearing." He went on to note that "Not much of the art that really seems to matter is being made in New York today ... Perhaps one of the positive results of the 1980s will be finally to clear our minds of the cant of cultural empire, of nostalgia for the lost imperial center. Under the present circumstances, a great artist can just as easily—and unexpectedly—emerge in Hungary or Australia as in New York."

When I read that, immediately I thought of Russell Chatham. That thought was reinforced during the summer of 1990, when I attended a thirty-year retrospective of Chatham's paintings at the Museum of the Rockies in Bozeman, and by the five weeks I spent in nearby Livingston experiencing the artistic renaissance that was transpiring not just there, but throughout the state. The fifty-one-year-old Chatham stood as artistic conscience to this renaissance—a "rebirth" in the sense of Harlem's during the 1920s—so invigorating that novelist William Kittredge famously dubbed Montana "the Last Best Place."

The principal celebration of Chatham's retrospective occurred the evening of July 21 in Bozeman, with a "Star Party Fund Raiser" to generate cash for the museum by selling tickets permitting the general public to rub elbows with "Russell Chatham's celebrity friends," the brochure read ... Montana intimates such as Thomas McGuane, Peter and Jane Fonda, Ted Turner, Harry Dean Stanton, Dennis Quaid, Meg Ryan, Jeff Bridges, columnists Alston Chase and David Quammen, Patagonia's Yvon Chouinard, fictionists William Kittredge, James Crumley, Rick Bass, and William Hjortsberg, composer Dave Grusin, director Sidney Pollack, musician Chris Rude of the Rude Boys, Hunter S. Thompson, and *Batman's* own Jack Nicholson and Michael Keaton. Keaton recently had bought a section of Tom McGuane's former ranch in McLeod, near spreads owned by Bruce Weber, Dave Grusin, Brooke Shields, and Tom Brokaw. Keaton and Peter Fonda were the lone film stars present when Chatham arrived shortly after nine-thirty, camera crews from *Entertainment Tonight*, *Today*, and *US* magazine sprinting to capture his entrance.

Chatham's massive figure was draped by a yellow sport shirt and white slacks, his gray hair hanging lank to his shoulders, his broken nose twisted sharply to the left. He looked worried. All day stars had been canceling. Meg Ryan called to say Dennis Quaid was distraught in Los Angeles after reading a cover story about himself in *The National Enquirer*, and that she must rush to his side. Jane Fonda and Ted Turner had flown to California for an impromptu meeting with President Ronald Reagan. Sydney Pollack begged off, as did Harry Dean Stanton. Jack Nicholson phoned asking to be excused because of early promotion for *The Two Jakes*. Hunter Thompson promised he'd fly up from Aspen only if Chatham provided "a Lear and lots of acid." Now Tom McGuane approached as camera lights flared, and he and Chatham shook hands. "You're the most famous person I know," McGuane quipped. Chatham grinned. A Mariachi band strummed, fans pressed for autographs, and behind (nearly forgotten) hung a dozen huge paintings capped by a 10 x 12 foot canvas titled *The Headwaters of the Missouri River in April.*

The series, dubbed "Seasons" by Chatham, had been commissioned for this gallery. It depicts changing seasons in the Missouri headwaters, a nearby region of historic and geologic significance, and one of great beauty. The paintings are landscapes, huge brooding river scenes mostly, containing not a figure nor a building. Chatham finished the last that morning. "It's still not finished," he protested. The canvasses are in the tradition of those by New World painters such as Albert Bierstadt and Thomas Moran, but also of more cosmopolitan artists such as Whistler, Ryder, Dove, and Childe Hassam. Chatham's more a Post-Impressionist than a Realist. In adjoining galleries hung a retrospective of one hundred Chatham paintings, and in an upstairs space a collection by California artists—notably his grandfather, Gottardo Piazzoni (1878-1945)—who strongly influenced him.

The paintings were what Chatham was about, not this party. "But this is my big shot," he explained, "to get a show in a *real* museum—someplace like the National Gallery." Despite over two hundred gallery openings, Chatham has been virtually ignored by the critical and curatorial establishment. As *Esquire's* Terry McDonell said, "The idea that everybody knows Russell Chatham's work except the critics is a dinner-party joke from Manhattan to Bel Air." He's had just one New York show, the reception to which cost him $10,000, and where he sold not a painting. A quarter-million dollars of his own borrowed money was invested in this exhibit, where nothing was for sale. "Dealers are mostly shysters, hyping bad art to people in museums which are filled with absolute trash," he's said. A sentiment that has not endeared him to the established art world.

But he was adored tonight. "Isn't it incredible we have this great artist in our midst, who's been working steadily all these years?" William Hjortsberg said. Becky Fonda slapped her neighbors with Star Party name tags as they gushed over

Chatham's paintings, many of which had been plucked from their walls. The Missoula contingent—Kittredge, Crumley, and Bass—drank excitedly with dinosaur paleontologist Jack Horner as Michael Keaton, in jeans and cowboy vest, hammed for cameras with Peter Fonda, who conducted a silent auction while the band played on.

Two weeks later Chatham sat in the Livingston offices of his Rebecca Fine Arts studio completing a sketch for a new landscape. Livingston, once home to Calamity Jane, is a town of seven thousand people, its two main streets dotted with cowboy saloons in false-front buildings a century old, flanked by the Absaroka Mountains and the Yellowstone River (*A River Runs through It* was filmed there). Since Chatham's opening, the Star Party had been featured on *Entertainment Tonight*, he'd been interviewed for National Public Radio's *Morning Edition*, he'd breakfasted at a Republican fund raiser in Billings with President Bush at the President's request, arranged to take Bush trout fishing (Chatham is a world-class fly fisherman), and negotiated the sale of a painting to the White House. "They want a big one," Chatham said, "for permanent display in the West Wing." Despite this success, Chatham's voice was muted, his concentration riveted on his sketching. Outside, muffler-less pickups rumbled through Livingston, hot rods downshifted, and tape decks blared from the street, but here in this converted dentist's office, the world was curiously inverted.

"I grew up surrounded by art," Chatham has written. "It was simply the most crucial thing. My uncle, aunt, cousins and especially my grandfather painted. Papa, as we called him, was a Swiss-Italian artist who'd studied in Paris then worked in San Francisco and on his ranch at the head of the Carmel Valley in Monterey County. That's where I spent my summers. It was an indescribably beautiful place. I saw Papa die there when I was five. He sat down at the table one morning, sipped his coffee, looked at me and said 'Goodbye.' His head fell forward. He'd had a massive heart attack. I remember feeling as if his spirit entered mine. And that my life would be filled with art."

As critic Chris Waddington's observed, "Piazzoni was a dominant figure in the burgeoning art scene of early 20th century San Francisco, counting Arthur Putnam, Ansel Adams, Ralph Stackpole and Diego Rivera among his admirers." His influence on Chatham was absolute. Russell began painting at age eight, and despite careers as an independent writer (he's published hundreds of articles on hunting, fishing, conservation and cooking, and three books of nonfiction), a publisher (his Clark City Press in Livingston creates fine books in limited printings, including works by Jim Harrison, James Crumley, Richard Hugo, Barry Gifford, and Rick Bass) and distributor of his own lithographs and paintings, has never stopped.

Chatham sat in a loose seersucker shirt and khaki shorts before a pine easel that held the 30 x 36 inch canvas he was painting. He'd taken it from nearly scratch, building on a sketch of ocher fields supporting dark green cottonwoods, below white clouds hanging in a tarnished silver sky. "It's a scene I spotted outside Bozeman," he said. "I started this canvas with a fence in the foreground that wasn't in what I saw, but since it works I'll leave it." The texture of light above summer fields was what he sought to capture. The mood of this painting was more airy than of those in the Bozeman show. He sat dabbing oil while we spoke, the room empty but for six other canvasses (one of black Angus cattle in a field, another of an olive-drab, nearly Expressionist landscape) in odd stages of completion. His wide easel stood on a flowered scrap of linoleum. Between strokes he squeezed his brushes methodically with clean rags, and mixed his oils on a simple wooden palette that held a tin pot of turpentine. Chatham's demeanor while painting was one of extraordinary calm.

It had not always been so. When he moved to Livingston with his second wife in 1972 he was broke and desperate. "I drove this 1949 Chevy pickup packed to the roof with everything I owned here from San Francisco," he said. "I had no job, no immediate prospects of employment. But I'd found a house—up the road from McGuane's at Deep Creek. When the landlord asked what I did, I hesitated at first then said, 'I'm an artist, but—' He stopped me and said, 'I knew it! If I waited long enough an artist would come along and rent that house.' He gave it to me for 800 bucks a year."

Chatham had met McGuane, Richard Brautigan, and William Hjortsberg while living in Bolinas in 1967. McGuane heard that Chatham, who'd recently broken the world's record for a striped bass caught on a fly rod, lived in Bolinas. "Because of the name," Hjortsberg said, "we thought he'd be this tweedy English gentleman. He was just another ragged artist like us." Chatham's principal mentor, the painter Richard Van Windergen, had died in 1970, so when McGuane moved to Montana he followed. Unconsciously, Chatham was seeking another mentor and he found that in McGuane, who influenced his writing, bolstered his dedication to art, and increased his self-confidence. "Tom had total confidence in himself," Chatham remembered. "All day we'd talk about fishing and art—how anything less than absolute commitment just wouldn't work. He said something I've never forgotten. He described the world as a safe—'keep tinkering with the lock and it's bound to open.'"

As McGuane continued working for the movies, he introduced Chatham to a succession of Hollywood associates. Jack Nicholson met Chatham and his close friend, novelist Jim Harrison, the same year. Harrison had become acquainted with Nicholson during the 1975 shooting of McGuane's film *The Missouri Breaks.* Nicholson gave Harrison $15,000 to write a book, *Legends of the Fall,* the sole condition of the stake being that he would get first shot at the product's film rights. Eventually he would purchase thirty Chatham canvasses. "Jack has a great love of art," Chatham said, "and he goes out of his way to buy and be around it. But I was stunned when I first visited his house. He has an extraordinary collection of paintings. I wasn't expecting that kind of commitment."

Commitment was what Chatham had been living, and he thought one needed to be broke to maintain it. His father was a lumber company executive in San Francisco, with literary ambitions, who had sacrificed his life to the family business and would die "the most unhappy man I've ever known," Chatham said. Papa Piazzoni had died broke but satisfied with his production of art. The choice for Chatham was clear. During the 1970s, selling only a few paintings a year, he subsisted primitively on Deep Creek without oil heat or often electricity, swapping art for firewood, medical and legal services, babysitting and rent. One fall the pipes burst and he spent four months hauling water from Deep Creek. He did a series of commissioned portraits of neighbors, but balked one day when a cowboy offered him fifty dollars to paint an Indian head on a circular saw blade. Though discouraged by his poverty, Chatham was spiritually content; Livingston's isolation was so similar to Carmel Valley where he'd spent summers as a child watching his grandfather paint, fishing with his cousins, and later painting alone at the ranch through one long winter, that he toughed it out. It was part of the Art Life. "I'd drive past McGuane's and think, '*Time* magazine's visiting him again,' when nothing critically was happening for me. Yet I'd idle there above Paradise Valley and get a terrific idea for a painting, which I'd start the next day. It was worth it. One night I stopped above Tom's and got so excited by a hole-in-the-clouds scene that I scratched it onto the truck's fender with a rock. I didn't have any paper."

Chatham was poor but he was not laboring alone. An extraordinary community of artists had followed McGuane to Livingston, a town which by 1979 sheltered Sam Peckinpah, Warren Oates, Rip Torn, Richard Brautigan, Jimmy Buffett, Margot Kidder, Dan Gerber, Jim Harrison, Dennis Quaid, Phil Caputo, Peter Fonda, Tim Cahill, "Gatz" Hjortsberg, and other less famous personages. Livingston was not Montana's only draw. Bozeman supported the novelist and nature writer, David Quammen, Missoula (a bellwether since Richard Hugo settled there in 1964) the fictionists Richard Ford, Ivan Doig, David Long, Ralph Beer, Norman Maclean, Rick Bass, James Crumley, James Welch, and William Kittredge, who would co-edit the 1,200-page, *The Last Best Place*, an anthology of Montana writing from Indian myths to contemporary poetry. Painters and photographers swarmed to the state. Something of Montana was in the wind.

It reached urban dwellers such as Chatham, Fonda, and Bridges who had fled California as its cities grew increasingly uninhabitable, and who wished to retreat to small-town, frontier values. It reached others who were reexamining America's primary myths in the wake of Vietnam, and who wished to experience westward expansionism on their own terms. It reached others who sought an artistic community where talent might be nurtured outside the cutthroat atmosphere of Los Angeles or New York. Yet Livingston "is far from being Aspen or Sun Valley," Chatham wrote. "It's essentially a community of ordinary, kind people, plus a few cripples, drunks, retired railroaders and thousands of members of a cult immodestly titled the Church Universal and Triumphant. To be frank, a little Hollywood creates a healthy mix...."

The accuracy of this was brought home to me two summers previous to the Star Party opening, at the biannual presentation of Livingston's Woolly Worm Review ... a tongue-in-cheek variety show, written and emceed by Michael Devine and intended as a midsummer dig at visiting fishermen. A 19th century band shell in Sacajawea Park had been decorated like an underwater grotto. Papier-mache fish dangled from the rafters, red, orange, green, and blue creatures, a river bank hung with branches graced the back wall, ferns lined the front, everything in vibrant color. Several hundred townspeople and trout fishermen, crunching popcorn and drinking pop, awaited this year's Review. Fifty yards east ran the Yellowstone River; the sunset layered Mount Baldy in pastel stripes. Backstage, Jeff and Beau Bridges (Jeff costumed as Neptune in a white toga) awaited cues. Cahill and Hjortsberg, in fishing vests, practiced lines. As did Alston Chase. They would banter with Devine, then read outdoor pieces. Bozeman poet Greg Keeler would recite poetry—"Ode to Duct Tape," others—and strum a few songs. Peter Fonda, who plays tambourine and sings backup with Devine's bar band, would present a taped monologue. Eventually, the Woolly Worm would close to generous applause, its $1,000,000 cast taking bows, then striking the set. A party was scheduled at Owl Bar, next to the tiny Empire Theater on Second Street.

Despite this sort of quintessentially small-town perk, Chatham by 1983 was itchy to become financially secure and professionally visible. "If only to be able to afford to spend more time in three-star restaurants." But he remained conflicted. His mother's uncle, Maurice Del Mue, had been a commercial artist responsible for images such as the Arm & Hammer baking soda box, the eagle for Ghirardelli Chocolate Company, and the yellow-robed figure on the Hills Bros. coffee can. Mue had been disparaged by the Piazzoni family. His work was not art in the spirit of Papa's. Chatham's own uncle, Carroll, had invented the Chatham emeralds—artificial gems grown in a kiln—a feat "which was true alchemy." He was disparaged as well. Nevertheless, Russell started his print and lithography business with his third wife, Suzanne, painstakingly learning the etching process in Seattle. He collaborated with McGuane on a project titled "In the Crazies," a portfolio of lithographs, paintings, and etchings depicting the Crazy Mountains near Livingston, combined with textual fiction. He created a half-dozen covers for Jim Harrison's novels. By the late 1980s, Rebecca Fine Art, in partnership with Clark City Press—his publishing venture, established to keep his own work and others of note in print—was flourishing. "Russell's the only landscape painter in the world with a downtown office and eight people working for him," McGuane joked.

At a time when critics warred over the notion of "quality" in art, and when conceptual, performance, and installation pieces thumbed their noses at the inflated prices of more traditional painting, Chatham quietly pursued his vision: one closer to the values of Japanese or Chinese landscape painting than that of the post-modernists. As critic Chris Waddington's noted, "Chatham's work reminds us that landscape is the original modernist genre." And as Chatham was fond of saying, "The real avant garde is always the oldest thing you can imagine." Yet his choice to remain outside the New York nexus baffled his associates. "When are you getting out in the traffic pattern?" Tom Brokaw needled. Chatham stubbornly declined; a big show in the East seemed improbable. "What are we to do with Chatham?" Harrison lamented in an introduction to the retrospective catalogue. "He has the soul of a Great Waif and his work doesn't belong anywhere, certainly not within the confines of post-modern art, which strikes one in permanent diaspora. Everyone in the critical apparatus points in a different direction or is building a different birdhouse, none of which has room for our Waif."

Then in the fall Chatham traveled to New York, day tripping to Washington for a meeting with Virginia Mecklenburg, chief curator for the Smithsonian's National Museum of American Art. Mecklenburg liked what she saw of his work and made plans to visit Livingston to view canvasses in progress. An exhibition was proposed. Brokaw forwarded prints to then-director Carter Brown of the National Gallery, and it looked as if a show might be curated there as well. The long journey from critical anonymity seemed at an end.

To hedge the bet, Chatham opened his own gallery in Livingston this year, and bought the 100-year-old, West Side School, which he planned to transform into a major museum, highlighting his, his grandfather's, and other artists' work. He's been commissioned by the National Park Service to paint four large canvasses to hang in Yellowstone's historic Old Faithful Inn. And shows are scheduled this summer in Livingston, Seattle and Minneapolis. These moves, combined with his critically acclaimed Clark City Press, has rendered

Chatham *the* mover and shaker on the Montana art scene.

He remains philosophical. "Painting for me has been largely an innocent obsession, an act of faith, a vocation," he wrote. "I don't know if I can ever become a great painter like my grandfather, but I feel worthy of him, and I believe my best work lies ahead ... by now my imagination has become so entangled with Papa's that his way of viewing nature's inner life has to some degree become mine, and my vision is frequently an almost unconscious homage to him."

Chatham's work is in the context of Montana's artistic renaissance and the commitment to both quality and to the Art Life that have distinguished its members. Despite celebrity friends, Chatham leads a modest existence, bringing the same passion to hunting, fishing, and cooking that he does to art. "They all come from the same well of feeling," he's said. Few people's work—neither McGuane's, nor Richard Ford's, nor Ivan Doig's, nor Jim Welch's, nor Richard Hugo's, nor that of Montana's numerous painters and sculptors—captures the state's essence as does Chatham's. This is because he deals almost exclusively with landscape: the inescapable elements of Montana's mountains, forests, and sky. His paintings embrace the spirit of vacancy. Displaying, as Harrison's noted, "the marrow of landscapes, where you will witness (in Buddhist terms) the natural antagonism between form and emptiness...."[66]

—1990

Postscript: Chatham died in November, 2019, after a long illness. In his last years, he had moved to Point Reyes, California, near his childhood home and not far from his grandfather's ranch.

---

66   This and published remarks quoted herein are from *Russell Chatham: One Hundred Paintings*, Clark City Press, Livingston, MT, 1990.

GLENN'S: THE ELAINE'S OF MONTANA

The Barnacles—grizzled regulars who've appended themselves to the horseshoe-shaped bar at Glenn's as if it were the hull of a listing freighter—glance dismissively at a birthday celebration toward the saloon's rear. But realizing it is for one of their own, return to their beverages and banter. These are served by their host, Glenn Godward, who rolls in his sailor's gait from bar sink to whiskey station with the poise of a sea captain ... no, a railroad conductor, as the barroom, with its length of paneled walls and the height of its ceiling feels more like a boxcar than a sailing ship. This is appropriate, as the establishment sits at 106 East Park Street, Livingston, across a modest stretch of macadam from the Montana Rail Link and BNSF tracks. The Barnacles, gray-bearded to a person, sip their drinks with Zen-like precision, lifting glasses in tandem, as if the movement were choreographed.

They are musicians, artists, writers, carpenters, fishing guides, a race-car driver, a dinosaur collector, photographers, lawyers, and business people—a cross section of Livingston's population and a clientele that has followed the seventy-year-old Godward from bar to bar, often for decades. "I've been seeing Glenn as a bartender since I first came here in 1968," the author Jim Harrison says. "He's very mannerly. I don't know if he is the last of his breed but there are certainly very few like him. He is my favorite bartender in the world."

Godward may have good manners, but this afternoon he's playfully goading the Barnacles, skidding coasters toward them and snapping, "What'll it be?" In every case he guesses, but a customer Godward's known since childhood blurts that he's just returned from San Francisco and could he get an Irish coffee the way it's mixed at the Buena Vista Café? "You'll get it the way I make it," Godward says, "and you'll like it." The customer laughs.

There's sincerity in Godward's remark. He's tended bar since 1966 and except for a three-year tour in the army, has had no other full-time job. His affability is innate. But as the cantankerous novelist, Peter Bowen, admits, "Glenn is the only bartender in Livingston I'm afraid to piss off."

———————

The history of bartending in the American West is peopled with larger-than-life characters. In mining camps and cattle towns, the saloon often was the first permanent building constructed. As Richard Erdoes writes in *Saloons of the Old West*, "The saloon was all things to all men." It was "an eatery, a hotel, a bath and comfort station, a livery stable, gambling den, dance hall, bordello, barbershop, courtroom, church, social club," and served other functions. Its proprietor was a man to be reckoned with. He had to be multifaceted, and to know his customers.

"You have to respect them," Godward says. "They're all good friends. I tell them it's their home away from home. And it is."

This morning Godward sits in a booth, mid-restaurant, awaiting a beer delivery. His soft features, beneath a head of graying hair, looks strained and his shoulders, draped in a light jacket are hunched with fatigue. He lives alone and admits, "I have terrible sleeping patterns. I think it was about three this morning I got to sleep, and by four I was wide awake. So I watched *Orangutan Island* and *Chimp Eden*." He sighs. "There's not much on at four in the morning."

He was born in Glendive but moved to Livingston with his four brothers at age two, when their father was transferred by the railroad. "Half of Livingston was the railroad. They used to say it was a million-dollar-a-month payroll here." Saloons were situated near the tracks and Godward worked in many, "cherry picking" techniques from the various bartenders to whom he apprenticed. "A lot of the older guys took pride in what they did. In those days bartenders wore white shirts and ties. Some of them had the old time aprons on. But I never did."

It could be a rough trade, and often barkeeps were roughest of the lot. "I worked at this underground club, The Cave, maybe two years. One night the guy who owned it, Bud Rapstad, was sitting shaking dice, and there was a pile of money on the bar. A couple of police officers came down looking for someone. Bud turned around, drunk, and said, 'Get the hell out of my bar.' The cops said, 'Simmer down, Bud, we're on our way out and we have no beef with you.' Bud said, 'Get your asses out the door before I gut the two of you.' He'd been cutting meat and had this bloody apron on. They left, but they took him with them—for disturbing the peace in his own bar."

When Rapstad was released, he chastised Godward for not having helped him whip the cops. "I said, 'Pay me off and I'll leave and that will be the end of it.'" He moved to the more sedate Guest House and began the first of several stints at that motel's bar. "It was quiet, but later on Sam Peckinpah stayed there. We got along well and bet on football games together." Godward thought he'd tamed *The Wild Bunch*'s director, but "then some Japanese film makers wanted to do an interview with him upstairs, so they got him drunk and thought it would be fun to see what kind of reactions they'd get. I'm in the bar and I look out and these Japanese fellows are running down the stairs, with Peckinpah beating on them all the way."

Godward had studied accounting at Montana State, but after three years in the army, "I never went back for my degree. I knew I didn't want to sit behind a desk the rest of my life." He'd been attracted to bars since he was young. His father had imbibed moderately. "I guess *his* dad was a drunk. We'd go for a ride with my father, but we'd have to sit in the car and drink an orange crush." Godward's parents divorced when he was in grade school. "I think the old man had a wandering eye. I'm sure the divorce affected me, but I don't know how. I just became independent as hell."

He was drawn to saloon life, not for the drinking so much as for the action. "It just looked like a lot of fun. The Murray Hotel bar was the first I ever went into. I worked there a couple of years, with Slim Fleshman and Chuck Tweed. They taught me the basics of it. They weren't pillars of the community but they were good people."

Godward had befriended creative types like Peckinpah and Harrison at The Guest House, and to a minor extent while bartending at The Pastime, a family-style tavern with a lunch counter and local clientele. But it wasn't until his tenure at the Livingston Bar & Grille, established in 1996 by the painter, Russell Chatham, that many of the nation's creative folk became his customers. "You never knew who you were going to wait on." It might be locals such as Harrison, Peter Fonda, Margot Kidder, Tom Brokaw, Jeff Bridges, and Michael Keaton, or it might be globe trotters such as Sam Shepard or Jane Fonda and Ted Turner. "It was a totally new crowd for Livingston. There were artists and writers and a few professional people. The oldtimers in town didn't know what to think of it. But I made a lot of friends."

"I couldn't have run the place without him," Chatham says. "His reliability is stunning."

Chatham sold the Bar & Grille in 2007, and though

Godward briefly tended bar for the new owners, he and two partners had their eyes on an 1883 building near the corner of Park and Main that had housed The Slack Knuckle, Orion's and Calamity Jane's pubs. Owning a business had never been a goal for Godward. "I can't stand debt and I never liked being tied down." But at sixty-five, having survived prostate cancer and a heart attack, the time felt right. The bar and restaurant opened in 2009 as The Park Place Tavern, but in 2014 Glenn bought out his partners and renamed the establishment Glenn's. It served good, inexpensive food, craft beers, and tasty cocktails. A television hung from the wall, but it rarely if ever played. Despite its media clientele, the saloon existed outside media time. It was up close and personal.

"Glenn *sees* you," the guitarist and photographer, Libby Caldwell says. "That's important. And there wouldn't be a Glenn's without Glenn. He's why everyone is here."

———————

Richard Wheeler's eightieth birthday party has attracted ten or twelve celebrants toward the saloon's rear, and they are an accomplished bunch. In addition to Wheeler, who soon will publish his eightieth novel, they include other writers, musicians, agents, and artists. A nearby editor says, "I realized the other night that folks at our table had written more than thirty books, produced half a dozen albums, produced music videos, published an award winning magazine, and dickered publishing contracts for a number of the country's top writers. I thought, where but Glenn's."

"It's the Elaine's of Montana," adds the literary agent, Bob Dattila.

Wheeler himself says, "It's as close to being a club as any bar I've ever frequented. Of artists, writers, and media people. And Glenn is well-read." Harrison adds, "He is very calm and intelligent and you don't hear any of that verminish tea party trash that you hear in so many bars these days."

The Wheeler tables nosh on Glenn's pub dishes: everything from Thai Chicken Salad to a Grilled Vegetable Platter to Surf & Turf. But up front, it's the height of the 4:00 to 6:00 P.M. rush, and Godward is kibitzing with patrons ranging from an Indianapolis Speedway driver whose race car has a decal of Godward's face on its hood, to a man who once owned a dinosaur museum, to a former member of the Church Universal and Triumphant, who's engaged in "inter-dimensional repartee," to a professional bullfighter, Raymond Ansotegui, who apprenticed bartending with Godward at The Pastime but as a boy worked with has father inseminating cattle. "Don't listen to this guy," Godward shouts. "He's a rodeo clown and a cow fister!" Ansotegui grins, saying, "I never did anything but push them up the chute."

Then Ansotegui waxes serious: "Glenn taught me to be a gentleman bartender. Look around. This is the *heart* of Livingston. And it's here because of Glenn."

By 7:00 P.M., a former Irish musician is talking to himself at the bar's southwest corner, emitting to passersby the occasional "Go away and die," but otherwise behaving. *Honkytonk Heroes* is on the stereo and a lingering Barnacle, the author Tim Cahill, explains to a visitor how in December he'd died for several minutes in a rafting accident on the Colorado, but was resuscitated to drink once more at Glenn's. "It's peaceful here," he says. "A good bar reflects its owner's personality. And Glenn's is tranquil."

"I used to be pretty hotheaded though," Godward counters. "You get people drinking and they get mad about something, you don't want to take it personal. I used to worry, but I had a heart attack and I made up my mind that I wasn't going to let it get to me. I don't even drink anymore." He shakes his head. "Migraines."

Soon Cahill departs. The restaurant tables coddle a party or two, and after supper a few Barnacles will return to linger beneath Edd Enders' expressionistic railroad paintings and to banter with Godward until nine or ten, when he will attempt to close. "Our deck's open late in the summer," he says. "That's a younger crowd, which keeps us busy." A regular appears, not one of the Barnacles but a businessman with a rap that Godward has confessed drives him crazy.

He serves the fellow politely, listens to his blather a few moments, then retreats to the bar's far corner. "I really can't complain," he says, drawing himself a Coke. "Everyone has his cross to bear."

—*Montana Quarterly*, 2015

HOUSE JUSTIFIED: SAM PECKINPAH
IN MONTANA

A half-dozen bullet holes pockmarked the ceiling in Sam Peckinpah's apartment at Livingston's Murray Hotel, holes the director placed there one night while tossing maniacally in a fit of drug-fed paranoia. A Duncan Phyfe table 14 feet long stood near a rough-hewn bar where Peckinpah cheered pals such as actors Rip Torn and Warren Oates with strong drink and stand-up arm wrestling. To its left, I remember, was a New Year's eve photo of himself and a man who appeared to be Henry Fonda—party fezes askew and tinsel dripping—captioned "Story Conference." Beyond was Western memorabilia: a potbellied stove, a windup Victrola that might scratch Spade Cooley foxtrots, and walls hung with posters from the director's films: *The Ballad of Cable Hogue, Straw Dogs.* To the right was a shrine consisting of an antique Remington typewriter, upon which Peckinpah composed screenplays, framed by photos of himself directing, of his cowboy-bodyguard Allan Keller, and of cast members from *Bring Me the Head of Alfredo Garcia.* On a shelf was his leather-cased pool cue with the inscription, "To Sam Peckinpah, the world's second-worst pool player," a royalty check from MGM for 50 cents, sake cups, an Oriental thermos, an autographed picture of Harry

Truman, the director's copy of Paul Seydor's book, *Peckinpah: The Western Films*, and a wooden ranch sign reading, "*Listo Para*, Sam Peckinpah. Al Garcia."

Peckinpah lived at the Murray from 1979 until 1984—when he died in California of heart failure. He wrote as well as directed, so it was appropriate that novelists Richard Brautigan, Thomas McGuane, and William Hjortsberg resided outside Livingston, as did the actors Peter Fonda, Jeff Bridges, and Margot Kidder. But it was Warren Oates (star of *Garcia* and a *Wild Bunch* outlaw) who brought Sam to Montana. They purchased property together on Six Mile Creek, near Emigrant, in 1976. At Oates' death in 1982, Peckinpah kept the cabin he'd built there—Dennis Quaid later owned it—but lived at the Murray as a recluse.

There he had offices for his Latigo Productions, slept, wrote, and indulged. During August of 1980, and in October of 1983, I lived one floor below him. He was rarely heard from, except for an occasional shot fired through the ceiling or a call downstairs to the bar. A sign on his door—THE OLD IGUANA SLEEPS, AND THE ANSWER IS NO—discouraged visitors. He appeared in public once that first summer. He bought into the Murray's poker game, laid $1,000 on the barroom table, lost $700, picked up the remaining $300, said, "Boys, you'll never get this," and ate it.

After Peckinpah's death, I moved to his apartment. It consisted of five rooms, with a kitchen and two baths. I lived there during the summers of 1989 and 1990. Downstairs each morning a woman played "Home on the Range" on an oversized Hammond. At night trucks rumbled up Park Street, and saloon patrons who'd been dancing to the Murray's jukebox since 11:00 A.M., might be gaga to a live band by eight. Bikers, bindlestiffs, or big game hunters could be seen in the lobby—such as those spied one afternoon, grimy with five days' beard, who'd spread a six-pack of Lucky Lager around two .30-.30s disassembled on the table for cleaning. Sundays it was hard to tell whether Angelus bells summoning the faithful emanated from church or the depot across the way. While engines clanged in the railyard, music sifted from the bar and the Old Iguana's boot heels beat time in memory.

———➤

When Sam Peckinpah moved to Montana in 1977, both his reputation and his health were in decline. *Convoy* —the film version of C.W. McCall's truckers' ballad—had been completed, and though it would prove the highest-grossing picture of Sam's career, it received terrible reviews. And delays due to his drug and alcohol use during its filming had resulted in his being blackballed by the industry.

He had grown up by the Sierra Nevadas—a mountain near his Fresno home was named "Peckinpah"—and his great-grandparents had been pioneers migrating west. "They became lawyers and judges," Peckinpah would say. "They got too respectable. But my granddad, Denver Church, had a 4,100 acre cattle ranch in the foothills of the Sierras ... my earliest memory is of being strapped into a saddle when I was two for a ride up into the high country. We were always close to the mountains ... we'd summer in them and some winters I ran traplines in the snow. We loved that country, all of us."[67]

Livingston was a return to that mountain West. He lived first at its Yellowstone Motor Inn, then at the Guest House, and intermittently at Chico. "He loved Chico," Mike Art, its owner then, remembers. "His stories were terrific. We cashed a lot of fun checks." Then in 1978, Pat and Cliff Miller bought the old Murray Hotel in town and began its restoration. Peckinpah moved his Latigo production company first into room 204, then to a large suite at the third floor's rear, once leased by Walter Hill, son of James J. Hill of the Great Northern Railroad. Hill had decorated it with crystal chandeliers and ornate French doors, but Peckinpah covered its walls in barn siding and built a standup bar in its living room. He added

---

67   *Playboy* interview, 1972.

a small wood stove—"The heating wasn't good back there," Pat says—and placed it on bricks above a pine floor. "He had a huge wood box and the living room was very cozy and interesting," Pat would write. "His floor-height sofa and chair had been on the set of *Straw Dogs*."[68] The sofa had been the one upon its female lead had been so controversially raped.

Violence of course was one of Peckinpah's themes, and he was known to be violent toward family, friends and lovers. Ex-wives attested to this, and Pat says, "He threatened his son, Matt. He'd make him sleep in a bag outside the door. He didn't want him inside with the drugs." Livingston's Joe Swindlehurst—who would remain his friend and attorney throughout the Montana years—met Sam professionally. "He got into trouble with a young female film-person. Didn't amount to much, but it was something that would have landed him in jail in 2016."

Before the *Straw Dogs* sofa, Sam built an entertainment center, with a screen for showing films, and a large TV. He decorated the walls with photographs, one-sheets and Western prints by the artist, John Doyle. Several of Peckinpah's six Picassos were hung. For security he installed a burglar alarm wired to the Livingston sheriff's office, and covered his skylights with bars. In later years, drenched in paranoia, he would sit in the suite's entranceway snorting cocaine and cradling a .44 magnum, as he blasted through the door at imaginary assailants.

"The shots fired through the ceiling were like that," says Pat. "That night he thought he saw demons. Or insects. He may have had the DTs. When the roof leaked over his bed, he complained. I told him, 'You shot through the roof, call a carpenter and get it fixed!"

Ten years earlier he'd been the New Hollywood's darling, garnering reviews for *The Wild Bunch*, such as this from *The New Republic*: "Peckinpah is such a gifted director that I

---

68   *Life is What Happens to You When You Are Making Other Plans*, Pat Miller, 1995.

don't see how one can keep from using the word 'beautiful' about his work. There is a kinetic beauty in the very violence that his film lives and revels in ... The violence *is* the film." And this from *Time*: "*The Wild Bunch* contains faults and mistakes, but its accomplishments are more than sufficient to confirm that Peckinpah, along with Stanley Kubrick and Arthur Penn, belongs to the best of the newer generation of American filmmakers." He'd upped that ante with 1972's *The Getaway*, then again with 1973's *Pat Garrett and Billy the Kid*. But in 1979, he was lucky to find work as a second unit director on other people's films.

He took the jobs, though. "I'm a whore," he explained. "I go where I'm kicked. But I'm a good whore."[69]

He'd had a heart attack in Livingston, a serious one that had required the insertion of a pacemaker. He spent two weeks at Livingston Memorial, recovering from the operation and from delerium tremens. Joe and Carolyn Swindlehurst picked him up the morning of his release. Doctor's orders were no cigarettes and no alcohol. He'd been living at the Yellowstone Inn, and rather than go to his room, he turned into the bar. He ordered a Ramos Fizz, drank it, gurgled "Arghh," and fell backward off the barstool. "We thought he'd died," Swindlehurst recalls. "Carolyn started to cry and we're looking at him. His mustache began to twitch. Suddenly he can't help it anymore and he starts to laugh."

"I just wanted to see whether you cared," Peckinpah said.

That sort of black humor endeared him to drinking buddies but not to friends and family. By 1979, he'd gone through three marriages and essentially was alone. Then he found the Murray.

The 1904 railroad hotel, enlarged in the 1920s, was straight off a Peckinpah story board. It was like something from his movies. Its four stories, once elegant, had been gutted after the 1978 sale. A Murray investor and poker partner of Sam's told him about the Walter Hill suite. Sam took one look and

---

69   *Playboy* interview, 1972.

booked it.

"He felt he'd come home," Pat Miller says. "He paid $700 a month and called me Boss Lady. There was never an edge to it."

She'd write, in a memoir, "We knew his health was very marginal. He walked downstairs. Someone always took him up in the elevator. I wanted him to run it himself but he declined with the excuse that he was not mechanical and if he got stuck between floors he would become suicidal. So we laughed and kept traveling in the 1905 Otis."

Peckinpah, like many alcoholics, suffered from depression. He'd discovered cocaine on the set to 1975's *Killer Elite*, where it had been prevalent. It seemed the perfect anti-depressant; Freud had been addicted, as had the fictional Sherlock Holmes. Its deleterious effects then were not widely known. The drug cheered Sam but intensified his paranoia, his personality shifts, and what may have been a bipolar disorder.

Fêtes in Peckinpah's suite became legendary; he was generous with his stash. "He'd make you snort it off the back of the toilet," a friend recalls. "You'd straddle the bowl and suck it up with a straw." The "loved him/hated him" dichotomy tilted toward "love" in Peck's place. "He was very charming," the businessman John Fryer remembers. "But he could turn on a dime."

"I think he was a split personality," Pat Miller says. E. Jean Carroll, who interviewed him at the Murray in 1982, recalls, "There were several personality changes" during their meetings. "He'd get in a mood and you'd get in a mood." In her *Rocky Mountain* profile of Sam, she describes a script chat with McGuane, where Peckinpah suddenly screams "Fuck you!" and invites Tom outside.[70] "He was a terrible human being," McGuane insists. "But most of his violence was theatrical." Despite the abuse, friends stayed loyal and unsuspecting journalists fawned. His interviews were famously caustic. Brandishing a weapon one night, he chased a Japanese film crew downstairs at the Guest House, where its bartender had

---

70   The challenge was an invitation to share drugs, McGuane says.

to restrain him. "He would blow up physically," Swindlehurst explains. "But at heart he abhorred violence."

Cocaine heightened his gun play, which was not solely directed at humans. "Sam had a couple of cats in the apartment," Pat says. "He wanted cats with no tails, so he tried to shoot their tails off. Shot along the edge of the floor. He didn't hit any. But there were bullet holes in the entranceway."

"He scared me with those pistols," Mike Art recalls. "He'd wave them around. When he drank, he grew whiskey muscles."

In addition to the .44 Magnum, Peckinpah kept a Bible by his bed. "The pistol laid on top of it," Pat says. "His Bible and his gun. I should have taken a picture of that." It was an image too loaded to have worked in his films, but it was redolent with the contradictions in his personality and of his past.

———————

"My father was a superior court judge," Peckinpah would say. "He believed in the Bible as literature, and in the law. He was an *authority* ... a deeply religious man."[71] He also was violent, striking Sam and his sister, Fern Lea, at any disobedience. His mother was an hysteric who bathed with Sam until he was four and slept with him each birthday night until he was fourteen.

"Mother, fortunately and unfortunately, was the most powerful figure in his life," Fern Lea told Peckinpah's biographer, David Weddle. "He got his creativity from her, though I'm certain he would have denied it. Sam was basically a woman, emotionally ... I think he was embarrassed by it because in our family, 'By God, the men are men!' ... he didn't want that side of him to show."[72]

Inevitably it did, and the Peckinpah males were troubled by Sam's delicate features and his prettiness. E. Jean Caroll,

---

71   *Playboy* interview, 1972.
72   *"If They Move ... Kill 'Em"*, David Weddle, 1994.

recalls, "He was tiny. He could have starred in *The Danish Girl*." His father "never understood Sam's theatrical ambitions, his writing," his sister-in-law, Betty Peckinpah told Weddle. "For me, the tragedy of Sam was that he spent his life trying to find acceptance from that family. The macho posturing ... that wasn't Sam. It was, but it wasn't ... It made him one of the saddest people I ever knew."

The sadness manifested itself in uncontrollable rages and in deep melancholy.

It persisted through military school, the Marine Corps, China during WW II, graduate school in theater arts, an apprenticeship in television and from the first, a precocious directorial career. Drugs, alcohol, and women abated it. But nothing proved its cure.

"I saw him that way," Pat Miller recalls. "I felt really bad because he was alone and there wasn't anybody in the apartment. One winter day he called down and said, 'Could one of the housekeepers come up? My kitchen's so dirty and I don't even have a broom.' I sent up my mother. She cleaned his kitchen, then said, 'He followed me around the whole time.' She had been a nurse. 'You know, Pat,' she said, 'he's pretty depressed.' He called me the next day and said, 'What you doing Boss Lady? I thought you might get some whipped cream and raspberries and give me a back rub.' I told him I'd take a rain check. He said, 'You'll take a rain check? Well, the offer will remain open.' He was very lonely. There aren't any raspberries in Montana in the winter."

The one place in childhood where his spirits rose was at his grandfather's ranch in the Sierra Nevadas. "It offered a vision of paradise," Weddle reported. "He watched the older men working the cattle in their leather boots and chaps and weathered Stetsons; smelled the wood smoke, sweat, and dust; watched the lariats whirling slow and weightless in the air, then flicking out around the head of a steer and pulling it taut and vibrating. He drank in the rough, raw sensuousness of it all." His grandfather had a rustic cabin "where a huge pot of beans, onions, potatoes, and venison was always bubbling." At night, "he listened to the tales the men told ... of cattle stampedes, desperate horseback rescues in mountain snowstorms, river crossings, prizefights, and wrestling matches...." The stuff of his future films.

He would have his cabin up Six Mile. If not a replica, then a reminder of his childhood Eden.

———

There's a scene at the opening of *Ride the High Country*, Peckinpah's second film, that is the view across Six Mile from Sam's cabin. It is of a mountain framed by tall pines, and it's of the Sierras. When Sam saw the high end of Oates' property by the creek he must have recognized it. He'd situate his cabin there—which would prove not an easy process.

The contractor and tipi maker, Don Ellis, was standing in a field when he first heard Peckinpah's name. "I was building a log house and this man—whom I'd seen drive by several times—stopped and said, 'How'd you like to build a cabin for Sam Peckinpah?' I said, 'Who's Sam Peckinpah?'"

The director had blueprints in hand, but what Ellis had to do was haul timber four miles up a winding dirt road, cut them on three sides and fit them to the architect's plan. A Polaroid survives of Peckinpah before the incomplete cabin, smiling. "He seemed happy enough," Ellis remembers. "I built the kitchen counters, and the first time he saw them he stabbed a knife into one." The cabin had a master bedroom facing the lower Six Mile meadows, a stone fireplace and conversation pit, a small guest room, a dining area and a kitchen facing the mountains. It was remote, had neither running water nor electricity, and "was a bear to take care of," Ellis says. Peckinpah's visits were sporadic. When there, he would drink with hangers on like the rodeo cowboy/bodyguard Allen Keller, his neighbor on Six Mile, Harvey Counts (who'd done time for pistol whipping a man) and his attorney, Joe Swindlehurst. "He loved the cabin," Joe says, "but after his heart attack he didn't go up there as much. He was afraid something might happen."

His emotional swings were wider and more frequent. Ellis recalls driving him to Cooke City, and on the way back "he started to hallucinate flying saucers. He wasn't drunk, but you never knew what he might have taken." He was writing a screenplay for a film about cannibalism in the Donner Pass. It wasn't going well. And the film projects he eventually accepted—second unit directing on the comedy, *Jinxed* and *The Osterman Weekend* —were beneath him or elegies to his paranoia.

Ellis was employed to hang barn siding on the walls of Sam's Murray suite, and built cabinets and the standup bar out of planks from a snow fence on the Millers' ranch. While the cabin remained Edenic, the Murray suite, with its burglar alarms and grated windows, its hiding places for drugs and cash, became a paranoid's fortress. "I used to check on him every afternoon," Pat remembers. "He was nocturnal, so about one I'd go upstairs and call for him. He would shout "Leave me alone," or "Get out of here," and I'd know he was all right." But some days, manager Ralph White, would say, "Don't go up there, Pat. He's sitting in front of the door with a gun." He had a brief marriage to Marcy Blueher (a woman Ellis later would wed) but his rages, the drug-fueled and alcoholic abuse, finished it. Then suddenly he got better. The last year of his life he was sober; he made amends, shot two music videos for John Lennon's son, Julian, and had contracted for a new film—from a screenplay by Stephen King, titled *The Shotgunners*.

Then he suffered a massive coronary in 1984 and, on December 28, died. He was fifty-nine years old.

"His lease for the suite had been up," Pat remembers. "A few days before he passed he called and said, 'Well Boss Lady, I just signed the lease for another five years. 'Will you be there?' I said, I will be, unless you want to buy the hotel. He said, 'Well, I'd love to buy it. If I could find the money, I'd buy it in a minute.' He did love the Murray," Pat says. "And to us, he was a friend."

One summer day in the early 1990s, I hiked from Warren Oates' former house near the mouth of Six Mile, up the dirt road to Sam's cabin. His son, Mathew, was in its yard, and we sat staring at the mountains and talking about Sam. What we said was inconsequential, but it was a moment. Mathew seemed to have settled with his father's legacy. As he'd tell David Weddle, "It seemed like we really came to terms, in a lot of ways ... He was trying hard not to be a crazy renegade, the wild son of a bitch that he'd been in the past. He'd call me up in the middle of the night sometimes and say, 'You remember that time up in the cabin in Montana when I said so-and-so?' I just want you to know I didn't mean it.'"

Two lines from Sam's films came to mind. One, a quote from Sam's father, that's spoken by Joel McCrea in *Ride the High Country*: "All I want is to enter my house justified." The other, probably written by Sam, is from *The Wild Bunch*: "We all dream of being a child again. Even the worst of us—perhaps the worst most of all."

I apologized to Mathew for having interrupted his privacy, and hiked back down the creek.

—*Big Sky Journal*, 2016

DAVID LYNCH: ALIEN

All afternoon David Lynch has been tinkering with *Dune*—the $40,000,000 extravaganza he is directing for Dino De Laurentiis—but now he's cadged a few seconds alone in his office, surrounded by five Woody Woodpecker dolls and a statue of Bob's Big Boy costumed as an extraterrestrial. There's an energy to this den, with Lynch's drawings about, his art books, his Laurie Anderson tapes, that misshapen rocket sculpture on the floor, the relief he's molding of Raffaella De Laurentiis ("a relief when it's finished"), the doodles and designs for experimental furniture that will double as sculpture. Downstairs at Van der Veer Photo Effects the minions may be laboring at numerous De Laurentiis projects—*Firestarter, Conan the Destroyer, Dune*—but here Lynch is telephoning the latest of his *Angriest Dog in the World* cartoons to the L.A. *Reader*, a free, alternative newspaper he won't abandon to his success. He's telephoning because the drawings never change, only their dialogue. The cartoon is a paradigm of constriction—a reptilian pup straining against his tether in a suburban backyard. This is, according the Lynch's standing caption, THE DOG WHO IS SO ANGRY HE CANNOT MOVE. HE CANNOT SLEEP. HE CANNOT EAT. HE CAN JUST BARELY GROWL BOUND SO TIGHTLY WITH TENSION AND ANGER, HE APPROACHES THE STATE OF RIGOR MORTIS.

"All set?" he asks his cartoon editor. "Here's number one— 'What are you doing with that gun' 'I'm going to load it and blow my brains out.' 'Man, you scared me ... For a second I thought you were going to use it on me.'"

The Angriest Dog growls. "Here's number two—"

Next door, Raffaella's office, with its plush furnishings and art, has a bit more of the $40,000,000 touch—but there are two odd, conceptual pieces by Lynch, his *Fish Kit* and *Chicken Kit,* both animals dismembered, photographed, and with "stitch kits for assembly." Lynch, after all, is the director who once singed the hair off a live mouse with Nair to study it. So Raffaella indulges him. Dino's thirty-one-year-old daughter and the producer of *Dune,* she is busy producing *Conan the Destroyer, Tai-Pan,* and Lynch's next film, *Blue Velvet,* a love-story/murder mystery which he's to start shooting this fall. Between editing *Dune* and thinking up cartoons, he's still writing *Blue Velvet*'s script. It will be a small film, more like *Eraserhead,* the 1977 midnight classic that launched his movie career.

Lynch is attracted to smallness. He likes minutiae; he can control them. Yesterday he endured a luncheon with the Universal brass, who had screened a rough cut of *Dune.* He is well aware that *Dune* could make or break him. With the art film *Eraserhead* to his credit, which colleague John Waters calls "one of the best movies ever," plus *The Elephant Man,* for which Lynch received two Academy Award nominations, he doesn't want to blow it. At thirty-eight, Lynch is the envy of every young director in Hollywood. But this afternoon he's fled to feed his subtler passions.

"Cartoon number three," Lynch says to the *Reader.*

The Angriest Dog heaves against its leash.

David Lynch was a painter long before he became a movie-maker. So there's this fantasy he harbors of leasing the Toluca Lake Bob's Big Boy, and flying Mary Boone or Leo Castelli in from New York to host a show of his more ambitious canvases. When Lynch dines here he checks Hollywood at the door. To him Bob's is a pinion of the American Art Life—he *thinks* here, sketches, and above all conceptualizes.

"The Art Life has been *real* important to me," says Lynch. "I read this book by Robert Henri, *The Art Spirit*. What I took from it was that art comes first. In the Art Life you don't get married and you don't have families and you have studios and models and you drink a lot of coffee and you smoke cigarettes and you work mostly at night. Your place smells like oil paint and you think beneath the surface of things and you live a fantastic life of ideas. And create stuff."

The director cocks his head, inhaling Bob's cacophony. The restaurant's brightness is startling to one acquainted with Lynch only through his movies—under lighted and clanking with industrial imagery, surrealist shop films of the soul. But Bob's glare seems to console him; it's an anodyne to his creative anxiety. Lynch's face, like a young Jimmy Stewart's on steroids, opens with a fey grin.

"I've had this *fear*," he says, "the fear of being restricted—in every way. And I used to be afraid to go to coffee shops, especially on my own. I was afraid to go out of the house. I couldn't face the world."

A curious statement from a director who, through his considerable charm, to say nothing of his talent, in eight years hiked himself from the cloistered anonymity of an American Film Institute fellowship to the helm of one of the most elaborate movies every made. But fear and creativity trot in double harness for Lynch. When one's mentioned, the other is right behind.

"The fear started in Philadelphia," Lynch says, "but it's got a lot to do with the city. Because I grew up in Idaho, with this perfect, middle-class childhood, city things scared me. My mother is from Brooklyn, and when I visited there as a kid, it always scared me. Later, at art school, my brother-in-law Jack Fisk and I lived next door to a morgue in a factory neighborhood of Philadelphia. *Eraserhead* came from that." In high school Lynch began painting seriously and rented a first studio with pal Fisk—director of *Raggedy Man*. He attended Corcoran Art School sporadically before graduating from Hammond High in 1964, then hit Europe with Fisk for a time "before realizing I was 7,000 miles from McDonald's" and that he was, passionately, "an *American* artist." He cut his trip short, returned home to various jobs to support his painting, and eventually followed Fisk to the Pennsylvania Academy of the Fine Arts in 1965. I was the late '60s before he experimented with filmmaking. His first films, *The Alphabet* and *The Grandmother* ("about a confused little boy who grows his own grandmother from a seed"), combined painting and film and were indeed adjuncts to his painting. The were eccentrically animated and included filmed shots of still canvases that were interspersed with bright color against black sets.

"I wanted to do a kind of film-painting," he remembers. "Using film as a painter would. I was interested in paintings that moved, sort of. And with sound."

He also was experimenting with film-sculpture. He constructed a sculptured screen with three-dimensional heads, upon which he projected a one-minute film on a loop, with six people vomiting—"their heads on fire"—that endlessly repeated itself. "The whole thing cost two hundred bucks."

Lynch carried his Academy vision to the AFI in 1970, where as a fellow in the Center for Advanced Film Studies he took five years to complete *Eraserhead*—a painterly work, somehow bridging the black-and-white worlds of Charlie Chaplin and Robert Motherwell. It established Lynch as a kind of one-man Ashcan School of film, terrifying audiences with its bleak humor and psychological intensity. The movie found some pocket of the American nightmare that hadn't been reached—not in the high-tech, suburban horrors of Spielberg nor in the historical allegories of Coppola. It was surrealistic, owing much to the surrealist painters' experimentations with film, but cinematically more in line with the mood pieces of a Hitchcock, Billy Wilder, or Jacques Tati.

Lynch so immersed himself in the Art Life during *Eraserhead*'s shooting that he lived on the set, in the bedroom of its protagonist, Henry—a weird yet sensitive dreamer with a mile-high '50s hairdo, a troubled wife, and a monster baby that he eventually kills. Lynch emerged each night for his *Wall Street Journal* paper route and for the shakes at Bob's. He was earning forty-eight dollars a week. He had run out of money on the film. His first marriage had broken up, and he had no place to live. "I'd lock myself in Henry's room in a way that from the outside it looked as if no one could possibly be inside."

By the time he completed *Eraserhead*, Lynch had come to see film, with its acting and collaborative activity, as a more direct route to the unconscious and as an extension of '50s action painting, his first love. But painting gnawed at him; he needed to return to it for sustenance, and for sure footing.

Between the completion of *Eraserhead* in 1976 ("my Bicentennial film"), its release in 1978 by Ben Barenholtz, father of the midnight movie, and the beginning of *The Elephant Man* in 1978, Lynch wrote *Ronnie Rocket*, a screenplay about "a little guy with red hair and 60-cycle, alternating current," and did little else but paint.

The point being that Lynch may be the first director of his generation to come from, and remain in, a painterly tradition. As an *artistic* director, he's something of an outcast in Hollywood, or at least someone puzzling to others. For one thing the man broods, and when things get heavy, he lightens up by visiting Bob's. "An awful lot is hidden in life," he says. "And it's pretty neat. But a lot of times, when things are dark, you start *thinking* about what is hidden. And you worry."

Lynch sips his fourth cup of coffee, begins to draw on a napkin.

There's no dark side to Bob's Big Boy," he says. "The dark side is in my mind."

———

"You really must show these," Gilbert Marouani is saying of Lynch's canvases. "They're *important*—a show in Paris, it can be arranged." Lynch and Marouani, his musical coordinator on *Dune*, have decamped to Lynch's Westwood apartment after a trying day. "*Jeelbear*," Lynch whines, "I just don't know." The two have been discussing Lynch's previous shows in Mexico City and Puerto Vallarta, but Lynch is edgy, anxious to break free of Marouani and work on the screenplay to *Blue Velvet*.

"*Daveed*, really—"

The director is barely coping. It's 11:00 P.M., and he's beat. Yet he looks quite uptown in this white-on-white duplex, with its zebra-skin rug and blue Art Deco furniture.

Conversation drones on. Finally Lynch surrenders and lays out scrapbook photos form the set of *Eraserhead*: snapshots of the director as young genius, affecting three neckties and a battered straw hat; photos of Jack Nance as Henry, with his "high-look" haircut; photos of Sissy Spacek, Fisk's wife, who helped briefly with promoting and ultimately with the film's financing; and of Spike, Henry's monster child.

Earlier tonight Lynch directed himself with the assistance of old-timer Jack Cardiff, in his screen debut. Lynch played a radio operator wearing goggles and a rubber trench coat, and he wasn't half bad. "Hitchcock was in all his movies—I've already missed two." Acting has capped a list of creative indulgences today that includes editing *Dune*, writing a script, composing cartoons, sketching, and directing.

He has fun intermittently with this project, despite knowing it's his megabreak and, with *Dune II* and *III* under contract, his future. Should he pull it off, he'll be among the most powerful directors in Hollywood. If that prospect seems odd in light of his character—dreaminess is his forte—it plays into people's awe of him. He quickly sheds whatever social nebbishness he displays, to rise to the business at hand. He is a calculating dreamer.

Earlier, at a poolside supper in Studio City, there had been an argument between Toto, the rock group scoring *Dune*, and Gilbert Marouani. By July the score must be completed, and Toto was negotiating for more time. Throughout supper, Lynch had told stories and jokes and lightened the mood with country-boy charm. Now everyone was tense. Marouani argued, "For every day this movie's late to Universal, it costs us $50,000 in interest." The musicians pleaded, citing artistic integrity. Lynch was torn—sound is so important to him ("50 percent of a movie"), as is the integrity of the smaller artist. Finally he said, "If this movie's not finished by August, Dino's gonna kill me." Everyone laughed.

"It's not so much compromise in directing," Lynch says now, "but finding the third solution. A director is a filter through which every decision passes. He holds the reins but must *have* reins too. That's the money people's job. I hate having reins, but I would go totally crazy if I was left alone. And Dino could take the picture away from me."

"Unlikely," Raffaella's personal assistant has said. "Dino and David embrace, they kiss. And this from De Laurentiis, with his reputation for terrible clashing with directors. But people *love* David, he's so much the artist. You know, the world is not reality for him."

—————

It is an odd period in Hollywood when a director like Lynch, more in touch with the horrors of subconscious existence than any filmmaker since Luis Buñuel, can win the trust of Dino and Raffaella De Laurentiis. "People ask if we've allowed David his creativity on *Dune*," Raffaella says, incredulously. "Would we hire a David Lynch and then castrate him?"

They might, if money were the issue. But Dino is too cagey for that. A cyclical producer, with films in his ledger as diverse as *Flash Gordon* and Fellini's *La Strada*, he heads possibly the richest of independent production companies, at a time when independent production is calling the shots. It's a moment of flux in Hollywood—not unlike those post-*Easy Rider* years—when major studios made huge investments in a youth culture they didn't understand, falling over backward to stake any independent who, by turning a dollar, could keep them current. These days the indies, from Dino De Laurentiis to the 16-millimeter kids, are being courted avidly by major studios desperate to supply an insatiable cable, cassette, and multiplex market with product.

It helps that established directors, like Francis Coppolla, Steven Spielberg, Sydney Pollack, and others in what has been called "the million-dollar-club," have nearly priced themselves out of the game.

And yet young directors today, anxious to work, are being hired not just for their lower fees but for the sensitivity to the traditions from which they're emerging: television commercials, rock videos, and cult films of a mildly exploitive nature. Each of these traditions is new, and each has changed the way Americans see film. Cult movies like *Android, Repo Man, Eating Raoul, Liquid Sky, Smithereens, Suburbia,* and *Eraserhead* share a contemporary vision and look, and are exploitative in that they mine the baser instincts of the American Dream. The cult directors' interests are those of their generation. And they are auteurs. De Laurentiis is smart, because David Lynch is the best of these, and Dino has him under contract. But Lynch is like his generation in other ways, too. Ways that might in the end undermine that Medici prince of Hollywood. Lynch's attention span is short. And, like so many of his legendary contemporaries, the idea of commitment makes him uncomfortable.

———➤

The Tuna steaks at Mortons are grilled just so, the asparagus is fresh, the flowers and exotic plants happily tended, and so many tanned grimace-smiles float through the shrubbery, it's like Lynch's canvas, *Smiling Boy Wallpaper,* come to life. There's Carol Burnett, there's Alan King, there's what's her name, Ernie Kovac's daughter, there's Arnold Schwartzenegger, there's Howard Cosell. But Lynch is oblivious—he's curled about a draftsman's pen, sketching examples of '50s atomic furniture for his guests.

"David makes an *unusual* husband," Mary Lynch said earlier, in their Virginia home. She's his wife of seven years, mother of their two-year-old son, and sister of Jack Fisk. "Our house is quite near Jack and Sissy's, but David's rarely here. What can I say? The guy's wanted to make films from day one, and I'm not going to be the person to stop him. But—he's still *real* interested in painting," she added hopefully.

"I never had that much luck in painting," Lynch says. "But in film, it was as if doors kept opening for me. A lot of it has to do with breaks. I have a limited life as a director—everyone does."

He orders a drink. Conversation drifts toward the '58 Packard Hawk he's restoring, toward a '59 Impala he drove as a kid, and toward how *Blue Velvet* will in part be a car picture. Lynch loves cars. Once, his mother, at a loss for praise during a women's club luncheon, exclaimed, "David's a very fine driver!" Lynch seems more at ease tonight, after what has been a troubling afternoon. There was another meeting at Universal. Lynch was either so distracted or so upset afterward that he skipped an important appointment to hang out at the body shop with his Hawk. But—it's *unsettled* him to see the car torn apart, its insides exposed, and his mind shifts with vivid, Lynchian imagery to a description of a child he's seen with a severely injured arm. It reminds him of his first memory of the movies, with his parents at an Idaho drive-in, watching *Wait 'Til the Sun Shines, Nellie.* There'd been this little girl, on screen, who'd strangled slowly on a button.

'My parents were *different*," he says, "and fairly quiet. I was ashamed of my parents for being the way they were. My mother liked a bit of a city, but I always said of my father, 'If you cut his leash he'd go right into the woods.'" Lynch tests his cocktail. "I'm not big on reality," he says. "I prefer a dream, but I've always thought there was something more to life than the surface. That's why I like factories." He brightens. "They *are* what's beneath the surface, they're the unconscious in a way. I've used them in all my films. Factories get me in my *soul*. It's the rhythm of their machines, the relationship of those different shapes, and all my favorite things: glass with wire in it, soot, steel, cement, fire, tremendously powerful sounds, and images. A factory *thrills* you, you feel the universe in it, as you should in a great film. To create or build something is the neatest thing in the world, and a factory is a place to build things. Yet there's decay—in everything."

Lynch stares hard at his glass. What he's just said seems to have moved him.

The waiter serves a second course. Functionaries scurry. "I started transcendental meditation in 1973," Lynch blurts, "while I was shooting *Eraserhead*. I'd had trouble with the isolation of painting. But I still wasn't happy. 'Why not?' I said. 'I've all these friends around, I'm making the movie I want to.' But happiness is a weird thing. I'm considering psychotherapy. I'm a sick person," he says, laughing. "I have this strange, recurring habit pattern, never mind what, that a doctor has got to examine."

Someone orders dessert. Lynch brightens.

"My films," he says, "don't have a lot to do with my surface life. Subconscious life, yes. I like surrealism, and to me a lot of the world is very absurd. I like alterations, and I like distortions. When I went to art school in Philadelphia, my world became smaller and smaller. I started going inside myself. And it was great. It was always night and always a dream. I was in and among ideas, swimming right near them, and able to study them. During *Eraserhead*, I was able to live in a world below the surface for *five* years. I haven't able to do that with *Dune*. It's too huge, with too many people. With *Eraserhead* I never had to articulate any ideas. They could stay closer to where I'd captured them. And keep their power. They maintained a purity and were very abstract. But if I'd articulated them, verbally or in writing, people would have said, 'What the hell are you talking about?' They were able to stay as film ideas. I was very safe."

The others chatter among themselves. Lynch draws closer. "There are tremendous gambles being taken with *Dune*, financial for Dino, artistic for me. I mean, Michael Cimino's *The Deer Hunter* is one of my favorite movies. I haven't seen *Heaven's Gate*, but—I know a film can get away from you. It just can. If he'd had Dino there it would have been different. We *need* boundaries. Dino's an expert at pressure, but I've learned the trick is to use it. A lot of people say, 'These bastards, if only I could get rid of them, then I could create great art.' But pressure forces you to think in much higher gear. It's hell, but it's *real good*."

Lynch squirms a bit, accepts his coffee. "Right now, after *Blue Velvet* and *Ronnie Rocket*, I'm set to shoot *Dune II* and *III*. All for Dino. He says, 'I've adopted you.'" Lynch chuckles uneasily. "I've got my work cut out for me."

The director stretches, looks about the room. He fidgets. He digs beneath his shirt collar. Suddenly he's digging seriously, as if for a bug or some terrible itch. His face contorts. Someone loosens his tie. He digs again and this time surfaces with an irritating label. He flips it toward the ashtray.

"I've *got* to get back to painting," he says.

——◆

There are any number of ways that Hollywood can kill you: blind adulation, too much exposure, not enough control. Another is by not letting you in.

In a run-down building off Venice Boulevard, Jack Nance, David Lynch's star discovery, Henry in *Eraserhead*, sits in the darkness and nurses a warm beer. His three-day growth of beard and close-cropped hair are for a small part in Richard Benjamin's *City Heat*. His apartment is darker than anything in Lynch's imagination, darker than Henry's place, so dark that no one but a mole or Jack Nance could navigate it.

Nance is forty. He looks sixty. His voice is gravel. His famous hair has grayed, and he wears a tiny cardigan sweater. Nance has a long list of theatrical credits, but he's worked in just three major films since *Eraserhead*. "I did some Chuck Norris karate things, too." His performance in *Eraserhead* was brilliant, and Lynch considers him the equal of John Gielgud and John Hurt. Nance strokes his stubbled chin. Outside, the Chicano kids crank up their ghetto blasters and kick at the walls.

This is the Art Life Lynch can always return to.

"I ... was on the street for two years," Nance mutters. "I managed this apartment building awhile."

He shrugs in the shadows, then gestures reverently. "But David—you know, he's a *born* director, he was born to the task." A pause. "He hired me for *Dune*." Another pause. "I was in Mexico a month and the guy—his *humor* is what does it, you know. But secretive. He's *the* most secretive and protective person of anything he does. *Viciously* protective. When we shot *Eraserhead*, he had to unlock the set every night with wrenches. One day the AFI directors, George Stevens and Toni Vellani, came down with some dignitary and Lynch wouldn't show it to *them*."

Nance manages a laugh. He sips his beer, then smacks his lips nostalgically. "But David. He took *care* of us on that film, *Eraserhead* has been a gold mine. Everyone got paid, shit, we're still getting paid. He's *devout*, you know. Hollywood's rough. But Lynch—hell, D. Lynch will survive."

—*Esquire*, 1985

Postscript: *Dune* premiered on December 3, 1984 and opened on December 14 to negative reviews. Roger Ebert gave it one out of four stars, and called it the worst movie of the year. Gene Siskell said, "I hated watching this film." Janet Maslin gave the film one star out of five, and generally panned it. The film lost approximately $15,000,000 at the box office, but was nominated for an Academy Award for best sound. Not having final cut, Lynch distanced himself from the project, saying later that "I started selling out on *Dune*. Looking back, it's no one's fault but my own. I probably shouldn't have done that picture, but I saw tons and tons of possibilities for things I loved, and this was the structure to do them in. There was so much room to create a world." He would return to smaller projects like *Blue Velvet, Twin Peaks, Wild at Heart, Mulholland Drive, Lost Highway,* and *The Straight Story*, re-establishing himself as one of Hollywood's finest directors. He would have his Leo Castelli opening, too. His paintings were exhibited there in 1989. Since then, he has shown widely around the world.

TWILIGHT OF THE DRIVE-IN

The view from behind the windshield is this: a 60-foot-wide screen upon which a geologist negotiates the digestive tract of a titanic alien, the action backdropped by a full moon and the darkened ridge of Libby's Cabinet Mountains. There are dozens of cars lined up like pigs before a trough, springs sighing as patrons neck or heave toward the concession stand for chili dogs or pretzels with hot cheese. There are couples in lawn chairs, kids hanging from tailgates or blanketed on the roofs of station wagons. And all around Montanans are mating. Then there's myself: a middle-aged guy in a red Porsche, a wallflower at the drive-in.

I finish my Hogburger and settle back, the 911's hood elevated on its rippled grade. The movie is *Evolution*, an end-of-the-world comedy that seems tastelessly apropos for Libby, the asbestosis capital of America. Actors pump Head and Shoulders up the posterior of a gargantuan extra-terrestrial, only to be sprayed with alien poop. The score emits Wagnerian strains below monsterly bellows. A hand reaches out; I jump. It's a boy with a squeegee, scrubbing my windshield for tips.

"Do girls look at you a lot in this car?" the ten-year-old asks.

"Not tonight," I say. He shrugs. I flip him a buck. Libbyans are nothing if not fatalistic.

Despite the town's reputation for asbestosis, my radio has declared that the EPA is now promoting Libby as "a safe place to live and visit," and that there's no "excess risk from asbestos pollution." This after a year of monitoring its vermiculite mine and related locales. KTNY's announcer was concerned about "undoing" the national coverage, and reestablishing Libby's status as a "safe and wholesome community."

I cut *Evolution*'s FM track and saunter toward the projection booth. It's cold this July evening—perhaps forty degrees. "No mosquitoes," owner Leo Huber brags, slapping his biceps. He's a fast talking guy, stocky, gray-haired and a bit stooped at seventy-three from a life of major work. He wears dark slacks, suspenders, a white windbreaker, cowboy boots. A former heavy equipment operator on the Kootenai Dam and Alaska Pipeline, Leo admits, "I didn't want to own a theater. My wife badgered me."

"I hated to see him gone," Emelia Huber says of the Alaska years. "I told him he had to quit."

She and Leo have run the Libby since 1980. Emelia's a courtly brunette in a teal blouse and glasses, who greets friends from a picnic table by the concession stand. She remains seated, having recently broken a leg. "Hi Emelia," folks say. Or, "When you gonna sell this thing?" She smiles enigmatically.

Libby is so far north that at 10:30 P.M. it's barely dark. Fifty miles from Canada and thirty from Idaho, this is a preposterous locale for a drive-in. But it's always done well, and at least one couple, Margie and Doug Ladely, has driven an hour east from Bonners Ferry to visit the theater—one of six remaining DI's in Montana.

"It's a family thing," explains Margie, who grew up in Alaska. "An outdoor experience. I'd hate to see it go."

Yet go it might. The Hubers have their drive-in on the market (as do two other proprietors of Montana DI's). The land that most theaters occupy is valuable. Pamida offered to buy the Libby's five acres of grass and speaker poles, but could not meet Leo's price. "He makes it hard for them," Emelia says, "because he doesn't really want to sell." An entrepreneur from California is on the hook. "I'd like to sell," Leo says, "for the right price. I'd like a young person to take over." He studies me. "*You* should buy it."

I laugh. I am touring Montana's drive-ins on a pilgrimage that with luck should take me from Plentywood's Sunset DI, to Terry's Prairie, down to Lewistown's Westernaire, north to Butte's Silverbow Twin, and up to Columbia Falls' Midway Theater to complete the circle. This trip is in part an exercise in nostalgia. But it's also one of fear. Of thirty-nine Montana drive-ins extant during the nineteen-sixties, these are what remain.

———

That decade saw the peak of the national market. In 1968, there were 4,700 theaters in the U.S., but the tally as of the year 2000, according to the Motion Picture Association of America, was 512. Given the relentless competition of multiplex theaters, DVDs, VCRs, cable and satellite TV hookups, that figure in 2002 certainly is lower.

It's hard to imagine a world prior to DI's, but such did exist. Not until June 1933 did Richard Milton Hollingshead open the first drive-in theater on a four-hundred-car lot in Camden, New Jersey—Walt Whitman's hometown. Hollingshead's DI was the first drive-in *anything*. He erected a screen on the roof of his machine-parts shop, graded his lot into ramped semicircles, set up a sixteen millimeter projector, and placed speakers beside the screen. He was acting in the throes of a powerful vision—one that illuminated America's growing obsession with the automobile and that haunting view from behind the windshield.

Drive-ins did not flourish until after WW II. By 1952, fifteen-million more cars were on the road than in 1946, and drive-ins increased proportionately. The Libby DI opened in 1948, as did its indoor "hardtop" sibling, the Dome, on downtown's Mineral Avenue. Lewistown's Westernaire opened in 1944, Columbia Falls' Midway in 1952, Plentywood's Sunset in 1952, Terry's Prairie in 1953, and Butte's Silver Bow as late as 1977. Nationally, hardtops were declining, causalities of television programming and a middle class flight from the cities. DI's, or "ozoners," rode the suburban wave.

From the first, there was an outlaw feel to the DI. "It was always a receptacle for the slightly disreputable film," critic John Bloom has said. "One that you couldn't show next door to *Snow White and the Seven Dwarfs* at your local six-plex." Drive-in owners denied that they were sleaze mongering. "They've been denying it since 1948," says Bloom. "You thumb through the old exhibitors' journals, and once a year you'll find an article which reads, 'Drive-ins Used to Be Passion Pits, but Now They're Family Entertainment Centers.' It's always *last year* they were passion pits."

Though Libby's back row seems crowded with occupant-less vehicles ("Leo wakes them when the movie's over," Emelia says), the contemporary DI finally may have morphed to family entertainment. *Pearl Harbor* was Libby's feature prior to *Evolution*, with the squeaky-new *Fast and Furious* upcoming. "I talked him into it," Emelia says, "but it's expensive. Now he doesn't want to let it go."

"I try to stay with PG-13," Leo says. "Because it's a mixed crowd." And that other crowd knows all else risqué is obtainable on video.

⎯⎯➤

Leo and Emelia are as close to step-grandparents as these PG-13ers are likely to get. In fact, the couple has five children and ten grandkids. Besides the two eleven-year-olds who wash windshields for one-to-five-dollar tips ("They take it all home," says Leo), teenagers run the concession stand and a sixteen-year-old, John Blythe—in his third year as projectionist—juggles the film canisters. "Leo hired him because he was on crutches," Emelia says.

Leo walks over to check a row of metal poles upon which old-fashioned DI speakers are affixed. "For cars without FM," he says. "The rest just dial up our frequency."

The Libby has spots for 264 vehicles, though by receipts he figures tonight only thirty-nine are present. Earlier, I'd stood by the tiny hexagonal booth, with its warning SLOW, DIM LIGHTS, as Leo sold tickets. "It's four dollars a person," he said. "Why drive to Kalispell to spend seven? I used to have five-dollar-a-carload nights, but it got dangerous because so many people packed into one car. And someone threw a bomb. Still, people hang under pickup trucks, trying to sneak in. I tell them, 'You know how bad you could get hurt doing that?'"

"You got to have an iron hand," Dave Weisbeck, the Libby's previous owner, has told me. "Otherwise kids will take over."

The Hubers' granddaughter Paige is visiting from Denver, and she kept us company as Leo distributed tickets. At fifteen, she's brown-haired, slender, and attractive. "I like your car," she says, smiling. "But I'm a Mustang girl."

Leo and I walk through the concession stand. The kids who work there are playing a Jewel song, "Innocence Maintained." The counter is raspberry-red Formica, a classic fifties touch, and the pizza, burgers, and ice cream are in the buck-fifty range. "We keep all we make from concessions," Emelia tells me. "Three or four hundred dollars a night."

She does the Libby's books. "We pay a percentage of the movie gross to distributors," she adds. "If you want a first-run movie, you must pay seventy percent the first week, forty percent for one that's two to three weeks old." She sighs. "A younger person could make it work."

Leo bends to retrieve a paper carton, then grunts. He clutches his back. In addition to opening the drive-in every night at nine, policing that, selling tickets and closing about two, he cleans the downtown theater mid-mornings, tallies its receipts, checks its projectors and otherwise prepares for that night's show. He's clearly overworked. "Usually I get a high schooler to help out," he says.

As a youth he labored in various lead and zinc mines, and for six months worked with asbestos, but doesn't attribute his shaky health to that.

"It's nerves," Emelia's told me. "And several years ago he fell off the drive-in screen while painting it. That's why he walks funny."

Yesterday I'd visited Leo at the Dome, a classic 1948 hardtop bought by the DI's founders, Rose and Glenn Woods from a family named Kenise. Leo was mucking out trash from between the aisles, a chore he performs alone, seven days a week. "The Kenises owned a batch factory," Leo said, "so these walls are solid concrete. I'll put this theater's sound up against any place's."

We tour the Dome's lobby, with its Moderne furnishings and Art Deco concession stand. Leo struggles upstairs, shows me the projectors and a glass-enclosed balcony with its sign, NO SMOKING IN THE CRYING ROOM. "The crying room is for mothers with babies," Leo explains. "The glass keeps things quiet."

In the summer, he said, the DI earns more than the Dome. "After school starts, it's the reverse." He grew up in northeastern Montana, near Sidney. His father raised sugar beets, and Leo farmed with him until 1966, when he came to the Kootenai Dam project. He operated heavy equipment there. He did the same on the Alaska Pipeline—for seven years. Emelia managed rental units, raised their kids, and taught school in Libby for thirty-and-one-half years.

She grew up across the North Dakota line, and as did Leo, attended Sidney's Roxy Theater. Emelia is genteel, university-educated; Leo is more solidly working class. "I come from a rough bunch," Leo admits. "Movies were important." I asked which ones, and he thought a moment. "*The Ten Commandments.*"

Then Leo performed a remarkable demonstration. Rubbing his gnarled fingers he said, "I never take pills. I work pain against pain." He clasped his arthritic hands and pressed hard. Then grimaced. "There," he said, relaxing. "Pain's gone." He walked to the Dome's wall. "I get headaches, too." And like Victor Mature in *Samson and Delilah*, pressed his forehead hard against the cement as if trying to push it down. "There," he said, relaxing. "Pain against pain."

———

"Local businesses are *irate*," growls KTNY's announcer, about reports of Libby's asbestosized climate. Yet as I cruise downtown, the shops vaunt a lackadaisical air. Signs promote the forthcoming "Libby Logger Days," to my right is a "Clear Cut" barber shop, and left on Mineral Avenue a hair-cuttery called the "Curl Up and Dye." Today I've driven north through Yaak Valley, a gemlike plot of wilderness the timber-folk can't wait to harvest, then southwest through Troy, with its "Booze'n Bait" concession and rowdy saloons, then southeast past Kootenai Falls to Libby. I shall wash the Porsche, grab a Hogburger at JD's Zip Inn, a classic 1960s road-cafe, then sprint to the Libby. A pretty blonde is making change at the Conoco. I ask if she ever goes to the drive-in. She eyes me suspiciously, but nods yes. I explain my mission, ask why, and she smiles. "Because it's cute and dark," she says. "And so easy to sneak people into."

I turn toward my 911; three little boys surround it, their bikes abandoned. "Mister, how much do these cars cost?" they ask, and "How fast will they go?" I answer patiently, explaining the new models are outrageously priced but that this is a 1987. They climb inside, shift gears, twist the wheel and beep its horn. They leave, satisfied. Libby is car country.

Negotiating Highway Two and approaching the DI screen, I am struck by how fitting that structure seems here. From inception, drive-ins linked freedom of the automobile to Hollywood's fantasy life. Libby's outskirts are gorgeous countryside, country that needs no embellishment. The roads are hypnotic. The Cabinet Mountains are a klick west and at twilight a cowboy moon rides high. Behind its faux-log fence, Leo's screen punctuates the horizon like the false front of a frontier mercantile. Behind its speaker field, ladies canter horses prettily.

This is, in many ways, a lost Montana. There's an innocence to culture here, removed from the blight of urban speculation and misconduct, its people in touch with nature and tradition. How ironic to think their lives might be threatened by asbestos, a byproduct of industrialization, a *buffer*, an *insulator*—as if Libbyans wanted insulation from anything.

The twilight is exquisite, and, waving to Leo, I rumble through his speaker field and approach the screen as if it were the north face of Mount Everest. I park, kill the lights and instantly am reminded of every girl I've ever kissed in an automobile. The view from behind the windshield is sweet. The only place Americans truly meditate is behind the wheel of their cars. And at movies. But here I'm outdoors. I feel suffused with freedom, with fantasy; my loneliness disperses. Colors flash and it's like I'm seated before a campfire.

I bask in its glow.

—American Film, 1983
—Big Sky Journal, 2002

DESOLATION JACK: KEROUAC
ON THE BRINK

In 1959, during my fifteenth summer, I worked on a ranch near West Yellowstone, Montana, where I pulled barbed wire, cleared pasture, rode fence line, and endured the musings of a near-psychotic wrangler named Ray as he spun yarns and sang murder ballads in the bunkhouse. Meanwhile, the ranch owner—daughter of a wealthy Long Island family—swilled martinis and shotgunned swallows from the eaves in Chinese pajamas, a silk turban, and Arabian slippers with the toes pointed up. It was a confusing time. I was no Huck Finn lighting out for the territories but a child of privilege with a roughneck job his parents had brokered. The two novels I'd packed were *Pride and Prejudice* and *The Dharma Bums*— the former, required reading at the prep school I attended, the latter all the bohemian rage. Jane Austen made me want to curl up and doze, but Jack Kerouac got my heart pounding and made me wild to be a writer.

Now, thirty-five years after his death, Jenn McKee's fine recounting of Kerouac's life, *Jack Kerouac*, reminds me of how deeply I yearned to emulate him. Not his hitchhiking, drug use, orgiastic sex, or gleeful boozing, so much, as his fierce dedication to writing. As William Burroughs said, "Jack Kerouac was a writer. That is, he *wrote*." And Allen Ginsberg:

"I don't know of any other writer who had more seminal influence than Kerouac in opening up the heart of the writer to tell the truth from his own secret personal mind." But in 1959, I had my ranch job. And this was Montana. As novelist Thomas McGuane wrote, "If you read Jack Kerouac and were of a certain age, you felt you owned the whole place ... He trained us in the epic idea that the region was America; and that you didn't necessarily have to take it in Dipstick, Ohio, forever just because you were there when your hour had come round ... It was called *On the Road*." I was prepared to meet Wrangler Ray as Dean Moriarty, but when I lobbed Jack's Zennishness at him, he stared like I was a Communist.

Eventually my writing took the form of participatory nonfiction, or the New Journalism, a genre where the author is at story-center practicing, as Ginsberg said of Jack's work, "[often] a kind of prose which is neither fiction nor nonfiction, but is actually the mind of the writer thinking about the real world." That practice led me to compose books about Dylan's hometown of Hibbing, Minnesota, about FBI drug stings in Manhattan, about glib survivors of the 1960s, and a reportorial memoir, *Saloon*, about four years on the road, searching for the Great American Bar. In West Yellowstone at fourteen, though, I identified less with Jack's road-fueled exuberance than with his writerly sadness—that exquisite melancholy that haunted him throughout his life.

As Ernest Hemingway said, the best early training for a writer is "an unhappy childhood," and Jack trained hard. He was the son of alcoholic parents, a non-English speaking French-Canadian in a working class, New England town, a Catholic boy tormented by his invalid brother's death, a guilt ridden omni-sexual and, as his mother's darling, the object of incestuous ministrations (she bathed him until he was twelve) and an enmeshment with her that lasted until his death. McKee observes, rightly, that the pain of these issues nudged Jack toward the cultivation of a rich fantasy life, manifesting itself in various dissociative practices—one of which was writing.

Much has been made of Kerouac's sociological impact—"When's the last time you created a generation?" Seymour Krim asked, in his preface to *Desolation Angels*—but I'd guess that *The Dharma Bums* and *On the Road* were as important handbooks to my generation of writers as *The Sun Also Rises* and *Look Homeward Angel* were to Jack's. They were tipsy with romance of the writerly life: one of kicks, companionship, brooding solitude, word-drunk prose, and a ceaseless examination of self. These are adolescent preoccupations, to be sure. But also those of many adult novelists.

There's a closet writer in every reader ("I can do that"), but none keener than in the Kerouac devotee. Ginsberg was his acolyte, and it's fitting that through Allen's and Anne Waldman's efforts, a writing program—The Jack Kerouac School of Disembodied Poetics—was established at Naropa. For my adolescent self, Jack's influence came with *The Dharma Bums*. His alter-ego, Ray Smith, headed west (I already was in Montana) in search of inspiration and adventure, finding much of that in the company of Japhy Ryder, (Zen poet and environmentalist, Gary Snyder), on the slopes of California's Sierra mountains, and in Washington's High Cascades. The novel featured wilderness backpackers, Frisco revelers, freight-train bhikkus, Tantric sex buffs, and scofflaw poetry ravers. But at its heart was an intense group of writers hanging out and *talking about writing*. (I would find my such group, later, in Livingston, Montana.) The book became a hearty bestseller—Jackie Kennedy Onassis was photographed reading it on *Air Force One*—a fact hard to imagine in today's literary climate.

Kerouac was technically a novelist, but as McKee points out, at heart he was a memoirist, using "the creation of his novels as his own, public confessional," enlightening his readers "about his own desperate, strained inner life with painful candor." And I believe his greater influence may lie neither with his celebration of the beat vision, nor with his invention of "spontaneous bop prosody," but with his recasting of the literary memoir. Today, I teach in an MFA program; memoir writing is ninety percent of what nonfiction students wish to learn. But during the 1950s, it was the fictive way or the highway, as it was illegal to identify real people committing outrageous or even quietly personal acts in a work of literature. Those restrictions eased with Supreme Court rulings of the 1960s, and literary nonfiction exploded with the New Journalism, the New Biography and the New Memoir. The impact of Jack's candor, energy and stylistic zest upon writers as different as Tom Wolfe, Annie Dillard, Robert Stone, Hunter S. Thompson, Bob Dylan, Sam Shepard, and Mary Karr is obvious. As novelist William C. Woods has said, "Jack claimed his life would be a legend, and had the literary power to make that claim absolutely real."

But by the late sixties, he was too drunk and dispirited to care.

The damage to Kerouac's psyche from alcoholism—what Tom McGuane's called "the writer's black lung disease"—has been understressed. Jack drank himself to death at age forty-seven, but booze first affected him at home, as the child of alcoholic parents. (Alcoholism is a family disease, injurious to a child's self-esteem, sense of autonomy, psychic integration, capacity to trust, and heightening his dissociative tendencies.) Jack struggled with its effects to the finish. His drinking had more to do with those American (and alcoholic) anxieties McKee calls "the perpetual interior battle between cynicism and optimism, anarchy and control, freedom and security, hubris and self-doubt," than has been noted. Paradoxical behavior, such as Kerouac's belligerent antisemitism, while cherishing Jewish friends, adamant gay-bashing, while sporadically practicing homosexuality, and reactionary conservatism, while living apolitically, is classically alcoholic.

During the summer of 1956, Jack's sixty-three day stint without booze or drugs, as a fire lookout on Desolation Peak, proved the one extended period of sobriety in his adulthood.

He wrote of it both in *Desolation Angels* and in *The Dharma Bums*. On Desolation Peak, he found something like serenity, "a vision of the freedom of eternity." The mountains, the rocky wilderness, "the void," as he called that landscape, became his higher power—a submission to which is indispensable for alcoholic recovery. Of that experience he'd write, in *Dharma*: "Desolation, Desolation, I owe so much to Desolation," and, "I have fallen in love with you, God. Take care of us all, one way or the other." If he'd nurtured that caring presence, rather than heading "down the trail back to this world," with its "humanity of bars and burlesque shows and gritty love, all upsidedown in the void," he might have survived.

On October 21, 1969, the news of his death reached me at home. I was typing the last pages of my Hibbing memoir, *Positively Main Street*, in which my character (a young writer in thrall to Bob Dylan) debated whether to mail off a magazine piece that would do much to dispel his hero's calculated mythos. This had been my first reportorial gambit on the road, and it had been wildly confusing. "Should I send it, should I send it?" I asked. I would, of course, but in the book's narrative, before leaving Hibbing and motoring east to Highway 61, I rummaged through my gear to find a Powr House blue denim engineer's cap I'd bought on Howard Street. It was my good luck hat. At that moment, or close to it, a newscast interrupted my writing to report that Jack had died. I sat there motionless. Then I scrolled up the page and typed, "Jack Kerouac Is Dead?" as my final chapter head. The question might have fit anywhere.

Foreward to *Jack Kerouac* by Jen McKee

Chelsea House Publishers © 2006
Reprinted by permission of the Publisher

NUDIE: HONKYTONK HABERDASHER

On Saturday, May 12, 1984, I sat by the pool at Los Angeles's Château Marmont and leafed through *Daily Variety*. Amid the pastiche of Hollywood news I spotted a report that Nudie Cohn, the legendary western tailor, had died and would be interred that afternoon at Forest Lawn. Roy Rogers' wife, Dale Evans, would offer the eulogy. Nudie had designed Roy's and Dale's film costumes, as well as those of numerous Hollywood and country music stars.

I was concluding ten days' worth of research on a magazine piece. Not much left to do for *Esquire* but lounge beneath the Château's palms, take a good meal in its restaurant, and enjoy the delights of Sunset Boulevard. Nudie's funeral would be a treat. Dale Evans' presence would be worth my trip.

The service was scheduled for the Lawn's Old North Church, a 20th century replica of Boston's 18th century, Episcopal structure, from which Paul Revere's "One if by land, two if by sea" warning was said to have been delivered. It seemed an odd venue for the funeral of a Russian-American immigrant, born Nuta Kotlyarenko in Kiev in 1902, but this was Hollywood.

Cowboy music seeped from speakers as mourners took their seats in the white-paneled pews. Rhinestoned and multi-hued outfits decorated the persons of family, friends, and associates. Western hats topped haphazardly barbered heads. I spotted Tony Curtis and a slouched mourner that might have been Elvis's manager, Colonel Tom Parker. Nudie had designed Presley's $10,000 gold lamé suit, as well as costumes he wore in the 1957 film, *Loving You*. Parker was said to have been Nudie's dear friend.

Dale Evans, dressed in cowgirl hat, western boots, a Nudie vest and prairie skirt, took the pulpit. "Roy had wanted to be here, but he's been ill lately and just couldn't make it." She consoled the family and said how important Nudie's costumes were to Roy's and her images, and to cowboy film and country music stars in general. After all, Tom Mix, Ken Maynard, Hopalong Cassidy, Jay Silverheels, Lash LaRue, Hoot Gibson, Tex Williams, Gene Autry, Guy Madison, John Wayne, Porter Wagoner, Buck Owens, Hank Williams, Hank Thompson, Mel Tillis, Dolly Parton, and even Ronald Reagan had been customers. Several had been or would be buried in Nudie suits. Listening, I knew he'd costumed many others, including John Lennon, George Harrison, Bob Dylan, Cher, the Rolling Stones, Jerry Garcia, Michael Jackson, Liberace, and Elton John. Nudie's mark on popular culture was wide.

Several Flying Burrito Brothers or Byrds sat in a forward pew, though I could not identify them. Was that Chris Hillman, Roger McGuinn, Michael Clarke, and Chris Ethridge? Gram Parsons, in 1969, had led the Burritos and subsequently a generation of country-rockers toward Nudie's shop. Nudie had dressed the Burritos for the cover shoot of their first album, *The Gilded Palace of Sin*. Nudie's shop had been a hangout as far back as Roy Rogers' day. His son, Dusty, would note, "It seemed like Dad was always stopping by Nudie's, whether it was for a cup of coffee or a fitting."[73] *Easy Rider*'s Peter Fonda had said that "Gram took me to Nudie's a few times. I went out with Dwight Yoakam, too. Dwight had several jackets and pants made for him out there. Nudie was

---

73   Debby Bull, *Hillbilly Hollywood: The Origins of Country & Western Style* (New York: Rizzoli International Publications, Inc., 2000), 86.

hilarious. I loved his Eldorado convertible with longhorns mounted on the front. Six shooters as door handles. He took us for a ride...."

A white Nudie Cadillac, with steer horns on its hood, hand tooled leather seats, and chromed-pistol details was parked out front. Parsons, sadly, was dead from fast times and the pharmaceuticals Nudie had depicted on his marijuana-leafed suit. Nudie's head tailor, Manuel Cuevas, would say, "Gram and I discussed his suit in detail for several months before I committed it to fabric. It wasn't until years later ... that I realized he wanted me to design the suit the way he would want to die. From the pills, the woman, the cross, the poppies, to the flames on the pants and of course in the end his body went up in flames in Joshua Tree..."[74]

I craned to see whether Burritos present sported the Nudies he'd made for them to wear on *Palace*. I couldn't tell.

As "The Last Roundup" played through Old North's speakers, congregants passed a casket where the old tailor lay. He wore a signature rhinestone suit, and the mismatched boots he'd affected since boyhood—to remind him of when he'd been so poor he could not afford matched shoes. Wasted from the cancer that had killed him, he resembled a tiny beaded Navajo doll.

His had been a long trail, from Kiev to Brooklyn, where his mother shipped him at age eleven to escape Czarist pogroms, and then to Hollywood. His father had been a bootmaker in Russia, and in New York, his son would shine shoes before the Palace Theater on Broadway, fight as the exhibition boxer "Battling Nudie," do extra work for silent films, and found "Nudie's for Ladies" during the early 1930s, where, with his wife Bobbie, he sewed lingerie for strippers, using rhinestones as glitter. Not until 1947 would he open Nudie's Rodeo Tailors in Los Angeles, but by then western clothing was popular. In 1949 a phalanx of cowboy stars made its

---

74   Kevin Smith, "The Rhinestone Rembrandt: Manuel." PunkGlobe. com. Punk Globe.

way toward television and Nudie's shop. He designed many of Roy Rogers', Dale Evans', and Gene Autry's clothes, and became famous.[75]

Roy Rogers would explain the attraction. He'd tell Debby Bull that "We never really got fancy until Nudie came out ... Nudie made me a suit with some rhinestones on it, and I'd come through [an arena] and the spotlights would hit me, and I just lit up the whole place."

My uncle had been a pioneer in 1950s television, and I remembered that westerns had been one its most popular genres. The Lone Ranger, Hopalong Cassidy, the Cisco Kid, and numerous western stars had shows. Their costumes were flashy interpretations of Mexican and Spanish attire—embroidery and silver ornamentation being part of that package. Kids' versions of these outfits were available, and we wore Hopalong Cassidy shirts, Roy Rogers boots, and Gene Autry cowboy hats proudly. The Woodstock generation's interpretations of cowboy and Native American styles carried this affectation into adulthood. Spangles, high boots, fringed jackets, painted faces, feathers, and beads were the hippie height of fashion. Nudie's clothes prefigured this trend.

As his head tailor and designer, Manuel Cuevas, would say, "The cowboys had a rough sense of copying the Native Americans. They wore overshirts and dresses like Daniel Boone and Davy Crockett wore. They traded with the Indians and bought big dresses and wore them as shirts. The arrowhead [pocket] design came from the Indians ... The Spanish conquistadors adopted it."[76]

As did my generation. On June 28, 1969, Nudie made the cover of *Rolling Stone*, then the counterculture's tabloid of

---

75   He would remain so. In 2009, a Roy Rogers shirt by Nudie would sell at Christie's for $16,250 and, in 2010, a Johnny Cash bicentennial shirt would sell at auction for $25,000. In 2012, his suits would be featured on *Antiques Roadshow*. And in 2016, his granddaughter, Jaime Nudie, would help open Nudie's Honky Tonk bar in Nashville, featuring a gallery of Nudie creations. His customized, $400,000 Eldorado would hang from its ceiling.

76   Bull, 37.

record. Jerry Hopkins (an Elvis biographer) wrote the story. Nudie told Hopkins, "My impression of an entertainer is, he should wear a flashy outfit to be fair to the public ... He shouldn't be wearing a sport coat like the people in the audience. The costume is the first impression and it should be flashy." Twisting a diamond-flecked gold ring, shaped like a saddle, he added, "My costumes used to be called corny ... Now they call us mod. I don't care. Country music has took over rock and roll. Doesn't matter to me who buys the clothes."

Hopkins mentioned "two pairs of ruby encrusted boots" that Keith Richards bought from Nudie. Country star Porter Wagoner owned 52 suits, costing between $11,000 and $18,000 each (his first in 1962 had been free). Nudie's shop was said to have put Johnny Cash in black. It even designed shirts for Salvador Dali.

"You don't have to have cows to be a cowboy," Nudie said.

Western clothing of the cowpoke ilk dated to the elaborate suits worn by 18th century Mexican *vaqueros*, and some guess to the "suit of lights," or *traje de luces*, worn by Spanish matadors. Those suits used sequins and gold and silver threading. But Nudie was credited with having been the first costumer to have sewn rhinestones onto clothing, which initially he did for burlesque queens' G-strings and pasties. The Rhinestone Cowboy look of country stars and actors evolved from that tradition. Rhinestoner Glen Campbell was a customer. And Nudie designed Robert Redford's eye-popping ensemble for *The Electric Horseman*.

Style was important to Hollywood, but it was the horseman's needs that contributed most to the cowboy's look. He required a hat with a wide brim, a wide bandanna, a snug shirt, a short waistcoat for riding, high-heeled boots that wouldn't slip through stirrups, cowhide or wooly sheepskin chaps, and tight pants that would not bunch in the saddle. Bright colors and intricate stitching were derived from Mexican and Native American clothing. The fancier the details the better.

Rose Clements was Nudie's stitching artist, and as she would say, "I did all the embroidery at Nudie's from the sixties on ... There are two different embroidery machines ... one is satin stitch, like a monogram machine. The other is chain stitch, or hand-guided." She designed clothes for Johnny Cash, Emmylou Harris, and the Grateful Dead. "George Harrison had a suit made, a red one, and he had me embroider his mantra around the collar: *Hare krishna, krishna, krishna.*[77]

The cars Nudie's designed were pure California—in the tradition of its custom car culture, its Chicano lowriders, and indeed the Mexican art of ornamental saddle crafting.[78] Silver highlights had decorated Mexican saddles for centuries, and it was a poor saddle whose cantle and stirrups held no engraving. Nudie's Bonnevilles and Eldorados featured longhorns on their hoods, but used chromed pistols as door handles, gear shifts and fender ornaments. Rifles decorated the quarter panels, and as many as 540 silver dollars were embedded in the tooled leather upholstery. A silver-encrusted saddle rode the transmission hump; its stock was engraved leather with embossed silver dollars. An elongated Pontiac Grand Ville, which Nudie designed for Buck Owens, hangs in the Crystal Palace bar in Bakersfield.

As I sat at Old North, it seemed all of western culture surrounded me ... from my childhood cowboy heroes, to my rock and country-rock idols, to icons of a car culture that had obsessed me since my teens. Dale Evans, queen of the cowgirls, had said that Roy Rogers, king of the cowboys, would have been here if he'd been able. Seeing him in the flesh would have been a thrill comparable to my having met the Lone Ranger as a child, or having ridden behind Peter Fonda (who considered *Easy Rider* a Western) on his motorcycle—which

---

77   Ibid, 104.

78   The Mexican, Manuel Cuevas, claims to have designed Nudie's cars. As he told Bull, "I did all the cars, all the Pontiacs ... I was with Nudie for fourteen years. I really never saw Nudie sit at the sewing machine or cut fabric or design."

the year before I'd done. Nudie had dressed his Hollywood stars as smartly as Lagerfeld and St. Laurent had dressed their Parisiennes, and Halston and Bill Blass had dressed their New Yorkers.

And he would be buried among friends. Forest Lawn was a Valhalla of Hollywood legends. Bette Davis, Gene Autry, Debbie Reynolds, Ricky Nelson, Liberace, George Raft, Sandra Dee, Lou Rawls, Buster Keaton, Andy Gibb, Steve Allen, and many others were, or soon were to be buried there. Nudie would be interred in a Courts of Remembrance wall crypt, its plaque reading, "Nudie, 1902-1984, Western Clothes Designer"—his only monument.

Except for these mourners' attire. As yet another ballad played, they began to exit, sad peacocks on a runway to extinction. I turned to join them when, before me, I saw Colonel Tom Parker. He wore a carnation in the lapel of his dark suit, and a misshapen cowboy hat. Instinctively, I stuck out my hand. "Colonel," I said, "I'm writing a piece ..." The old man nodded and I thought I saw a tear in his eye. He smiled grimly and took my hand. I asked about Elvis's gold lamé suit, the one for which in 1957 he'd paid $10,000, and which Nudie said he'd earned "about a $9,500 profit." The Colonel confirmed the story, and smiled again. Not knowing what else to ask, I moved away.

A photographer bearing a Speed Graphic approached.

"You want a picture of yourself with the Colonel?" he said.

"You took one?"

"It's twenty bucks."

"Sure." I gave the man my address and peeled off a bill. This was, after all, Hollywood.

When I looked back, the Colonel had drifted away.

2020

XENIA

Whenever I spot odd jewelry on hipsters in the mountain West, I think of Xenia Cage's red bicycle-reflector ring. She wore it not in the 1980s or 1990s, but during the staid 1940s, when—married to the experimental composer, John Cage, she made surrealist art in New York and oversaw my fledgling attempts at painting. Xenia was a friend of my grandparents, who lived a half block from the salon of her friend, Peggy Guggenheim, and that of the surrealist, Max Ernst. An Alaskan by birth and a Californian growing up, Xenia moved to Manhattan in 1942 and played brake drums and flower pots in Cage's discordant ensembles. She was the first to see promise in my childish scratchings, and presented my watercolor—"A Funny Toby Thompson at the Beach with Red Chapped Lips"—to Ernst as a gift. Reportedly, he was delighted.

She was a born teacher and Village-style bohemian, participating with Cage in various ménages a trois, trying psychedelics, and crashing in group houses with other artists. She affected black dresses with colorful handmade jewelry and was, in the 1940s, a walking piece of performance art. She had a withered leg; despite it, Edward Weston photographed her in the nude. His portraits of Xenia hang in the Metropolitan Museum of Art.

When I was five, she asked what I would like as a gift. "A painting," I said. "Of what?" I handed her a comic book whose cover showed a greenish space maiden being attacked mid-air by a winged dragon before a range of Martian Alps. "Oh," she said. But she copied the illustration dutifully, pasting stars to the galactic backdrop and a banner to the highest peak reading, "Toby's Mountain."

Her serious work consisted of balsa wood and-rice-paper mobiles, such as those chosen by Ernst for Guggenheim's 1943 show. *Exhibition by 31 Women*, at The Art of this Century gallery. That show introduced work by Frida Kahlo, Louise Nevelson, Djuna Barnes and oddly, the stripper Gypsy Rose Lee. Xenia fashioned surrealist sculptures and watercolors, but her life and friends equally were her art. That coterie included Marcel Duchamp, André Breton, Ernst, Guggenheim, Merce Cunningham, Jackson Pollock, and Joseph Cornell.

The tension between East and West that complicates so many artistic lives complicated hers. Born Xenia Andreyevna Kashevaroff in Juneau in 1913, she was the youngest daughter of Andrew Petrovich Kashevaroff, the Archpriest of the Eastern Orthodox Russian-Greek Church of Alaska. He was a musician and scholar, but his father had been a Russian sea captain who married a woman of Alutiiq (or Tlinget) ancestry. Xenia was one-quarter Native and this heritage contributed to her exotic look: high cheekbones, a wide nose, and brownish-blonde hair. Ernst, who had a long-standing interest in Native culture and its art, was captivated by her.

As was the young John Cage, who met Xenia in Los Angeles in 1934. She had attended high school in Monterey and had been studying painting and book binding in Carmel. One day she walked into an arts-and-crafts store where he was working. "It was love at first sight on my part," he said. "Not on hers."[79] They became involved and, as Cage wrote to a friend, "Her world is almost without limitation: for she

---

79   Kenneth Silverman, *Begin Again: A Biography of John Cage* (New York, Knopf, 2005) 22.

includes, from her mother (an Eskimo) an animal, pre-historic, primitiveness; and from her father (a Russian priest) the rich and organic mysticism and instinctiveness of Russians."[80]

These qualities of West and East were compromised once they moved, nearly penniless, from Los Angeles to Seattle to Chicago and then New York. Xenia was far from innocent. As a student in California (and later at Reed College) she'd had affairs with various lovers, including Edward Weston (who thought her "a grand person to love ... most delightfully unmoral, pagan"[81]) and the biologist Ed Ricketts, who introduced her to threesomes. She enjoyed a flirtation with author Joseph Campbell, whom she met near Sitka, Alaska. She recalled sunbathing topless, one day, as from the surf "came this heavenly, naked Joseph Campbell, glistening with cold icy water."[82] Purportedly their friendship was platonic.

But Peggy Guggenheim's salon (of which Campbell was part) proved something else. Experimentation was the rule in thought, art, and in life. Anton Gill wrote in his book, *art/lover*, that "One evening, toward the end of a drunken party, someone suggested a game that was designed to test the players' indifference, or lack of it, toward one another. The Cages, Max, and Duchamp stripped, while Peggy and Frederick and Stefi Kiesler looked on ... Max immediately failed in the indifference stakes, as his eyes took in Xenia's naked body ... The game ended in an orgy of sorts, in which Cage took Peggy to bed while Max did the same with Xenia."[83]

She, in a letter, described the scene (or another) differently. Asking to choose a costume from Guggenheim's closet, she donned a pair of "chartreuse-and-purple lounging pajamas," the top of which was open in back. Ernst told her she had it on backwards. She flipped the pajama's back to the front.

---

80   Ibid, 22.

81   Ibid, 21.

82   Ibid, 21.

83   Anton Gill, *art/lover: A Biography of Peggy Guggenheim* (New York, Harper Collins, 2003).

Subsequently, she wrote, "John and I and Max and Peggy and Marcel had a whale of a time, which can't be described because of reputations etc."[84]

New York's experimental years (during which Xenia, Cage, and the West coast dancer Merce Cunningham shared affections) coincided with those in which I met her. My uncle, William Nichols, an actor, writer, and musician, knew her through his friendship with Cage. When Xenia's marriage to Cage dissolved (he left her for Cunningham), she moved to Guggenheim's house at 39 Beekman Place, near my grandparents' building. Through my uncle she met my parents, and through them, me.

Xenia was not the first artist I'd known. In my uncle's circle I'd met others—Aaron Copland and Boris Karloff were two—but Xenia, though the consummate New Yorker, was the first Western-born artist. An accomplished percussionist and key member of Cage's performing group, her forte was crafting things—primarily mobiles. She'd created one that hung onstage at a 1941 Cage Percussion Players concert, which author Susan Gilbert describes as "a large balsa wood and rice paper mobile beneath which the musicians, including Xenia herself, performed—the movement and shadows cast by the mobile [being] an intrinsic part of the show."[85] She'd shown her mobiles not just in Guggenheim's space but at New York's Julien Levy Gallery, which championed modern art, including that of Giacometti, Tanning, Ernst, Magritte, Kahlo, Man Ray, Noguchi, Cornell, Motherwell, and Gorky. The author and artist Penelope Rosemont categorized Xenia as being on the "cutting edge of surrealism in sculpture."[86]

---

84   Xenia Cage to Ruth Shaw, August 22, 1942, Newberry Library. As quoted by Silverman, 53.

85   Susan Gilbert, "Xenia Cage; the 31 Women number 20, her birthday is 28 August," (Sugswritersblog, August 29, 2013).

86   John Sheey, *Sculptor of the Surreal, Whacker of Flower Pots* (*Reed Magazine*, Vol. 96, Number One, March, 2016) Online edition. Penelope Rosemont's book is *Surrealist Women: An International Anthology* (University of Texas, 1998).

She collaborated with Duchamp on his *Boîtes-en-Valise* series and with Cornell. She made a chess table for Ernst's contribution (a surreal chess set) to 1944's *Imagery of Chess* exhibit. She practiced bookbinding, costume design, and curating—at the Metropolitan, the Whitney. and the Cooper-Hewett museums. But by 1950, when she painted Blue Bolt for me, her solo career was in decline.

As a five-year-old, I was captivated by art of a different sort than that practiced by Xenia. I loved cowboy comics and films. Television was in its infancy and, from the first, Westerns were its staple. The cowpoke superheroes Hopalong Cassidy, Roy Rogers, Gene Autry, and the Lone Ranger were my favorite characters. Comic book westerns, of course, predated TV and were spinoffs of dime novel, radio, and film productions. More imaginative dramas, such as those featuring Superman, Captain Marvel, and Blue Bolt had been popular during WW II. Their heroes were kin to the good-marshal-bad-outlaw staples of western narrative.

Xenia knew of my interest in cowboys and at one point fashioned me a western kerchief. She also made me a tiny necktie, sending fabric samples for me to choose from. She wrote, "My dear Toby, I don't know if you ever wear a necktie; but if you do, I would like to make a special one for you ... Here are some colors, and if you would pick out your favorite color that you like the best and send it back to me ... I'll make a Toby Thompson Necktie." In another letter, to my mother, Xenia expressed her frustration at the Blue Bolt assignment:

> I must say that I feel like a criminal making a picture of Blue Bolt—but he obviously must have some quality unknown to me. And since I'm an 'artist,' I'd be ashamed of myself not to be able to reproduce such a masterpiece. I can't gauge when Blue Bolt will be done, but I'll try to make it soon, so Toby won't have forgotten, and say 'What is *this*?'

After a New York visit, she wrote, "My dear Toby—I sure

was glad to see you … I will soon send you my picture of Blue Bolt shooting the dragon with his lightning gun, and saving the Green Sorceress. Usually I paint the way you do—I mean I make up things instead of copying other pictures. That is more fun to do, don't you think? I will finish the picture tomorrow after I buy some yellow, then I'll send it to you."

I received the picture, which I found mesmerizing—she'd eliminated the cover's graphics and emphasized the combat as well as the provocative figure of the Sorceress—clad in a bikini. As a present to Xenia in return, I sent several of my drawings and watercolors. Later she wrote: "Dear Toby— I'm glad you liked my picture. Thank you so much for sending me all those wonderful pictures you did. I think they are great, and I liked the titles too."

In another letter she wrote,

> I was pleased to get the beautiful painting you sent me called 'A Funny Toby Thompson at the Beach with Red Chapped Lips.' It's a wonderful picture; I like its bold style. And I liked your fine letter; thank you for inviting me to come see you … I have never been to Washington, and you could show me all the fascinating places. The Valentine you sent me makes me very happy; it's so original it makes me think you made it yourself. Thank you for sending me all those pretty things.
>
> I hope that the next time you are in New York you will come see me at my house. Although I am not a painter like you, I would like you to see my mobiles. Or at least we could have a drink together.
>
> Love to you and Roy Rogers, Xenia.

This came from 550 Hudson Street, New York, the address if not the apartment she'd shared with Cage before their divorce. Friends reported that she had been distraught after their breakup and the revelation of Cage's year-long, solo affair with Merce Cunningham, whom she admired and found "very beautiful and exciting and marvelous and dances like a god only better."[87] She had started psychoanalysis. With her leg crippled from tuberculosis and time spent in a sanitarium, she had known a troubled childhood. But why she took interest in me is a mystery. Perhaps it was because she had no children; early in her relationship with Cage—being advised her condition made her a poor candidate for motherhood—she'd had an abortion. Undoubtedly, with me, she felt her maternal instincts surfacing. And as an artist knew the ultimate creativity was manifested in bearing children.

Her Blue Bolt painting was copied from the cover of an April, 1950, edition of *Blue Bolt Adventures*, by the artist L.B. Cole and the writer Joe Simon. Blue Bolt, in the series, had been the young Fred Parrish—who during football practice, one day, was struck by lightning. On a small plane, seeking help in a remote area, he was struck a second time and went down with the craft. He was found and healed by a scientist, Dr. Bertoff, who treated him experimentally with radium deposits. These harnessed the electricity in Parrish's body and gave him super powers. Armed with the name Blue Bolt and a lightning gun to contest the evil Green Sorceress (who developed a crush on him), Parrish was transformed.

His metamorphosis from ordinary to extraordinary was similar to that which the cowboy heroes Paladin, Cisco Kid and the Lone Ranger made from average citizens to knights errant. That phenomenon has been exhaustively described— but not so completely the comparable transfiguration of many western artists. George Catlin, Thomas Moran, Paul Kane, Charles Shreyvogel, Seth Eastman, Alexander Gardner, Frederic Remington, N.C. Wyeth, Jo Mora, and others came to the West primarily to make art, but also to test themselves—against warring tribes, outlaws, ranch life, and a fierce environment. They were tenderfoots when they arrived but frontiersmen when they left. And metaphorically, by late in the century, Rooseveltians. Teddy was no painter, but a prolific author who never relinquished the survivalist values

---

87   Silverman, 61.

he learned on a North Dakota ranch. So much so that he recruited his Rough Riders largely from Southwestern cowboy, miner, and rancher stock.

Many artists, like Xenia, John Cage, and Merce Cunningham, reversed the journey and emigrated from West to East. This was not always a happy choice. But acceptance by New York's galleries, concert halls, and critics—then as now—spelled success. Manhattan was the new gold rush.

After her divorce, Xenia briefly moved back to California, but eventually returned to New York. As Kenneth Silverman reports, she was not happy. She "sometimes felt a profound loneliness, and sometimes wept ... her future looked bleak." She predicted, "Probably a furnished room. Or a kept woman."[88] Her discontent can be seen in the difference between photographs taken between her 18th year in California, and her 30th in New York. The former (by Weston) shows a girl of serious but open demeanor, posed in a country dress that is almost 19th century in design. The latter shows a New York woman in a Savoy Ballroom hat and a black dress before a surrealist mobile of geometric shapes. The Western portrait evinces innocence; the Eastern is all attitude.

Xenia visited my parents' house in the mid-1960s, and reclined on a couch, boozing at midday, she spun sentimental tales of high times with Peggy Guggenheim ("It was late and I was tipsy, so I slept on the white fur rug before her fireplace"), but flashed her bicycle-reflector ring and oozed charm. Later, Silverman reported, "she often seemed bitter. She hated New York, a living place she once loved, and told Cage she wanted to get out of this 'dreadful city' ... He offered her money to explore the possibility of moving to the West Coast ... Sometimes he sent invitations to events featuring his music or himself. Despite his concern about Xenia's well-being, her 'barby' wit made him wince: 'if I telephone her or write to her, I take my life in my hands.'"[89]

---

88   Silverman, 63.
89   Silverman, 392.

I saw Xenia once more, in the 1970s, in Manhattan. I dropped by the Cooper-Hewitt on a whim and asked for her. She emerged from the museum's basement where, since 1968, she had worked as a cataloguer and conservator. She was dressed in an artist's smock and looked well. But none of her frivolity was on view. We chatted; she was polite but reserved. Our enthusiastic times as protégé and mentor had passed. I told her a bit of my career, of my recent Bob Dylan book which I had tried to dedicate to her, but at the last minute couldn't. She smiled her Xenia smile and we said goodbye.

Since her death in 1995, tributes to her have trickled forth. They include portraits in the Cage biographies, a Wikipedia entry, a profile in the Reed College bulletin, and various blog posts. She is remembered as an under-appreciated artist who had the misfortune of being married to a celebrated man. As Gilbert notes in her Sugs Writer's Blog, "She is one of those talented and versatile women who are routinely ignored, their careers over-shadowed by famous male partners ... The full extent of Xenia Kashevaroff Cage's career as a visual artist remains obscure, her own art works have proved very hard to trace ... One small painting by Xenia is in a public collection in her home state Alaska, any other works which survive are either in private hands or possibly attributed to someone else."[90]

It's ironic that the Blue Bolt painting is one of but a few of her works to exist. It hangs in my house beside another eccentric piece—a note from Harry Truman, solicited by my parents at a White House function (on a night I was sick) that reads, "Hope that Toby will soon be well and have a long, happy life." Both artifacts coexist in a place of honor. Also cherished is Xenia's copy, sketched in conté crayon, of a

---

90   Gilbert, August 29, 2013. Gilbert notes that "Xenia Cage has been acknowledged as an artist in three exhibitions since her death: Siobhan Conaty's 1997 exhibition, *Art of This Century: The Women*, Pollock-Krasner House; Larry List's 2005 October-March 2006 *The Imagery of Chess Revisited* The Isamu Noguchi Museum; 2005-06 *Accommodations of Desire: Surrealist Works on Paper*, from the Julien Levy Collection."

Paul Klee painting. My uncle commissioned it from Xenia, in 1949, to illustrate the cover of a recording he made for me. These are the pieces of Xenia's art that remain. She might have cringed at the thought.

Xenia died in 1995, at the age of 82. Campbell's wife, the dancer Jean Erdman, paid for her funeral. Xenia was buried in the family plot in Juneau. Finally, she had come home.

2020

TWENTY-FIRST

TOM MURPHY:
BACKCOUNTRY MYSTIC

The images float before the viewer's eye, strange and otherworldly—like photos of the Crab Nebula from Hubble, or mixings from a hippie light show. They might be satellite shots of the Mojave, cell-section studies from an electron microscope, or hallucinatory paintings from a would-be Jackson Pollock. In fact they are nature photographs made by Tom Murphy, taken largely in Yellowstone Park and often of objects no more than 10 inches square.

He calls them Abstracts. "In a lot of ways I don't care what scale they are. I'm looking at graphics. I'm looking at the shapes and colors and textures."

Murphy sits not by his "silly blue tarp," beneath which he was photographed snow camping in the PBS film, *Christmas in Yellowstone*, but before his computer in a warm studio on a crisp December day. He is the author of seven books of photographs, a contributor to *National Geographic* and the *New York Times*, the director and/or subject of several films, the acknowledged expert on Yellowstone's backcountry and a man who has skied across that park three times, including "once solo, which is crazy," in 1985, and with companions in 2016—at age sixty-six. Today his shoes are off and his socked feet are crossed as he sifts through Abstracts.

These are not the wildlife shots of foxes, bison, and bears that have made his reputation, but dreamier fare. An image of white circles on a gray and tan background, striated with white, pops up. It might be a canvas by the painter Robert Motherwell. In fact it's a miniature titled *Brown Mud Ice*.

"This was taken on Blacktail Plateau," Murphy says. He jabs at the screen. "In the daytime you get melt, and these little pools of water. Then at night it freezes the surface of this pond or puddle and the water soaks into the ground and leaves these bubbles. You're looking at maybe four inches here. It's a simple story; it's a pane of ice over some mud."

Another shot is more conventionally beautiful. The screen fills with an image that appears to be of some exotic fabric. "It's hoar frost and lichen," Murphy says. "Hoar frost builds into the wind. But when it grows it forms these feathers. These little crystals are probably about half an inch to three-quarters of an inch long. And they are moving, fluttering. So the movement caught my attention."

A third—of an undulating field of white—suggests the curves of a woman reclining. "But they're snow pillows. They could be thirty inches tall or thirty feet tall. It turns out they're about ten feet tall."

Asked to define the parameters of an Abstract, Murphy says, "It has to be sort of unrecognizable. You don't have to know what it is, but you have to be intrigued. Good composition involves textures and shapes, and how the eye moves through an image. It's not just snow, it's how does the snow lie there ... what's the bigger and broader story."

The story of Murphy's life seems juxtaposed to the abstract footage of these stills. Raised on a cattle ranch in "the dry, prairie landscape of western South Dakota," and with six siblings, he nevertheless grew up "a loner," outside and multi-talented. He and his wife, Bonnie, moved, in 1978, to Livingston "with $300 between us." Murphy drove a school bus and dug post holes, while Bonnie clerked at the Yellowstone Motor Inn. "The reason I wanted to move to Livingston was because of Yellowstone Park," he says.

He taught himself photography (in which, since 1985, he's instructed others "from all over the world"), studied anthropology at Montana State University, and backpacked in the park. "I'd already fallen in love with the place." He worked a variety of jobs. "I can do all kind of things—I can overhaul engines, I can help build houses, I'm a practical guy capable of doing what people consider macho things." Yet he possessed a dreamy side that verged on the mystical.

"I like to have a mystical experience every day," he admits. "I'm not embarrassed about that." What such an experience promises, Murphy says, is "a surprise—a new realization. It's not hallucinating, it doesn't come from drugs or pain or starvation. It's just going and sitting on a hillside and calming down. Just watching is a meditation for me. There's stuff going on all the time."

During his fourteen-day, solo ski across Yellowstone in 1985, he endured minus-thirty-degree temperatures and a grueling trek. "You suffer. It's not fun. I don't do a ski trip because I like to ski. I do it because I want to see the country."

The payoffs, in terms of contemplation, were extraordinary. "I had so much solitude that all human sound went away. I could hear my heart beating for most of that trip. That was probably the most amazing part ... clearing out my head so that I was really there—truly part of this place."

Oddly, his Abstracts are reminiscent of the closeup photography that Zen philosopher Alan Watts included in his 1962 book, *The Joyous Cosmology* —about experimentations with LSD. Murphy has never used psychedelics, yet he's been accused of teaching photography "like Zen—if it looks good, it is good. I don't care how you did it, if you can get people to look at your photographs and want to walk around and learn something, that's a successful image."

Though he has traveled the most remote corners of Yellowstone, it's not just its distant reaches that intrigue him. He clicks on an image titled *Pallete Springs, Mammoth*.

"I was always intrigued by Mammoth, because of its amazing array of abstracts. It's winter in this, and conditions are changing constantly. The steam is moving around so fast—bam, bam, bam. As it moves through these trees, the shadows come through, the light comes through. Steam swirls from below and through the branches. It's kind of frantic. I see it, bam, and it's over." He sits back. "Some of this stuff is not contemplative. I'm just being overwhelmed. It's a matter of trying to stop the world for a second."

"Beauty" is a word Murphy is not hesitant to use, nor is "awe."

"I don't know how you define what's beautiful," he says. "But there is a universality to what people recognize as beautiful. I think it comes down to somehow reaching people's sense of awe. It's having people say, 'oh, that's interesting.' A cancer cell beneath a microscope, you can say, is scary ... but on the other hand, it's part of the universe. And all the universe is beautiful, on some level."

Murphy considers beauty and the art that captures it useful as a conservation tool. "It's making people care. William Henry Jackson and Thomas Moran, at the very beginning of Yellowstone, helped convince Congress to make it a park because of the beauty they brought back. Ansel Adams and other photographers and artists have made a big difference. Because a lot of the best art comes from nature."

There is the question of whether his backcountry mysticism derives from experience— he has skied some 2,000 miles in the park, hiked perhaps 5,000—or religiosity. A striking moment in *Christmas in Yellowstone* is when Murphy, dusted by snow before stark lodgepoles, looks around and says, "It's my church, my cathedral."

"I think my definition of God is whatever life is," he adds, "the force of life. Everything, I believe, has an equal right to live as me. And I try to give them beauty and truth, and therefore value, by demonstrating that they do deserve to live and they are beautiful. I believe in the value of other creatures.

I believe that everything has an equal right to live. And is equally beautiful." He turns from his monitor. "The basis of my approach to the world is that it's a beautiful place, full of all kinds of amazing, wonderful life. And it's a good place to be."

—*Big Sky Journal*, 2017

GATEWAYS

The gates swing open. One passes through and it's as if a hail of discarded ranch tools and auto parts fill the air: a sawtoothed blade, a cast-iron meat grinder, a draft horse hame, leaf and coil springs, an augur, elongated drill bits and picket pins, open-end wrenches, gears, horseshoes, pliers, thick chains, railroad spikes, and, almost as afterthoughts, a pair of treble clefs and a guitar. At one gate's bottom is a tiny bison, beneath which is written, "Black Buffalo Ironworks, Bob Dylan."

These gates, "Untitled II," are a pair exhibited with six other pieces of Dylan's iron sculptures, displayed in 2013-2014 at London's Halcyon Gallery, where a new show of Dylan's art will open this fall. The songwriter has sketched and painted for decades, and has exhibited his paintings at the prestigious Gagosian Gallery in New York, and in continental Europe. But Mood Swings, last year's exhibit at Halcyon of his gates, a railing, and window screens, was the first public showing of Dylan's efforts in metal.

Framed by rectangular bands of steel, their suspended wrenches, wheels, calipers, shovels, pliers, pulleys, gears, cogs, tongs, star braces, chisels, stretchers, spanners, horseshoes, snaffle bits, vises, motorcycle chains, pistons, carpenter's levels, and a steel roller skate, hang like exclamatory symbols in cartoon bubbles. In another way they are like the detritus of Dylan's mind, of his creativity. As with the junkyard as-semblages of Robert Rauschenberg, the black-and-white art films of David Lynch, the mixed-media constructions of Red Grooms, and like Dylan's most surrealistic, neo-Dadaist lyrics, they speak above the factory-like din of the unconscious.

Yet they are hung with rural implements. As Andrew Kelly wrote in the Mood Swings catalogue, Dylan's "unbridled cre-ativity has shown reverence for the past, for industry and ag-riculture of the kind now being consigned to the past in the developed world ... his faith is still in the soil and the hand and the tool." And as the London-based critic, Sarah Hamp-son, has written, "the gates are clearly Dylanesque in their sympathies, rooted in American folklore and blue-collar eth-ics. But they are also indicative of the man himself, someone who [in his multifaceted songs] has always been a welder of sorts."

Dylan has resided in Los Angeles since the mid-1970s, and owns a ranch in Montana. Yet he grew up on Minnesota's Iron Range. He has said, "I've been around iron all my life ... I was born and raised in iron ore country—where you could breathe it and smell it every day." His father and uncles ran an appliance store in Hibbing, the town surrounded on three sides by the Hull-Rust-Mahoning Mine, once the largest open-pit iron ore mine in the world. Dylan's paternal grand-parents were working-class immigrants, laboring daily with tools similar to those decorating his gates. But by the 1950s, Hibbing's WW II mining boom had fizzled. As Dylan would write in liner notes for *The Times They Are a Changin'*: "the town I grew up in is the one / that has left me with my legacy visions / it was not a rich town / my parents were not rich / it was not a poor town / an' my parents were not poor / it was a dyin' town ... " Dylan fled Hibbing in 1959 for college at the University of Minnesota, then to pursue his musical career in New York. But the iconography of rural life never left him. It peppers his songs, his movies and books, and illuminates his art.

He'd drawn since his early years in Greenwich Village, but he began painting during the late 1960s in Woodstock. He'd suspended touring after a motorcycle accident and, while still writing songs, found time to paint. He illustrated the covers of both the Band's first album, *Music from Big Pink*, and his 1970 collection, *Self Portrait*. It wasn't until 1974, after a long-awaited comeback tour, that he apprenticed himself to the New York painter and Ash Can School acolyte, Norman Raeben, who taught a group of students daily in an eleventh-floor space above Carnegie Hall.

Dylan has said that Raeben's unorthodox methods taught him "how to see ... by putting my mind and my hand and my eye together, in a way that allowed me to do consciously what I unconsciously felt." Dylan, in his songs, had long scoffed at boundaries, but Raeben's teaching permitted him to relinquish linear time, and as Dylan historian, Sean Wilentz has written, "to understand the artistic possibilities of pulling together the past, present, and future." Scolding Dylan, Raeben called him "an idiot," and one day, in criticizing a painting that seemed monochromatic, spat, "You're tangled up in blue!" Dylan brought in lyrics to that song a few days later. As he'd explain, "I was just trying to make it like a painting where you can see the different parts but then you also see the whole of it ... that's what I was trying to do ... with the concept of time."

Dylan sketched while on tour, and in 2007 he took 322 of those drawings and added color to them—in gouache and watercolor. The result was his Drawn Blank paintings, 170 of which were chosen for his first museum show, at Kuntsammungen Chemnitz in Germany. A second major show, The Brazil Series, appeared at Copenhagen's Statens Museum in 2010. The Asia Series premiered at Gagosian in New York in 2011. These paintings were broad-brushed and expressionistic in color, but showed real talent. As Diana Widmaier Picasso (the painter's granddaughter) wrote of Drawn Blank, "The themes touched on by Dylan ... are divided, however schematically, along three main axes: the portrait, the landscapes and the nude. The influence of the group of German Expressionists known by the name of *Die Brucke*, or The Bridge, can certainly be found here."

The gates are bridges of sorts. Like those in songs like Reverend Gary Davis's "Twelve Gates to the City," Dylan's "Gates of Eden," and films like Michael Cimino's, *Heaven's Gate*, they are passageways or station stops to grace and spirituality. Iron gates adorned the entrances to medieval cathedrals and a rockabilly pair adorns Graceland, the Elvis pilgrimage site in Memphis. One hesitates to mention Dylan's gates in the context of judgment day, but he admits, they "appeal to me because of the negative space they allow. They can be closed but at the same time they allow the seasons and breezes to enter and flow. They can shut you out or shut you in. And in some ways there is no difference."

When Dylan began sculptural work in iron is uncertain. He wrote in his 2004 memoir, *Chronicles I*, that he kept arc welding equipment at his Malibu estate, and had been making "ornate iron gates ... from junk scrap metal" since the late 1980s. In the late 1970s, he told the *Minnesota Times* that "I like to blast sculpture out of metal." About then, a musician who was teaching Dylan classical guitar was heard to say, "One afternoon Bob arrived in his pickup truck loaded with every sort of scrap and said, 'Look at all this great junk we collected today!'" Salvaged car bodies dot his property, and a studio with shelving marked "Auto," "Plow Parts," and "Misc.," stands nearby. Dylan writes of iron, in the Mood Swings catalogue, that, "I've always worked with it in one form or another."

Or perhaps against it. I recall walking Hibbing's streets in 1968, while researching a book about Dylan, and watching autos coated with red ore dust pass, rail cars loaded with raw iron lumber by, then drinking in Hibbing taverns beside miners coated with rust-colored grit. In Hibbing, one worked in the mines or for the businesses servicing miners. It was get out or choke. Art, in the form of music, was Dylan's ticket to ride.

Paul Green, president of Halcyon, has said that he visited the L.A. studio in 2007, and convinced Dylan that he should show the gates. "I didn't know he was sculpting things," Green says, "but he had been making these gates for himself and for friends." Dylan spent three years completing iron work for the Halcyon show, and all pieces sold, reportedly for as much as $415,000 each.

Despite their size, (one is 68 x 61 x 10 inches) and considerable weight, the gates are airy. And they are simply beautiful. Their shapes, circular or rectangular, are mandala-like, suggesting a rust-belt spirituality. They seem in part to synthesize what Dylan has attempted with painting, poetry, and song.

In 1975, a year after studying with Norman Raeben, he released a song titled, "When I Paint My Masterpiece." In it he recalled a trip to Rome and a chilly night on the Spanish Stairs. He'd rushed back to his hotel room where, he imagined, Botticelli's niece awaited. "She promised that she'd be right there with me," Dylan sang, "when I paint my masterpiece."

Perhaps that promise should be amended to include sculpture. For the forging of these pieces constitute the most elemental of Dylan's endeavors. Born of flames, fumes, and molten iron they are Vulcanic. And they are his closest encounter with the rough manual labor that surrounded him as a boy and that he has revered in song but fled in life.

At Halcyon this November, Dylan will show a new collection of watercolors and other paintings, as well as seven ironworks. One expects the latter also will be expressions of rust-belt spirituality. For as he sang on the 1974 album, *Planet Waves*, "My dreams are made of iron and steel / With a big bouquet of roses hanging down / From the heavens to the ground."

—*Western Art & Architecture*, 2015

BLUE MONTANA WALTZ

The quest for dancing as art might have commenced in mid-May at the Miles City Bucking Horse sale, Corb Lund and the Hurtin' Albertans having wowed the crowd on Thursday, and three bands dispersed along Main Street keeping saddle bronc and bull riders dancing before the Montana, Bison, and Trails End bars on Friday and Saturday nights. Or it might have kicked off near Montana's western tip, in Troy at the Home Bar, loggers in wide suspenders clogging to ragged bluegrass. But it started dead center in Bozeman, at the Have Fun Dancing studio of Lauren Coleman, who has taught there for over twenty years, and who coached me in the nightclub two-step, a tricky move that a dancing friend suggested I learn.

Coleman, between tunes, reminisced about the immense growth in popularity of ballroom she'd seen in recent years. "Part of it's due to shows like *Dancing with the Stars* and *Ballroom Bootcamp*, but the disco craze took off in the 1970s with *Saturday Night Fever,* and the two-step craze in the 1980s after, *Urban Cowboy.* Then, in the 1990s, there was the comeback of the Lindy hop. Tango and salsa grew with a rise in the Latino population. Country-western has always been popular, but that craze may have peaked. "

Like most things cowboy, it started in Texas. In 1866 the

first cowpokes herded cattle up the Bozeman Trail from Texas to the Montana mining camps, and later to Miles City. They carried dancing with them. When women were scarce, they cavorted together, bandannas on the arms of the "ladies" who were "heifer-branded." They danced two-steps, waltzes, polkas, and schottisches. The vogue never abated.

Nineteen-seventy-two was my first Montana summer dancing, largely in saloons along the Bozeman Trail. To paraphrase Elmore Leonard, I spent most of my cash on hoofers, horses, and honky tonks—the rest I wasted. What I recall are three-piece C&W groups with names like The Dischords or The Rapelje Redhots, and cowboy jitterbugging that was more like demolition derby than dance. And later, during my years at the Murray Hotel in Livingston, boogieing sweat-drenched in its bar until 2:00 A.M., then limping to my room and showering its smoke from every stitch of clothing except my boots. During the 1980s, I knew manic nights at Stacey's in Gallatin Gateway, at the Chico Saloon in Pray, at the Long-branch in Livingston and in far-flung dives such as the Bar 19 in Lewistown, where one New Year's Eve a vacationing Rockette kicked so high I thought she'd tap out the lights.

But such rowdiness was fading. Merle Travis Petersen, of the band Cold Hard Cash, told me, "Sadly all the real country dance bars I grew up with are closed. No more boot-scootin', line-dancin', honky-tonkin', as far as I can tell. The only place I know that has a real country-dance scene is the Do Bar in Great Falls, on Sundays. All the old dance couples come out. The gig at the Do is like going to a museum, a cool museum."

I called the Do Bar and a bartender told me, "We quit the Sunday afternoon thing. Just not enough folks coming out."

The search for a great C&W dance club began on June 13. My friend, Nancy Milligan—a willowy brunette and fine dancer—rode with me to Missoula, where a pal was gigging at the Top Hat with a Tom Petty cover band. Instinct told me that pay dirt would be found at smaller venues in smaller towns. But the Top Hat—a former dive on Front Street—that summer would host name acts like Ricky Skaggs and Lucinda Williams, had a first-rate sound system and spacious dance floor. We were the only two-steppers, and until the boogieing started late, its only dancers.

On a March trip, we had danced for hours at Missoula's Sunrise Club—a premier C&W venue, with lessons on Wednesdays and good bands on weekends. That night, couples had twirled in stylized unison, the women in ruffled prairie skirts, the men in black hats and vests, their boot toes polished. The band had been slick, interspersing hits with classics from Willie, Waylon, or Dwight. This was big-city dancing with couples performing elaborately choreographed moves—what I'd dubbed Cowboy Kama Sutra. But enough sketchy characters, biker types from the karaoke bar next door, wandered past to keep me on edge. The band kicked off "Bluebird Wine," and a patron hooted, clogged, and fell to the floor. The bouncers lifted him by his belt and rushed him to the exit. The stylized couples spun as the band segued into, "Cherokee Fiddle."

I longed for the country.

In fact, I sought something undefined. The few large clubs left would prove exhilarating, and Nancy and I enjoyed two-stepping with different partners. But the small spots were exhilarating, too. We'd waltzed at the Kountry Korner Café in Four Corners to an acoustic duo, the two of us gliding between tables, the only couple doing so. In January, we'd two-stepped to Muzak in the restaurant at Mammoth Hot Springs, and had danced on frozen Trout Lake and before the Buffalo Ranch in the Lamar Valley, ravens and coyotes our only band. There were few places we hadn't danced, moving together, in hotel corridors or in parking lots as the mood struck.

We hit the road with misgivings. The Three Forks to Chico strip was so rich. There were bands at the Murray each night, weekend dancing at the Sacajawea Hotel, Stacey's, Chico, at the Pony Bar, at the Eagles in Bozeman and other spots. But late in July we drove back roads to Great Falls, through the missile-silo country of Judith Gap and Harlowton, and through the Little Belt Mountains to the O'Haire Motel and its fabled Sip 'n' Dip. That bar was not a dance club but its singalong organist and mermaids in the pool were diverting. That night we hit the Flamingo, the Celtic Cowboy, and the Club Cigar, but the Montana State Fair was underway and bars were virtually empty. The Flamingo had a wide dance floor, a mechanical bull, and bands each weekend but this; dutifully we two-stepped to its DJ. The Do had a rock band but hundreds of rowdy youngsters; the same for the Cigar Bar. At the Other Place, a mom-and-pop joint on Ninth Street, I practiced my night-club two-step, and we enjoyed our best Great Falls experience. But frustrations built.

There was no dance club in Fort Benton, so we strolled by the Missouri, performing one jitterbug turn on its steel-truss bridge, and touring the city's hotel—a more than adequate venue, should it wish to host C&W hoofing. We drove southeast, past high buttes of the Shonkin Sag to Lewistown, where I'd partied with that Rockette a decade previous and years later polkaed to Montana Rose at its Eagles on a night when a trapper brought a wild marmot into its bar and released it behind the Joker Poker machines. But this night the Central Montana Fair was underway, and no band played in Lewistown. At the Montana Tavern we argued over a pool game and sulked.

Next afternoon we found the Red Ants Pants festival underway at White Sulphur Springs, and there in a field before the Big Belt mountains we two-stepped to Kelly Willis and the Nitty Gritty Dirt Band. But something was amiss. Our trips and my statewide research had yielded few gems. Nancy would travel the following weekend to Columbia Falls' Blue Moon Saloon, and would post good reports on that club. It offered C&W dance lessons, its floor was wide, "the couples good dancers," and its band that evening—The Bus Driver Tour—could not have been better. "But the couples left at midnight," she said, disconsolately. Nancy lived to dance.

She was one of the best C&W dancers in Montana.

Everyone said so, and she tolerated my inexperience with the more complicated moves stoically. She was like a feather in my arms, moving easily to and around my missteps. We'd had good nights at the Murray, where some evenings we were the floor's only couple, waltzing to a trio from North Carolina or a guitarist from Texas.

One afternoon, we drove the 46 miles from Livingston to Manhattan, a town of 1,520 people midway between Belgrade and Three Forks. Manhattan had several bars on its main drag and American Legion Post 87—with a log cabin facade and spacious interior barroom. It hosted dances each Sunday from one to five (a raffle at halftime) and that week featured the Sugar Daddies, a good Bozeman band. A vet collected our $8 covers and we'd entered a room as close to Merle Travis Peterson's ideal of a "cool museum" as probably existed.

Couples circled the floor and there was an instant sense of déja vu.

Nancy wore her turquoise *vaquera* dress, mid-calf boots and a weathered straw. She looked like a hip cowgirl from the last century. She and I triple-stepped, then broke off to dance with other partners—Nancy with an eighty-to-eighty-five-year-old foxtrotter who she said had "lots of different moves." The VFW's couples twirled, but without elaborate foot-and-hand work common in trendier venues. "We don't like people who've had lessons," I heard one woman say. Patrons varied in age from their early thirties to their nineties. I danced with a petite gray-haired woman named Harriet De Witte, who wore an embroidered vest and black jeans and was a fine two-stepper. "I'm eighty-four," she said, and coaxed me into a spin.

Harriet had written an article titled "School and Public Dances from Days Gone By" for *The Pioneer Museum Quarterly*, and she started to tell me about it. But we were interrupted by her grandson and his wife who were visiting from Dillon, 100 miles southwest. Other couples had traveled to the American Legion from as far as Butte, Anaconda, and Helena. One man wore a black derby and a purple vest, another a Buffalo Bill coiffure and goatee. No one seemed drunk.

"These American Legion sessions are the best," said Dave Carty, a Bozeman-based novelist and competitive ballroom dancer. "It's the mix of old and young, country and city—how bars in Montana used to be."

He and Nancy began a nightclub two-step and, with graceful footwork and elaborate hand moves, showed the crowd how it ought to be done.

"These are all good dancers at the Legion," Sugar Daddies drummer, Rick Philipp told me. "And they want variety. We have to mix the two-steps with cha-chas and polkas."

Harriet introduced me to Mike Hammond, a seventy-two-year-old Vietnam vet who, with his wife Judy, had started the Manhattan sessions in 2012. "We contract for the bands a year in advance," he said. "Everyone gets a vote as to which bands they want. It's democratic."

Hammond was a retired graphic artist who'd grown up in West Yellowstone. "They still had barn dances when I was a kid," he said. "Then during the 1950s in West there was Doc's Bar, the Stagecoach Inn and others. In the late 1970s, country-western came back to Bozeman. Judy and I visited the American Legion four years ago and offered to help organize. We were met with some skepticism. The four bands they alternate are the Sugar Daddies, the Country Tradition, Paul Ray, and TNT. Usually we have eighty to eighty-five people."

He introduced me to a man named Carl Ross, who was ninety-five. "I've been dancing here since it started," Ross said. We chatted a moment and he took the floor.

I sat back. As Nancy glided past with a succession of partners I felt transported. John Fryer, of Sax & Fryer in Livingston, had told me that his mother, Susanne—teaching in 1924 at the one-room schoolhouse in Cooke City—had so loved dancing that on Saturdays she would ski 29 miles to parties at the Buffalo Ranch near Tower Junction, or find a ride to Gardiner where she would dance all night then catch the mail-sled home to Cooke. Susanne Fryer had been a glamorous woman; I remembered her from my first summer in Livingston. Nancy owned glamor, and we had two-stepped in the snow before Yellowstone's Buffalo Ranch. My head began to spin.

I saw the past of summers spent dancing—both mine and the oldsters' in Manhattan: Harriet De Witte, whose first memory of a dance, she'd report, "was at West End in a bar/dance hall called Midway on top of the Bozeman Pass … I was very small and wound up asleep on a bench under a pile of coats" … and at junior high dances in Bozeman's Emerson gym, the girls placing shoes "in the middle of the floor and the boys had to pick a shoe and dance with the owner." She'd known "sock hops, spinster's sprees, and Sadie Hawkins Day dances." Then as an adult, events "at the Springhill Pavilion, the Fort Ellis school house, the Rose Creek, Pass Creek, Dry Creek," and other school houses. I thought of Mike Hammond dancing "at Borden's in Whitehall, at the Belgrade Lounge, Jackson's Barn, the Cartwheel Club, the Karst Ranch, the Steer Inn and the Norris school house." Gone, all gone.

The Sugar Daddies played something raucous … I was slipping through the cracks. Nancy walked toward me, smiled, and said, "Snap out of it."

We took a hiatus from dancing toward summer's end. I watched her boogie in an extraordinary white dress at the Livingston Hoot, but felt no desire to cut in. Our trips had both elated and discouraged us. But on August 16 we came together at the Chico Block Party, that resort's annual shindig held in its parking lot, with Montana Rose presiding. Few talented couples danced. Nevertheless we twirled on the macadam as Claudia Williams sang "Waltz across Texas," then rested on a hay bale.

"Dance is an expression," Nancy said. "A lost art."

"Not tonight," I said. And touched her hand.

—*Big Sky Journal*, 2016

MARIANA BOTAS: PANORAMA

A traveler sees the country with new eyes. Perhaps how he's imagined it, perhaps as it is. The Argentine photographer Mariano Botas may have dreamed Montana's open landscapes and time-roughened cityscapes, but he captures their authenticity with a sober directness.

It is dawn in his cityscapes. The streets are empty of people. Cars, parked or abandoned, wait for drivers who may not come. Something is about to happen. Or something may not. If it is evening, light fades and the probability of night is uncertain. Nothing human is evident. If people are present, they look away. Buildings stand implacably, as do the mountains and fields. They endure. Man's ephemera, his street signs, motels and car washes, totter in decay. They shine with this promise.

Montana is deluged with contemporary photography, but no artist with Botas' fixations comes to mind. Pictures of the American West often involve landscapes (monumental, paradisaical) or cowfolk and colorful roughnecks. Botas avoids these cliches for the loneliness of architecture, of commerce. He is the Nan Goldin of the abandoned grain elevator, the Bruce Davidson of the touch-free car wash. His pictures are bright, cheerful reminders of human impermanence. We are here but a moment. No one will remember. But the monuments to our happiness, our folly and striving, remain.

There is a bit of Hopper in Botas' compositions, his brick buildings, his roadside diners. One could live there. During the summer of 1976—my first in Livingston—I lived at an old hotel and weathered the squalls of a broken marriage. Sundays, or at dawn, I walked streets that Botas has photographed here. I marveled at the buildings' isolation, their indifference. I dined at his Beefburger cafe, washed clothes at his laundrette, wept in his bars. On happier days, I hiked the nearby mountains, danced in the cowboy saloons, and visited new friends. A novelist, Richard Brautigan, and I walked Main Street and shopped in its dime stores. At one, past the overweight salesladies and cane-shuffling patrons, Richard found a collection of tiny cowboy hats. They were doll-sized and he bought them. "These are for Rancho Brautigan," he said. Then he took me to a restaurant near the small town of Cokedale, in a landscape dotted with brick coal ovens. Inside, I looked past the deer heads and beer signs and saw, on high shelves lining the walls, a collection of miniature shoes. Brautigan laughed.

Botas would have appreciated those hats and shoes. He might have photographed them.

To view these pictures is to wander Livingston's streets at dawn, to drive Montana's highways after a sleepless night, and to meet strangers who look aside. Disoriented, but not displeased, the traveler brightens—having encountered the real.

Introduction, *Panorama*, 2007

STREAMSIDE VOWS

On August 1, beside the Gallatin River and beneath a rising moon, an odd mix of New York and Los Angeles museum folk, Parisian friends and Western artists, gathered to watch Charlotte Vignon, associate curator of decorative arts at the Frick Collection in Manhattan, and Joseph James Godla, chief conservator there, exchange vows at Rainbow Ranch near Big Sky, Montana[91]. As clouds raced across a cobalt-blue sky and the wind bent pines on the red-dirt mountain behind the wedding arbor, a guitarist played "Light My Fire" and a dog howled from a pickup truck across the road. The couple shared a kiss.

"We never considered getting married in New York," Godla said afterward. "Last November we were out here and I drove Charlotte down to show her this venue."

"I loved it," Vignon said.

"And because I've had other weddings," Godla added, "I

---

91   Vignon wore an off-white gown of silk gauze by Orlane Herbin of Paris. Her shoes were by Miu Miu. She carried a bouquet of Montana wildflowers by Leslie Lukas of Bozeman, and Godla wore a boutonniere of matching flowers in the lapel of a blue suit. He wore a white shirt with an open collar. The officiant of their marriage was Beth Renick, ordained member of the clergy of the Church of Spiritual Humanism. Music was performed on guitar by Craig Hall.

wanted to make sure this one had a taste of both our personalities."

In fact, Godla, age fifty-six, has had three previous marriages, each ending in divorce, and has enjoyed a twisting career path—from sculptor to luthier to cabinet maker to restorer, with a stint at the Montana State Prison, supervising its furniture shop. "I built a crew of murderers, which prepared me for dealing with curators," Godla said, jokingly. His variegations do not trouble Vignon, age thirty-six, who studied cello seriously as a girl, and has both a law degree from the University of Toulouse in Haute-Garonne, France, and a Ph.D. in Art History from the Sorbonne.[92] "I am maybe worse than him," she said. "I could have had many different careers, I could have been married many times before, and I end up here marrying Joe. Montana called me. It's so big. I was driven by that."

Godla, a stocky, balding man who grew up in Bozeman, Montana[93], and the slim, blonde Vignon, born in Paris and raised in the south of France, were introduced by Godla's former wife—Cynthia Moyer—his third, at a reception at the Metropolitan Museum of Art, where Vignon was a fellow in the European Sculpture and Decorative Art Department. "You're going to love her," Moyer told Golda. "And she was right," he said. Within a year, Vignon had moved to the Frick, where she and Godla worked together and became best friends. As each lived on the West Side, they began walking home across Central Park together.

The moment when friendship turned to love happened there. Vignon remembers, "We were lying down on the grass.

---

92   Vignon is co-curator of two current exhibitions at the Frick, "Gold, Jasper, and Carnelian: Johann Christian Neuber at the Saxon Court" and "White Gold: Highlights from the Arnhold Collection of Meissen Porcelain." She is an adjunct professor of history of European decorative arts and the history of collecting at the Bard Graduate Center in New York.

93   Godla graduated from Johnson State College in Johnson, Vermont., and received a master's in art conservation from Antioch.

Nobody that I'd been dating would take the time to be on the grass. It was a beautiful blue sky of Manhattan with the trees, and we're talking about the trees and about nature and about mood and about stuff. I was not thinking about what I'd have to say or that he would judge me."

"We were lying in the grass like a couple of kids."

"I was feeling like a teenager again," Vignon said.

They became lovers the night a business trip to Miami was canceled by a summer storm, "and we had drinks at this Moroccan bar on the West Side," Vignon said, "this weird place with curtains and a woman serving you. Very exotic. Aprhodisiacal."

"I asked if I could kiss her," Godla said.

"And I said yes. That was when we got together." Within two weeks they were crawling under chairs at the Vizcaya Museum in Miami, "to see if they were authentic," Vignon recalled.

"And what's more romantic than that?" Godla said. Their affair began in earnest.

Godla, whose father, a mining engineer, had run talc companies in Montana and Vermont, has "a great family," he said, but Vignon's childhood had been complicated. Her father has been out of touch with the family for twenty years. "Mentally he rejected us early on ... he was not there, and that was one of the reasons that I never wanted to get married. Marriage has never been associated with happy things ... Joe showed me that I could be happy in love with someone."

What Godla shared with Ms. Vignon, which he hadn't with his previous wives, was "a passion for the field of 18th century craftsmanship in French decorative arts," Vignon said. At the Frick they worked and taught seminars together, but kept their romance secret. "We tried as much as you could imagine to keep our professional life and our private life totally separate," she said. The Frick "is a small institution, it's a family by itself. We felt we have this relationship and it's not going to be for others. Nobody at work knew for almost a year that we were dating. We lived together and people didn't know. We were really good."

Their shared passion for furniture occasionally was trumped by other passions. But there were no office shenanigans. "We can't kiss in the Frick!" Vignon said. "But that makes it more romantic. We had to work all the time together, and see each other and have this burning passion. We met at the Met, but the Frick is where we had our courtship."

Surrounded by Rembrandts, Vermeers, and Corots, and within a distinctive Fifth Avenue mansion, their love did not bloom as readily as it had in Central Park—or in Montana. "It's not a romantic house," Godla said. "Not at all," Vignon agreed. "When you're there you feel power, money, social tradition … nothing that we are."

In the days after their wedding, the couple toured Yellowstone Park, seeing Old Faithful, the geyser-pocked Firehole River and the vast Lamar Valley. "We saw a grizzly," Godla said, "and wolves chasing each other. We saw a black bear."

"And magical light," Vignon said. "Enormous beauty, difficult to take because it's such a spectacular landscape and wild nature. We had people at our wedding from the Getty, from the Cleveland Museum of Art, from the Yale Gallery, from the Met, from the Frick. People who are exposed to the best art ever created. We were all here having the same shock. There's this absolutely magical wonder made by nature and not by human beings. I have like two or three persons, very sensitive persons, that were in tears from a landscape like that. It just takes your entire body. You let your intellect go. You're *taken* by it."

Despite their shared love of art and landscape, there is their nineteen-year difference in age. "I had a triple bypass when I was fifty," Godla said. "And I'm pretty convinced it was largely stress-induced. I was negotiating my divorce, while breaking up with the woman that I'd locked onto. And I was working through some things at work. I was extremely depressed a good while after that. And climbing out of that was a several year process for me."

"But I helped, huh?" said Vignon.

"Yeah," Godla said, tenderly. "When I got to the point when I could be open to something, luckily it was Charlotte … I'm not proud of my failures. If I have reluctance about even the announcement of our wedding, it's saying to the world, 'Yeah, I screwed up three times.' But I want to give it another shot."

Vignon said, "Life is short. And he's fifty-six. He probably will die before me. And I know that our love has to be *now*. And *today*. And we cannot wait and we cannot plan … we have no time to lose. We have to live every single minute, for many years to come. But it's a risk. To see yourself at thirty--six and think, 'Yes, one day I will be by myself. And maybe I'm not going to have kids." And that's something. That's why I want to be very, very happy now."

—*The New York Times*, 2012

TOM RUSSELL: THE ROSE
OF ROSCRAE

The singer-songwriter Tom Russell was a man who, as of January of 2016, had released thirty collections of songs, some of which had been recorded by Johnny Cash, Ian Tyson, Nanci Griffith, Lucinda Williams, and others, and whom Bruce Springsteen, Bob Dylan, and Grateful Dead lyricist Robert Hunter considered one of the most accomplished songwriters working. Annie Proulx called him "an original, a brilliant songwriter with a restless curiosity and an almost violent imagination," and John Swenson of *Rolling Stone* cited him as "The greatest living country songwriter … he's written songs that capture the essence of America, a trait that can only be matched by the country's greatest novelists." Lawrence Ferlinghetti said that "Tom Russell is Johnny Cash, Jim Harrison and Charles Bukowski rolled into one … he is writing out of the wounded heart of America."

That January, I met with Russell in his home near Santa Fe. At its door, he said, "What's the password?" I blanked. "Dylan!" he roared, and ushered me through.

I was there to jaw about Bob Dylan—a Russell obsession—and to discuss Tom's latest album, *The Rose of Roscrae,* which by any standard was an exception to the rule of contemporary songwriting. *Roscrae* was a "frontier musical," he said, released the previous year in an extraordinary two-CD set which, even though in the Americana vein, the *Los Angeles Times* listed as one of the top ten albums of 2015 and which, in a theatrical format, Russell hoped to see produced on Broadway. The album contained fifty-two tracks and multiple parts sung by artists (living and dead) as varied as Russell, Cash, Tyson, Jimmie Dale Gilmore, Maura O'Connell, Guy Clark, Joe Ely, Tex Ritter, Augie Meyers, Leadbelly, Moses Platt, Ramblin' Jack Elliott, and Walt Whitman reciting "America" from a wax cylinder.

Russell's folk opera told the story of Johnny Dutton, or Johnny Behind-the-Deuce, an Irish emigrant who leaves Roscrea (its proper spelling—Johnny is dyslexic) to wander the late 19th century, American Southwest "like Odysseus," Russell told me, "searching for a way back home."

In a sense, Tom said, this had been his journey. Raised and educated in California, with a master's degree in criminology from U.C. Santa Barbara, he had spent a year teaching in Nigeria[94] during the Biafran War before relocating to Vancouver where he played eight sets a night in its skid row honkytonks, then moved to Austin, San Francisco, and eventually New York, where he spent years camped in "the bunker," a boarded-up Brooklyn storefront, writing songs and performing.

In 1997, impulsively, he moved to Texas. "Here's your plot," Russell said. "A guy comes out of a storefront in Brooklyn, wants to escape the big time, moves to the most outsider place in the world—El Paso, Texas—and concocts this massive, weird, dark, folk opera on the West. What was that Raymond Chandler line? 'Nobody cared whether I died or went to El Paso.'"

He explained that "after seventeen years living the [New

---

94   Of Africa he had written that it "left me with the overpowering notion that art was tied in with deep magic, and a blood and bone hoodoo and drum music. Art was a spirit which transformed, elevated, and preserved cultures." *Blue Horse, Red Desert: The Art of Tom Russell* (Bozeman: Bangtail Press, 2011) 12.

York] bohemian-musician-cowboy-band lifestyle I'd come to the end of it. I saw a photo of an old adobe in *Texas Monthly* and told myself, that's where I want to be: Texas, Juarez, the desert. My songwriter vision was formed by Marty Robbins' 'El Paso,' which is huge in the American canon ... a gunfighter ballad that sounds like an opera. The other song was Bob Dylan's 'Just like Tom Thumb's Blues,' with the line 'when you're lost in the rain in Juarez and it's Easter time too ...'"

Russell was a big man with a gentle face and an engaging smile. But with his basso voice and build could be an intimidating presence. He was unapologetically male, and one could readily see him in the cantinas of Juarez. In 1998 he'd bought a 1930s adobe house across the border in El Paso, but drank in the Juarez honkytonks (his songs, "When Sinatra Played Juarez" and "Jai Alai" come from this period) and attended a bloodless-bullfighting school. "Not on any Hemingway trip," he said, "just to have fun. And to understand the culture. The bars in Juarez were unbeatable for vibe. My best friend was Tommy Gabriel, dead now, who had played piano for Sinatra in Juarez in the 1940s and 1950s, when it was the Vegas of the West. That lasted until the drug wars started. Thousands of dead bodies. They tore down the bull ring and most of the good bars. It was over."

While living in El Paso, Russell released ten albums and wrote 100 ballads, some about pop culture heroes traversing a spiritual desert that included Orson Welles, Bill Haley, Bobby Driscoll (the voice of Peter Pan), Mickey Mantle, Sterling Hayden, Elizabeth Taylor, Dave Von Ronk, and the young Dylan. Ian Tyson had a hit with "Navajo Rug," a song he and Russell co-wrote. Tom appeared five times on *Late Night with David Letterman*. One evening Dave introduced his song by saying, "You listen to this CD once and you'll saddle up and ride to Babb [Montana] and knock off a liquor store." Another night Letterman said, "How great is Tom Russell? Isn't he tremendous? Always the best. I'd like to quit my job and travel with him—if the money can be worked out."

Russell established an international reputation as "the best songwriter you've never heard of" and "the man from God knows where," producing an album by that title.

All this was warm up for songs that would find their way onto *The Rose of Roscrae*. These were traditional ballads ("the bedrock of American music") which included "Bury Me Not on the Lone Prairie," "Sam Hall," "Old Paint," "The Streets of Laredo," Leadbelly's "When I Was a Cowboy," and corridos from a Swiss Yodel Choir, paired with originals such as "She Talks to God," "Hair Trigger Heart," "He Wasn't a Bad Kid, When He Was Sober," and "Resurrection Mountain" that were among the best songs Russell had composed.

As the snow fell over a coyote fence in his New Mexico backyard, the sixty-nine-year-old Russell said, "I grew up on this Broadway-show tradition they called frontier musicals—like *Oklahoma!* and *Annie Get your Gun*. I was fascinated by the way songwriters treated the West ... the Tin Pan Alley cats were great, but really had no foothold in the real lingo and soul of the cowboy West. So I thought I might write a frontier musical with more authentic songs, dialogue, traditional songs, slang, and all of it."

He picked up an old Gibson, fingered it distractedly, then said, "I began hanging out with my cowboy brother and his second wife, who grew up on a 30,000-acre, Spanish land-grant ranch in central California. I listened to her family history and the way the local cowboys talked. My brother had run off with a local waitress, and my sister-in-law was left to ranch alone. She shot two bears inside her kitchen. This is a ranch just 200 miles from L.A., but linked back through eight generations to a deep Western past. Back to Texas and Ireland. So that's where *Roscrae* started."

The spiritual search of Johnny Behind-the-Deuce is the musical's most intriguing element. Caught in a hay loft with his rose of Roscrae, he's beaten by her father and vows to leave Ireland for the American West, to "become a cowboy," like those he's read of in dime novels. In Texas he becomes a gunfighter and an outlaw hounded by a medicine-show-preacher-lawman named Augie Blood, who drives a prairie schooner pulled by "four gospel mules," Mathew, Mark, Luke and John, and who pursues Johnny as Javert did Jean Valjean in *Les Miserables*. During his wanderings, Johnny hears music—Scots-Irish, African-American, Indian, Swiss, Mexican—that lays the foundation for what will become American song ... which is, as Russell saw it, a footing of the American character. Imprisoned at Angola, where he hears Leadbelly and Moses Platt, Johnny eventually is released and makes his way home to Ireland, where he and Rose are reunited. "Love is the Last Frontier," is the song that speaks to that reconciliation. Johnny has had to climb "Resurrection Mountain" to find his way home, but he's made it.

Russell had climbed that mountain, emotionally and professionally. After a series of relationships he categorized as train wrecks, and a brief hospitalization in El Paso for depression ("Hoyt Axton had dried out there—I felt instantly better"), he married Nadine Russell, a thirty-two-year-old Swiss-German whom he met after a performance in Switzerland and who "runs my life," he admitted, "keeping me fit with good food and exercise, and handling the business side of things." And ever since 1980, when he picked up Robert Hunter while driving a cab and sang him his cockfighting song, "Gallo Del Cielo," which Hunter loved and was moved to invite Russell on stage at a show in Greenwich Village, he had dedicated himself to the creation of fine songs.

But commercial success had proved elusive. "I would think if there's an angle to this story," Russell said, "it would be The Last Songwriter, the guy living in the middle of nowhere who's been hailed critically by everyone, but is way outside ... and who wrote an opus that summons up the roots of Americana music." Possibly. But it was enough to say that Russell enjoyed quoting Flannery O'Connor's remark that "We must push as hard as the age that pushes against us."

What *The Rose of Roscrae* spoke to as art was a passing of the folk era, the birth of a contemporary roots movement, Russell's role in it as elder statesman, and the dearth of quality lyrics being created by younger singer-songwriters. Russell, who painted expressionistic canvasses (critic Bill Reynolds would call him "the Edvard Munch of the West"[95]) wrote both fiction and nonfiction. A collection of his essays, *Ceremonies of the Horsemen*,[96] would appear the following summer; he had edited a book about songwriting with Sylvia Tyson, had published three other books (including a novel) with a memoir promised the following year. He wore one of Gram Parson's desert-scorched bones (excavated at Joshua Tree) in his hat band and felt adamantly that songwriters had lost their way.

"There are no more Dylans," he said. "Dylan is Van Gogh … in Van Gogh's book of letters and sketches are endless rough drawings—hundreds of working sketches of potato eaters, farmers, sowers, prostitutes, fishermen, weavers, and endless attempts at sunsets, fields of flowers, and on … all leading up to the final masterpiece paintings. The art begins wild, sometimes off balance, but ends up powerful and complete. I see the same processes in young Dylan in his collection, *The Cutting Edge*. Dylan is Van Gogh. We are receiving art that is forged in deep time, created by possessed souls— and does anyone have the guts now to trek that wilderness road again? Certainly Dylan hammered the point home in his [recent] Music Cares speech. The bedrock of his art lies in the study, and assimilation, of 10,000 folk songs steeped in myth, deep poetics, and mystical melodies—which he borrowed heavily from, and then carved into his own modernistic visions."

Russell fingered his guitar distractedly. In a way, *Roscrae* and Russell's wish to see the musical produced on Broadway were retreats to New York. To that end, he played several new

95   Russell had a show, the following month, with Bob Dylan and other songwriter-painters, at the True North Gallery in Ontario; he has a Santa Fe gallery and has exhibited his paintings in Europe.

96   With its pieces about songwriters, rodeo champions, old Martin guitars, muleskinners, and drunk saloon artists, one of the best books written about western culture.

songs, one inspired by *The New Yorker* writer Joseph Mitchell, and by his collection, *Up in the Old Hotel*. Russell began to sing, and as a light snow fell through the New Mexico sunset, we were on Manhattan's South Street in the building above the old fish house, Sloppy Louie's. He barked the song's refrain:

> The ghost of Joseph Mitchell came stumbling down the hall
> "I've got nothing more to say, folks, I believe I've said it all."
> And who could argue with a ghost? Because he said it so well...
> In that book he wrote called *Up in the Old Hotel*.[97]

With *Roscrae* and a fulsome canon, Russell just might reign as the Joseph Mitchell of western song.[98]

2016

---

97   Thomas George Russell, "Up in the Old Hotel." Lyrics. *Folk Hotel*. Frontera Music, ASCAP, Bug/BMG, 2017. Used by permission of TGR.

98   Since *The Rose of Roscrae*, Russell has released four albums: *Play One More: The Songs of Ian & Sylvia*, With two bonus tracks performed by Ian & Sylvia; *Folk Hotel, Old Songs Yet to Sing*, and *October in the Railroad Earth*, the title of which is an ode to Jack Kerouac. ORE was number one on Americana lists for two months in 2019. Russell's book, *The Ballad of Western Expressionism: Tom Russell Art*, was published during the fall of 2019.

BOWEN'S LAMENT

So I wrote the first Du Pre in 1994," Peter Bowen is saying, "and the sequel was to be my Assassination of the Livingston Writers Community book. Because after I got this perfectly marvelous, wonderful review in *The New York Times*, and bearing it proudly in my hand, I stood in the door of the Owl Lounge, where all of my good friends stood up from their stools and screamed, 'Out!' And I thought, 'I'll get you, you sonsofbitches.'"

Peter Bowen laughs. It's a magnificent laugh, starting somewhere around his kidneys and rising past his belly to resonate in a chest deep as a wheelbarrow. He tips back his straw, wiping tears with the back of a hand. The Du Pre of which he speaks is *Coyote Wind*, the first of those mysteries featuring Gabriel Du Pre (*Stewball*, the twelfth, was published by St. Martin's in April) a Métis brand inspector and sleuth, whom Jonis Agee, in her *Times* review, called "an original creation made up of as many complex parts as his Métis (French-Cree-Chippewa *voyageur*) ancestry," with "the soul of a poet, the eye of a wise man and the heart of a comic," adding that, "as only the best literary novels are able to do, *Coyote Wind* brings many worlds together and hones the language to create a fresh, memorable character and a profound vision." If that weren't praise enough, the *Times'* mystery columnist,

Marilyn Stasio, characterized Du Pre as "a solid man with lusty appetites who loves red meat, liquor and tobacco, plays a smoking fiddle, and is faithful to his woman," categorizing the novels as "strange, seductive ... haunting ... blunt and crude, soaked in whiskey and raspy from laughter, but still capable of leaving echoes."

Absent the whiskey, she might have been describing Bowen.

"Actually, I'm very fond of Livingston and the people there," he says. "All of its writers are geniuses and none of their significant others are psychotic." More laughter.

In Ovando, an hour east of Missoula and sufficiently distant to warrant refection, the sixty-year-old Bowen is seated in a borrowed kitchen before a black and silver woodstove, rolling smokes and swilling iced tea. Bracketing his silver-blonde hair and beard are cabinets he's built, part of a renovation deal he's made with the owners that has allowed him to live for the past four years in one of the property's outbuildings. Bowen is practiced in such arrangements, for despite the fifteen novels he's published (including four in the Yellowstone Kelly series), life is pretty much hand to mouth.

"I can live on about $1,000 a month," he says. "The Du Pres earn me about $10,000 a year and the rest I make off carpentry jobs."

Most of his repairs-for-lodging contracts have been around Livingston, of whose writers' community he's very much part. Occasionally he rents (once, a room in a house owned by author David McCumber, next to songwriter/poet Greg Keeler's room, in a melange of bachelorhood dubbed, "The Bent Fork Rod & Gun Club"), or he'll crash at Keith Lawrie's cabin up Deep Creek or in Dobro Dick Dillof's caboose up Suce. But there's been a woman in Boston—Christine Whiteside, his longtime companion—with whom he's lived for several winters, and this Ovando property, owned by former state senator Dorothy Eck's family, to which he's retreated intermittently since 1989.

"It's kind of isolating here," Bowen admits, shifting gears.

"I grew up in Bozeman, and this is on the western side of the divide. As an old rancher I worked for as a kid once said of Missoula, 'Son, you be careful over there, them people ain't like us. They eat things ain't got *legs* on 'em.'"

Ovando's noted for its fishing—the Blackfoot River runs through it—and it's a tiny hamlet off Highway 200, not far from Lincoln (where Ted Kaczynski holed up), abutted by wealthy ranches and the Bob Marshall Wilderness. With its false-front buildings, angler's shop, tourist café, museum, and tiny post office, it's more a Williamsburg miniature than Du Pre's Toussaint, Montana, with its three seasons of "snow, mud, dust," its hardscrabble barflies at the Toussaint Saloon, where Du Pre inhales whiskey ditches, wolfs cheeseburgers, plays music and rolls his own smokes. Ovando has its Trixi's Antler Saloon, but Bowen has dodged it.

Instead he's cooked us a supper of pork shoulder, potatoes, and no vegetables ("vegetables was what you *fed* to food," a cowboy's told Du Pre) and now we're relaxing in his appropriated kitchen. Spread about are copies of *The Economist, The New Yorker, Scientific American,* and the Sunday *New York Times,* and scattered across the table are three University of Montana library books—on the Iraq war, on WW I, and on Einstein's theories. A taped documentary of Ramblin' Jack Elliott's life flickers across the television screen.

"I fired Jack once," Bowen says. "I ran a coffee house in Ann Arbor during the late 1960s, and while singing 'Rock Island Line' he just walked off stage and out for the night. Not sure he's ever forgiven me."

Like Du Pre, Bowen's a serious musician. Performing is another of his tools (with carpentry, drawing, and guiding) to keep the wolf at bay, and music's a great love. One of the first times we met, Bowen was triple billed with Elliott and Dobro Dick in a folk concert at Livingston's Murray Hotel. Elliott seemed to have forgiven him, until Bowen's deep baritone blew him offstage.

"When I was at the University of Michigan," Bowen says,

"I'd ride the train to Chicago and go to Pepper's Lounge on the South Side. Heard Howlin' Wolf and Muddy Waters there. Muddy called me 'Cowboy.' I was with Arthur 'Big Boy' Crudup the day Elvis died, and he said, 'That Albert Preston stole all my music and never paid me a dime.'"

Bowen, in the late 1960s, was at the end of a flighty academic career that included an apprenticeship as a potter, too much drinking (he no longer partakes), a brief fling with the Air Force—"We disliked each other and agreed that perhaps it would be better if I went away"—and a lifelong struggle with manic depression, that "just frogged up everything." He hadn't yet started writing. "I wouldn't begin until I was thirty-five—it's actually wonderful that I've managed to write anything." He returned to Montana in 1973, "banging around to jobs which were for many purposes just a waste of time," and eventually taking fiction-writing courses at the University of Montana. "After several quarters, I got a letter from the department chairman which said I was 'insolent and arrogant and frightening,' and that after due consultation, they had obliterated every trace of my ever having been there, and that if I ever said that I *had* been there, they would sue." Uproarious laughter. "I thought it quite a vote of confidence."

In subsequent years, he's written thirty-five novels, nineteen of which have yet to see print, and twelve of which, the Du Pres, already are classics. The four Yellowstone Kellys—satirical takes on a picaresque, 19th century scout—have their charm, but as Bowen's friend, David McCumber, author of *The Cowboy Way* and now managing editor of *The Seattle Post-Intelligencer*—says, "the Du Pres "drip with authenticity and are better than anything else in the genre—Peter's up there as an artist with Charlie Russell." George Witte, editor-in-chief of St. Martin's in New York, adds that Bowen "writes in an utterly distinctive voice: lyrical, sly, intimate, at once terse and relaxed. He sounds like no other writer, and his vision of the West—what it was, and what it's become—is steeped in history without being in the least sentimental."

He's both prolific and fast. He wrote *Coyote Wind* in six days, and typically spends no longer than two weeks on a Du Pre, producing twenty-odd pages at a sitting. "I write two novels at the same time," he says. "On alternating mornings. Then afternoons I'll work on the Assassination of the Livingston Writers Community book, when I'm tired and cranky and don't really care about anybody's feelings."

Describing his childhood (which was scattered) Bowen grows uncharacteristically tight lipped. Born in Georgia in 1945, he lived in Colorado and Indiana before moving to Bozeman at age nine, where his Ph.D. father taught education at MSU and coached sports, and his mother helped organize the Museum of the Rockies. They were bookish and "gentle" parents, "but I," he admits, was "an obnoxious kid, a poisonous little wretch, and fairly feral. I used to take off gaily for school and disappear up into the mountains." His father was not an outdoorsman, but "we went camping and stayed in cabins up on the Gallatin River, and he taught me how to build a fire and further how to do it safely." And he was an accomplished athlete. "When people are talking fathers and what they did, I have them all trumped. I wait until the last possible moment and say, 'I don't care about your Navy crosses and honorary degrees from Oxford, *my father wrestled in a carnival for a man named Ten Cent Jack.*' Which he did, while working his way through Iowa Teachers College."

As a boy, Bowen considered both MSU's library and its campus his private reserve. "If I had a question about something I was bold enough to track down some poor overworked professor in his cubicle and ask, 'What is this particularly interesting bug, or rock or whatever?'" And he loved to read. "Fiction, nonfiction, anything I could get my hands on. I even loved browsing through *The Encyclopedia Britannica*." He ran errands for his mother at the Museum of the Rockies. "She was from Pierre, South Dakota, and in the West, she told me often, it does not matter who your family is or how much money you have, it matters only who you are."

His mother's message suffuses the Du Pre series, whose subject is the integrity of a culture (the Métis' and old Montana's) threatened by variously malignant incursions: yuppie "envirodweebs," an overweening government, low-fat diets, new-age cultists, moral relativists, preachy teetotalers, anti-smoking zealots, champions of wolf reintroduction, "Californicators," all Texans, Japanese businessfolk, the FBI and ATF, the religious right, Lewis and Clark Journal counterfeiters, drug runners, Hollywood fascisti, and the poisonously ubiquitous "trust fund snots." In the midst of these, Du Pre maintains his dignity, taking guff only from his women (Bowen's sturdiest characters) knowing "the strength of the Métis was the men's humility, but the backbone of the tribe was the women," and that ritual was the path to spirituality—the latter personified by Benetsee, a boozy sweatlodge shaman, part spirit, part seer, who interprets signs and shapeshifts, but, as Du Pre muses, is "family, too. Spooky old man, lived on nothing, people brought him food, fixed his window it got broken." Again, a situation akin to Bowen's.

Despite his various patronages, there's anger at the heart of Bowen's writing that is both populist reactivity and a kind of boho snobbery. Like many artists, he distrusts wealth's intentions: "Wealth was a sign of a bad heart," Du Pre reflects, in *Coyote Wind*. "The more power you had, the less you owned." Yet earlier we'd driven his two Labradors across a half mile of neighboring ranchland, for their afternoon swim in a cattle tank by the Blackfoot's south fork. The property was rich and immense, "fourteen or fifteen sections," its gate locked, but Bowen had the key. He shrugged off this access. "It's owned by friends," he explained, "whose family's been here since 1872. I'm rebuilding an addition to their cabin, and they're kind enough to give me a key to their gate."

We stood by the river as his dogs played and he explained the complicated ecological difficulties the Blackfoot faces, "having nothing to do with agriculture, mining, logging or anything else. It's a biologically weak river with a really high siltation rate." This raised the touchy subject of environmentalism, the most controversial motif in the Du Pre novels, which again circled back to class anger: "Environmentalists are merely the new bourgeoisie," Bowen snipped, "a common mess of over-moneyed, selfish, and vicious jerks who wish to reorder the Mountain West into some sort of squalid suburb abutting wilderness." He called the moneyed playgrounds circling Yellowstone Park—Jackson Hole, Cody, Red Lodge, Paradise Valley, Bozeman, Ennis—"the bathtub ring," saying, "that which the gods wish to destroy they first make hip," then shrugged that the Park itself was "perfectly worthless for agriculture or grazing, so I don't really care."

Despite such comments, as *Playing God in Yellowstone's* Alston Chase has said, "Peter's a staunch Democrat who conscientiously votes—though from his books you'd think him an anarchist to the right of Attila the Hun." And he's an ardent conservationist: "It's the old argument between the followers of John Muir and those of Gilbert Pinchot," Bowen explained. "If you have something, do you want to just keep it 'pristine and untouched,' so you can have a natural cathedral in which to worship, or, if it has things that are of use to human beings, should you use them and take care of it at the same time? I prefer the second. We have a huge wilderness area north of Ovando which is deteriorating very rapidly. But if you were to suggest to these little nitwits that perhaps pit toilets and permanent camping structures back there might be a good idea to preserve the place, they'd have twelve cows apiece." Muted laughter.

Back in the kitchen, he brews tea to be iced. The Ramblin' Jack video has been replaced by a PBS documentary on roots music, and I'm reminded that some of Bowen's best writing is of Du Pre fiddling at hoedowns, festivals, and in Montana roadhouses: "Du Pre got his fiddle, tightened up the bow, tuned. He began to play, 'Baptiste's Lament' ... Benetsee pulled a willow flute from his coat, stuck it in the corner of his mouth ... the fiddle and the willow. River bottoms, the wagons full of meat, new babies in the bellies of the women ... The old *chansons*." As I watch, Bowen rolling smokes in a sleeveless cowboy shirt and jaunty straw, I can't help but think that Du Pre's and Yellowstone Kelly's dilemma, of being modern men "dragged kicking and screaming through history, forever getting stuck between the tectonic plates of historical motion," afflicts Bowen. As he's written of the Duke of Wellington, "He would not have liked the 20th century, and, well, no sane man does." And like many writers outside their time, Bowen's role seems that of a literary gadfly nipping at the smugness of a Last Best Place culture, muttering, "We still could blow it."

That gadflyism has not always won him friends, and it's contributed to his isolation. Which is fine: "Literature does not proceed from everybody holding hands around the fire at Camp Lit and singing 'Michael Row the Boat Ashore.' It is a solitary effort, always has been, always will be." Yet he's made noises about moving back to Livingston, and I ask whether, financially, he's more flush. "No, things are customarily grim. When I get back down there, I'll have to look for part time work. But what the hell. I'll go on writing, go on living my life."

Methodically, he inserts the day's rolled smokes into an empty Camel's pack. I recall lines from an essay he wrote, ten years past, that now seem prophetic: "I've pretty well contrived to avoid any semblance of responsible behavior in life. I will be an old bum, loved but unrespected. I have written [thirty-five] novels, which is all a writer can do. They will all see print someday, but that isn't up to me. I have done that work—my end of the bargain."

Despite this output, I risk asking what might be on the back burner. Without flinching, he says, "I've got a fictionalized memoir of my childhood, I have a book about Daniel Boone's last journey, when at age seventy-six he walked from the upper Missouri into Yellowstone Park, where he stayed ten months, then floated home to Kentucky. And I'm at work on a novel about Montana in 1923 up on the Hi-line, the year that Dempsey and Gibbons fought for the heavyweight title in Shelby and three banks failed and their officers had to take to the hills, because they used their depositors' money to put up the purse." Laughter. "Magazine work has pretty much dried up since 9/11—my last piece was for Forbes *FYI* on 'Trout Flies of the Rich and Famous'—but there's *Stewball*, the new Du Pre, which is based in part on Montana's brush races, those below-the-tax-man's-radar horse races out in the boonies."

Stewball's one of his better novels, and *Publishers Weekly* has written, "As in previous Du Pre books, the fast-paced narrative offers ample doses of local color, evenly spaced bursts of violence and an unforced, laid-back style," with *Booklist* adding, "The 12th entry in the Du Pre series is as consistently entertaining as its predecessors. Gabe, ever skeptical of the modern world and its institutions, places his faith in people, the land, a hand-rolled smoke, and the occasional ditch-water highball." There's been no review in *The New York Times*.

I pose a delicate question: does this bother—and, furthermore, when his "more serious" novels are rejected for publication, does he lose heart?

"I try never to stop working," he says, "It's sort of defiance: 'Well, alright, you sonsofbitches, you're not going to make me not work.' Some of my novels I know are unsuccessful, and I keep them because UM's Mansfield Library, which will archive my manuscripts, wants the failures as well as the successes. Which I think is perfectly legitimate. They were honest efforts and if they turned out poorly, well that's entirely my fault. God forbid that after I'm dead and gone there might be some poor English professor who's turned out into the street because I didn't leave sufficient material for him to quarry a doctoral dissertation." Raucous laughter. "I mean, we *do* have responsibilities to one another."

Does he take more than two weeks to write novels like the Daniel Boone one? "Oh, yes," he says. "They're, for one thing, longer. I'll work on one for a while and perhaps go do something else. I try to have several things going, if one is not really occurring to me—then I can always go back to The Assassination of the Livingston Writers Community book, and beating up my friends."

He smirks. "You, for instance, are doomed. Your reputation will not recover."

—*Big Sky Journal*, 2005

MARGOT KIDDER: STATUESQUE

Margot Kidder got the idea for the rollicking Statues of Liberty in June, while she was having an MRI. "My joints were killing me, and I was listening to NPR through headphones, when I had a vision of all these dancing Statues of Liberty," Kidder recalled. Her activist group, Montana Women For, had plans to march in Livingston's Fourth of July Rodeo Parade—a staunchly traditional event—but other than being *for* peace and *for* justice and equality, did not have a catchall theme.

"Then I saw us marching in aqua-green costumes with foam crowns and torches, and dancing to sixties music," Kidder said. "We'd have a float that would carry a long banner with our name, and a ten-foot-tall statue of the Statue, flashing a peace sign."

"It was her Joan of Arc moment," said Diane Kamp, an activist and rancher from Big Timber, who like the fifty-six-year-old Kidder, stood Saturday on Washington's Constitution Avenue with nine other women dressed as Statues of Liberty. They carried a seven-piece wooden sign, reading MONTANA WOMEN FOR PEACE over a colorfully painted mountain mural.

Sixty-eight statues had marched in July's Rodeo Parade, but only these few could afford a trip to the capital. Even

Kidder was staying with friends. Widely known for her role as Lois Lane in 1978's *Superman*, Kidder—who has a long history of activism in this country—had marched, limping, with pinched nerves in her neck and spine, against the first Gulf War in Washington. On Saturday she again limped, this time from severe osteoarthritis. "My knees are really hurting," she said, "but I'm determined to make it."

This was the Canadian-born actor's first protest march as an American citizen. She'd been naturalized on August 17, after living for thirty-seven years in the United States, most recently near her daughter and grandchildren in Livingston. 'Now I can vote against each and every elected official who supported the [George W.] Bush administration," Kidder said. "And I'm free to protest this administration's policies, without fear of getting deported." She frowned. "My grandkids need me."

Earlier, at a rally on Pennsylvania Avenue, the Statues were invited onstage, with their sign, to stand near Gold Star mother, Cindy Sheehan and behind Joan Baez, as the latter energized demonstrators with song. Afterward, Kidder was invited to speak. She introduced Montana Women For, explaining that they'd won Best Patriotic in the Rodeo Parade, "with a peace float," and that she'd recently become an American so she "could protest this war with full credibility." She added, "I really don't want anyone coming up to me and saying, 'I'm so discouraged I want to move to Canada,' because that's chickening out. We need every single person who yelled at the television about Bush to get off their butt and into the street."

"I feel that strongly," Kidder said on Constitution Avenue. "And to become an American at a time when the world hates us, is a really serious thing to do. I've torn off a Canadian-citizenship band-aid that's protected me from having to identify with the bad things about the United States. I was always able to say, 'That's not me, I'm Canadian.' Now I have to say, 'It's us.'"

Kidder was seated on the asphalt massaging her knees when the crowd began to move, and had to be helped to a standing position. She hoisted her placard. The word "Montana" on the Statues' sign, and its mountain mural, already were attracting comment. "Montana, all right!" shouted fellow demonstrators, while angling for photos. And, "That's what America's supposed to look like." Surrounded by Code Pink demonstrators, some of whom carried signs reading, "My Bush Would Make a Better President," or "Sixty Million Bucks to Investigate a Blow Job?" the crowd began chanting "We're Women, We're Marching, We're Not Out Shopping." Slowly the Statues angled left on Fifteenth Street and marched north past the Treasury building.

There, an elderly man dressed as Uncle Sam and carrying an aluminum cane, spotted the Statues and cried, "Montana! I was born in Cascade." He shuffled toward them, demanding his picture be taken before their banner. The entire march halted as this was affected. Only a few people recognized Kidder.

She seemed transported, though, marching briskly and breaking rank to direct the Statues' movement like a grandmotherly drill sergeant. Turning up Pennsylvania Avenue toward Lafayette Square, she said, "My God, what a beautiful city. How would we react if someone bombed it? As a citizen, now, of a country that has bombed a lot of breathtakingly beautiful places, it *is* a thought."

The march slowed in front of the White House and camera crews, positioned there, descended upon the Statues. Still-photographers posed them. Film crews jostled for shots. An Australian sound man asked, "What do you think about democracy?" And one Statue, Belinda Winslow, said, "Democracy is wonderful, and I support it 100 percent. That's why I'm here—because Bush doesn't."

Statue Diane Kamp shouted, "In Montana, we say, 'Instead of following the herd, it's time for our voices to be heard.'" And in an aside, "The only time you should follow a herd is if a cow's at the lead and she's yelling, 'Sale!'"

The Statues made it past the White House, but Kidder's knees blew out before the Executive Office Building and the women stacked their placards. "It did seem to be mostly women marching," Kidder said. "I think that's due to motherhood." Seated on a wall off Lafayette Square, the Statues already were planning their next campaign. "We'll organize women all over Montana," one said. "We'll hook up with Cindy Sheehan and Code Pink and take it to the nation." And, "It's a show that needs to stay on the road."

Despite her aching knees, Kidder radiated happiness. "This was like a giant vitamin B-12 shot," she said. "Every citizen needs that. And for an actor, it was like a great opening night."

2005

Kidder died in May of 2018 at her home in Livingston, Montana.

THE REAL DEADWOOD

The latest microcosm of America that is not America is *Deadwood*, the HBO series that takes the Wild West excesses of every auteur from Sam Peckinpah to Quentin Tarantino and does them twelve better. I say "microcosm that is not" because, as creator David Milch observes in John Ames' *The Real Deadwood* (Chamberlain Bros./Penguin, $9.95), 1876 Deadwood was "not part of America. They were an outlaw community and they knew it." Yet the program's themes of misguided greed, intractable racism, sexual exploitation, casual violence, and rare tenderness on the frontier are entrenched in American art. So it was inevitable that a historical cheater—a kind of Cliff's Notes to the series—would appear.

Hamfistedly subtitled "True Life Histories of Wild Bill Hickok, Calamity Jane, Outlaw Towns, and Other Characters of the Lawless West," *The Real Deadwood* is an informative and gripping account of the gold camp's misdeeds, written by an honest scholar (Ames has published fifty-six novels) with a firm grasp of his subject. We learn that Al Swearengen really did like to swear, that as proprietor of the Gem Hotel he served also as pimp, casino boss, murderer, thief, and white slaver, earning between $5,000 and $10,000 nightly; that

Sheriff Seth Bullock was a conservationist admired by Teddy Roosevelt, and that Calamity Jane preached free love, was "a pioneer in the arena of women's rights," probably whored, died of alcoholism, and had the largest funeral ever said for a woman in town. We read that early Deadwood rivaled Tombstone and Dodge City for its violence, averaging one-and-a-half murders per day (10 percent of its yearly population); that its Civil-War-veteran diggers suffered "soldier's heart" or PTSD, and "that meant a lot of armed men with impulse control problems" ... that its Main Street was "a thick gumbo of mud, night slops, tripes, all of it attracting a shifting black blanket of flies"; that its gambling houses weren't shut until 1947 and its bordellos until 1980; that "there was no hellhole quite as hellish as a gold camp" and, as wrenched from the Sioux's homeland, "Deadwood wasn't just lawless it was illegal ... A white man's town on Indian real estate."

Ames is most compelling in his disparagement of "the Robin Hood as avenger mind-set," that romanticizes killers like Wild Bill Hickok and Wyatt Earp, hypothesizing that "Perhaps the criminal-romanticizing excesses of the French Revolution also shaped the frontier mythos." Certainly Deadwood's life was horrific, "an unevenly mixed cocktail of sheer terror and maddening monotony." And despite Bullock, it was effectively lawless. As David Milch notes, Deadwood was "the equivalent of the first amphibians coming out of the primordial ooze. Not only was there an absence of law, there was a premium on the continued absence of law.

—Big Sky Journal, 2005

ELMORE LEONARD:
A WESTERNER COMPLETE

Elmore Leonard's milieu, in crime novels such as *LaBrava, Get Shorty,* or *Freaky Deaky,* is that of South Florida, the deal maker's Hollywood, or mobbed up Detroit. But eight of his forty-two books are Westerns, and with publication of a 546-page, *The Complete Western Stories of Elmore Leonard* (Harper Paperback, $15.95), that number has been raised to nine. Leonard began these stories in 1950, publishing the earliest in journals such as *Dime Western, Zane Grey Magazine, Argosy,* and *The Saturday Evening Post.* "I looked for a genre where I could learn to write and be selling at the same time," he says in the preface: "I chose Westerns because I liked Western movies." It would not be long before several stories, "Three-Ten to Yuma," "The Captives," and "Only Good Ones," were sold to Hollywood, and Leonard could quit as a copywriter on Detroit's Chevrolet account and turn exclusively to fiction.

The thirty-one offerings in *Complete Western* demonstrate from the first how dedicated he was to craft, and how much he'd learned from predecessors like Bret Harte, Mark Twain, and Walter Van Tilburg Clark. His plots are intricate, but serve to develop characters as quirky and complex as any in the modern novels. Leonard's stage set is that of the Arizona and New Mexico territories, and half a dozen stories feature cavalry posts during the Indian wars. "I liked the Apaches," Leonard says, "because of their reputation as raiders and the way they dressed, with a headband and high moccasins...." None of his players are stereotypically good or evil, but display both traits (plus fear, coolness, and the occasional stupidity). They are templates for his modern criminals and cops, and for outlaws and deputies that appear later in this collection.

Perhaps the finest story is "Three-Ten to Yuma," its style owing much to Hemingway's, but its pace so cinematic that, unsurprisingly, a second movie will appear this fall, starring Russell Crowe (the 1957 version starred Glenn Ford) and Peter Fonda. In "Three-Ten," Deputy Paul Scallen escorts outlaw Jim Kidd to Contention, Arizona, where they are to ride a 3:10 train to the penitentiary at Yuma. Kidd runs mind games on Scallen ("How much do you make, Marshal?"), and a contest of wills rages while outlaws wait to brutally wrest Kidd from custody.

There's more than a little bloodshed in *Complete Western*. Leonard's first story, "Trail of the Apache," finds a rancher hung head-first over a fire, "the black rawness creeping from this portion of his body upward to where his hands were tied tightly to his thighs; there the blackness changed to livid red blisters ... death had come slowly." In his mature fiction, Leonard would undercut such violence with humor, but laughs here are scarce. Later selections provide some respite—"Saint with a Six-Gun" is perhaps the first hipster Western—but smiles won in *Complete Western* are from reading apprentice tales deftly wrought, and from watching a young genius master his craft.

—*Big Sky Journal*, 2007

JIM HARRISON: LIVINGSTON SUITE

ater has coursed through Jim Harrison's writing, all of his novels and much of his poetry—in *The Theory and Practice of Rivers* and *Braided Creek*, most notably. His latest book of verse, *Livingston Suite* (Limberlost Press, $25), with illustrations by Greg Keeler, is no exception, though the Yellowstone River, which flows through Livingston and these twenty-seven ambulatory poems, is a leitmotif to be both embraced and feared.

A boy has drowned, his body gone missing, and as Harrison walks the streets of Livingston (it's July, 2002), the river and what it holds are unavoidable: "None of us wants to find the body / but then it's our duty to look," he writes. "Each morning I walk four blocks/to this immense river / surprised that it's still there, / that it won't simply disappear / into the ground like the rest of us." He detours to Livingston's alleys: "Maybe it's where poets belong, / these sub-streets where the contents of human life / can be more clearly seen, our shabby backsides / disappearing into the future." But there, inescapably, he's drawn toward the past: "Under the streets are the remnants / of an older town with caches / of Indian skulls ... I'm back home in Reed City / over fifty years ago when trains were steam but the cows / and alleys were the same." He admires Livingston's prim lawns, noting that "A community can drown in itself, / then come to life again. Every yard seems / to have flowers," but admits that "All my life / I've liked weeds. Weeds are botanical / poets, largely unwanted," and sees that "the strange cool odor / of sprinkler water / [creates] its own little breeze / in the Livingston Park." He walks his dog, Rose, gazing "at the wide eddy with a slow but inexorable whirlpool," where the boy died, realizing that "You can't row or swim upstream on the river. / This moving water is your continuing past / that you can't retrace by the same path / that you reached the present." He laments "the eyes that were given us that we don't wish to use / for fear of madness ... After years of practice / I learned to see as a bird but I refuse / to do it now, not wanting to find the body." Eventually, he flees to Michigan, and "in a cabin beside the river," learns that "It was my wife who found the body while walking / her dog Mary beside the river at Mayor's Landing ... I wish it wasn't you, I said. 'But it was,' she said. / It had to be someone. Why not me?"

This set of poems, with Keeler's precise line drawings of dogs, alleys, and the Yellowstone, is a lovely contribution to the town literature of Montana. While in the vein of Lorca's *A Poet in New York*, Kazin's *A Walker in the City,* and much of Whitman, Harrison's strolls are idiosyncratic and wholly original. Residing two blocks from where he wrote many of these poems, this reviewer experienced the city anew. If one of poetry's ambitions is to make the familiar seem fresh, *Livingston Suite* succeeds wonderfully.

—*Big Sky Journal,* 2005

AMBER JEAN: THE ROAD
TO WINEGLASS MOUNTAIN

The road, in late December, is snow-covered, icy and treacherous. It climbs one thousand feet in elevation, and three miles to Amber Jean's property, itself cloaked in nearly a foot of snow, its tree branches bent from pillowed fluffs, and with a gibbous moon in a too-close sky. I park by her studio, where prayer flags dance and no light shines, then hike a forest two-track 100 yards to a cabin, nestled into the mountain like a fire-lookout's perch. The 4:00 P.M. glow of Livingston, below, is a distant promise.

"You made it," she says, smiling. "That road is steep." She invites me in, where her collie, Tala, leaps and the kettle for tea is bubbling.

Amber is a striking blonde in her early fifties, muscularly fit but with a face that's open and soft, with distinct vulnerability. She wears a dark fleece and bluejeans with a hint of rhinestone bling; her face is cut by a smile that shows cottontail-like incisors (her trademark is the rabbit). She reaches for tea mugs, and I see that four of her sculptor's fingers are encircled by rings. Dressing for her is creativity.

But it's not art. "I've started working again," she says. "For the first time in months."

She's returned to Montana from Bhutan, to which she was

invited by its prime minister to carve a figured entranceway to the Great Room of the king's palace retreat: a log house constructed by Bozeman contractor Ken Ryder after a Bhutanese hotelier visited Montana and became enthralled by its log structures.

"The prime minister commissioned Ken to build a nontraditional retreat," she says, "a log house for the king, and Ken recommended me to provide carvings."

She's made three trips to Bhutan, and the finished piece—an entablature with images of a mountain lion, a snow leopard, snowcapped Jomolhari peak, rhododendron for the queen, heavy stones, and "a rabbit for the king's young son," she says, "who was one."

But, as she's written, "Bhutan kicked my ass." Despite the country's beauty, its Gross National Happiness Index, the people's openness and the challenge of her work, she's come home depressed. She returned to the memory of several recent deaths and the trauma of a pit-bull attack during a bike ride in Paradise Valley, from which she still suffers.

Her dog, Tala—attacked in a separate incident—has helped in her recovery. As Amber has blogged, "We are healing. Improving. I purposefully pick less-peopled places to ride ... I have biked since the attack but never with Tala. Sometimes I biked and cried. Sometimes I froze in fear while meeting dogs. A few times fear sickened me 'til I puked. But I have kept riding—bits and pieces."

Anxiety has been a fact of life for her, for as long as she can remember. Sleeplessness has haunted her, and despite a life of adventure that includes ice climbing, whitewater kayaking, mountain backpacking, and joyous cowboy dancing, she lives with trepidation. "Fear is an integral part of life," she's said. "But I refuse to let fear run things."

Making art is a comfort, particularly woodworking, which involves not just the raw material of lumber, but salvaged trees. She presented a TED Talk in 2013, focused on her relationship to forests. It spoke movingly about her creative process, and about ways in which she identifies with trees.

"They're a lot like people," she said. "Each tree has its own spirit." She spoke of her early work on trail crews, fighting fires, and of her stints as a wilderness ranger. She had studied at the Pennsylvania Academy of the Fine Arts, but despite her life in Philadelphia, "I found I was increasingly drawn more to the wilderness. I felt less lonely, sleeping alone beneath the stars, surrounded by trees, in the wilderness of Montana."

An epiphany for her happened at the base of a tree. It "had been struck by lightning. It was half dead and half alive ... These nakedly dead limbs intermingled with these life bearing branches, like lovers who refused to be torn apart. And the live parts of this tree were clinging to the dead parts, like a mother would cling to its dying child. This tree stood there ... triumphant. I had tears running down my face, and I thought, 'If I could do that, if I could create art that would touch those inner places, if I could create art that would speak emotions, if I could illuminate the human experience, with all of its contradictions, the dark and the light, and the love and the loss, and the life and the death, if I could do that, then I would be an artist."

She named a series related to that epiphany *I Never Promised You a Rose Garden*. She created it after her father died, in 2010, of pancreatic cancer. "He and I had a difficult, challenging relationship," she told her TED audience. And "This 100-year-old barbed wire found its way into my *Rose Garden* series."

Her father had been a ranch hand and salesman who had grown up on a Nebraska farm with nine brothers and sisters, "in a house so poor it had a dirt floor." He contracted polio as a child; one leg was shorter than the other. Amber's mother was one of twelve children and better off. "She was a beautiful person," Amber says. In 1967, when she was born in Gillette, Wyoming, her father worked "selling drill bits for Howard Hughes" in Rock Springs. The family lived in a trailer park. Amber was adventurous: "From the first, my mother told me,

I'd find ways to climb from the crib and ... explore." Her curiosity contributed to her sleeplessness—"I hated to miss anything"—but her anxiety and periodic depression no doubt came from her relationship with her father. "He was difficult in *most* ways," she says. "He didn't like women, though he loved my mother. He didn't like his mother or sisters, and he believed in the limitations of women. He was hard on me. We had difficulties from the beginning. He thought reading was a lazy activity. I was beaten for reading. He took my night light away, so if I saw the moon I would climb up against the window and read in the moonlight." He would strike her for any infraction. "A punch was a 'love tap.' He wouldn't hit me in the face, but he'd wallop me off the couch."

There was no way she could please him.

The family moved to Montana when she was four, and from the first "I loved being in the woods." Her father was not a woodsman, but by then sold life insurance in Bozeman. Her mother worked as a homemaker. Amber did well in high school, gaining acceptance to the Academy, from which she would graduate with honors. Summers she took forest jobs in Montana and reignited her love affair with trees. In 2010, her father was diagnosed with cancer and given two weeks to live. She was with him when he was told. "I'm glad I was there. He lived six weeks. He was so darn tough."

She began what she calls her reliquary series after experiencing the emotions she felt at his death. "In spite of his faults," she says, "he did the best he could." She's written of the series, "A reliquary is essentially a house for a relic. It's an architectural term that talks about the space created to show a piece that's a relic. That's imbued with a spiritual energy or an object that people have reverence for." The large reliquaries are eleven-foot-tall sections of Douglas fir, salvaged from burned timber stands. They have been sawed lengthwise, then hinged together, she says, "like a book," "a shrine," or "an intimate space" that can be opened to the viewer. "By opening the tree and allowing the viewer in," she creates a "space that elicits a more spiritual response in the viewer ... what I discover when I open the logs and I pay attention to the energy ... it's a real spiritual process for me ... mined from my subconscious and strong storytelling symbols. The message is very intimate...."

The fire-damaged bark of the trees is left intact and their interiors are stained, painted, or carved, then decorated with winding tree branches and vertical strands of barbed wire. On one side of each reliquary is an arched Gothic window that frames a relic: exemplified by crystal necklaces, glass shards, carved spider webs, lingerie, and in one, the collar of a deceased dog. Smaller reliquaries (7 x 5 inches) consist of windows framing the skulls and feathers of birds. Each reliquary, large or small, plays a duet between life and death, spirit and form.

Their effect is breathtaking. Joseph Godla, chief curator at New York's Frick Collection, has called Amber's work, "Audacious"—an understatement. The sliced-open trees are portals to subconscious fears and moments of wonder that can only be described as existential.

The strands of crystals, Amber's said, "are like tears. Or replenishing rain. Either way, they catch the light ... I believe grace helps us through those rough places." As does her process with trees, which she's described as a dance. "Each tree is like a new dance partner. Sometimes the trees lead, and sometimes I lead." Splitting the tree is akin to opening up people: "There's so much inside that's impossible to see on the outside."

Her outdoor activities have brought significant pause to her creative ones. In the spring of 2015, she was bicycling near the Yellowstone River when she was attacked by three pit bulls, one of which, at 140 pounds, bit her thigh and hung on, trying to pull her from the bike. "I tore my leg from its mouth," she said, "and kept pedaling. The other dogs knocked into each other trying to get at me—so I was able to ride away." She believes that if the dogs had pulled her down she might have been killed. She was treated at Livingston's ER and released. "But I had puncture wounds you could put your fingers in." Over the next few days, she developed septicemia and was hospitalized. Lawsuits proved inconclusive. What lingered was a major case of PTSD.

"I couldn't sleep, I was terrified of dogs, other people and their dogs, and I *love* dogs. I couldn't work. I sketched a few drawings of snarling dogs with big teeth, but they weren't very good. The fear wasn't about individual dogs, It was about the pack."

Her trauma intensified from the memory of a similar attack by a German Shepherd when she was two, and possibly from memories of her father's violent outbursts. But she had been healed from his abuse, in part, by a remarkable friendship with a man named Cliff Denham—who had built the cabin in which we sat, and sold her its land.

"I met Cliff in 1994," Amber says. "He was interested in romance, but I wasn't. What developed was a relationship that was the most important in my life." He was a logger, twenty years older, who "loved me more than my family. Unconditionally. Not for what I'd *accomplished*. He fully accepted me. And knew me better than anybody," including lovers who had visited the mountain.

"My father wouldn't let me cry," she adds. "Cliff didn't like me to cry. He'd say, 'Oh, honey,' but he'd permit it. He gave me all the space I needed. He was rock solid."

Denham died in 2016, days before Amber's wedding. He was to have walked her down the aisle. She walked it alone. It was a spectacular July afternoon, with hundreds of friends present on Wineglass Mountain, and her mother there for the last celebration of her life. She would die of complications from Alzheimer's ten days later. Amber's aunt would die that fall.

Amber's bridegroom and the man who helped her process those deaths was Raymond Ansotegui, a land reclamation scientist and rodeo bullfighter whom she describes as "a passionate soul and one of the kindest men I've met," and who, when the invitation came for her to work in Bhutan, supported her decision to go—and what's more, to stay through three long trips. "You're carving for the king!" he said, when she wavered.

Amber says, "I was in Bhutan by the October after my marriage. I had no plan for the carvings, no idea beforehand. And I was to work beside a carver who had had very rigid training. Bhutan had not seen a female carver before. So there was the question of whether I could do it.

"From the beginning, the plan was for my carving to be a central focal artistic element to elevate the 'retreat cabin' into a palace fit for a king. I didn't know what the subject matter of the carvings was going to be, but the central placement of my artwork in the great room had been decided early on. I had seen blueprints and was later shown photos of the progress, including detailed photos of the interior. The placement and importance of my artwork was clear from the beginning (but not the subject matter). I trusted my ability to feel out the culture to decide how best to create a piece that would totally wow them, while also being absolutely accessible to the Bhutanese people and respectful to their culture and king—while capitalizing on pushing boundaries of what they may think possible, and to create a connection between our cultures, while also representing the "West" (which in my opinion has to do with a 'do not fence me in attitude.'"

Though the weather was freezing and the living conditions difficult, she would later write, "The project for the king of Bhutan gifted me with space, place and purpose during a time of deep grief. A magical country steeped in tradition, color, kindness—and feral dogs ... Three trips over the ocean to live within the majesty of the Himalayan mountains during various seasons, but even the warm seasons were 'unseasonably cold'—brutal when spending long days carving outside."

The Bhutanese paid for her plane fare and "my housing," Amber says. "That was it. The governor was very supportive in the beginning, he approved of my design and was very pleased to have non-traditional carving in the palace. He dealt with the budget, and eventually became critical of me. Why was I taking so long? And I was pushing boundaries; the Bhutanese have a strict carving tradition and I worked outside of that. The governor became hostile between my second and third trips. Part of it was financial, and part of it was because I was a woman. It was very stressful. I couldn't please him, and that hearkened back to my father."

Eventually the finished product won over the governor. "With the colors, which carvers don't use in Bhutan, he began to see figures emerging. He said, 'It looks so real!' He accepted that it was art. And he became my biggest advocate. He held a dinner for me, and said, 'I am sad not more people will be able to see it.' Because it was the king's palace. I was so thankful. Once again, I saw the power of art."

That power traveled home with her to Montana, and has infused her latest miniature series, which she calls *Queen of the Night*—from a novel of the same name by Alexander Chee. She began it this fall, after returning from Bhutan, when "depression hung a heavy wool cloak onto my cold tired body." She describes it as "the series I completed during the darkness. Like the people of Bhutan who pilgrimage to monasteries perched like bird nests on cliffs, each piece in the series is a step in my pilgrimage toward the light."

I find the miniatures singular in Amber's artistic development, nearly surrealistic in their abstraction, and powerfully evocative. Only 5 x 7 inches in size, they retain the Gothic window motif, and are a mixture of contradictory media. One, titled "Color of a Wound," has a flesh-pink and bruised-purple foreground, to which is appended a long green feather, and a dark red one. The whole is framed by bloodied barbed wire. Another miniature, titled "The Undoing," shows the tiny figure of a ballerina, floating in a Chagall-like dreamscape of a stormy blue sky dotted with moon-like spheres. Another, titled "Permanent Dusk," retains the flesh-wound and barbed-wire motif, but adds feathers that, in their arrangement, move toward hope. And the bird imagery of "I Sang the Far Edges," "The Gift Called Hunger," "Bawdy and Plotted," and "Sprawling, Soaring," takes positive flight.

Each miniature was named for a quotation from Chee's novel, and was created in the massive studio near the foot of Amber's drive—a space that houses several of the eleven-foot-high reliquaries, winches for lifting them and other objects, power tools, hand chisels, paints, and dyes, a kitchen and a crow's nest for naps. She spends twelve-hour days working, and it's in this studio, or its previous incarnations, where she has created pieces that include paintings and bronzes (one a spectacular buffalo-bench for the Bozeman airport), that have been shown from Arizona to New York to Bhutan, and which have earned her fame. She has been named one of "America's Wood Working Greats" by *WOOD* magazine and at Grand Rapids' ArtPrize, showing her reliquaries, made the top twenty-five of the show's fifteen-hundred contestants from fifty-three countries.

I excuse myself to use the cabin's bathroom, itself a work of art. Its cabinets are hand carved and a clawfoot tub faces a picture window, through which deer and occasionally moose can be seen. Returning, I think that it's in this cabin that art and love have combined, in a mood that even to a visitor feels sublime. Of Ansotegui she says, "Raymond is a super gentle, bighearted soul. After my attack, he dressed my wounds multiple times a day. He's deeply rooted to the earth and to mother nature. He's immensely supportive. And he's multi-faceted." I think that their cabin is not so much in the forest as of it. It combines the dual elements of Amber's ruggedness and femininity, and Ansotegui's quiet machismo. It's purely functional, yet feels as if it were constructed to showcase Amber's furniture. Many of her pieces (a dining table with carved rabbit pedestals, a colorful frieze, a reliquary-like totem, a carved linen chest, a stained-glass window) decorate the space, which despite its rusticity is markedly ethereal.

"When I first moved to the mountain," Amber says, "this house had no electricity, running water, or toilet. I was living then in what would become Cliff's house. A bear had it's den a half mile up the hill, near my privy. I had to pass it every day, which was frightening. But one morning the bear was gone, so I did my business in its den." She laughs. "It never came back."

I ask about her inspiration for some of this cabin's furniture. "Most of my ideas come from experiences I've had," she says. "Or thoughts and feelings or a strong emotional reaction to a situation or a memory ... the function [of the piece] usually comes as an extension of the experience of a feeling I'm trying to portray. So instead of thinking about decorating a piece of furniture, it becomes a piece of furniture so that I can invite people in to a certain reaction to the piece."

Beneath us, across the snows of Wineglass Mountain and the trees below, shine the lights of Paradise Valley. I can't help thinking that, through her work, Amber has dug for the roots of her anxiety and depression, without reaching their true source. Yet she continues to dig. As she told the TED audience, "I'm honoring the vow I made to myself at the base of that lightning-struck tree. I will continue to dive into those unknown, dead places, and I will celebrate the tiniest little light catchers ... I believe the invitation is in the opening. And the purpose is to awaken, and to touch those inner places."

2020

T.C. CANNON: THE BALLAD
OF SOLDIER BLUE[99]

He was a folk-rock painter, enraptured by Bob Dylan and as much an artistic experimenter as were his Native American counterparts in sixties music—Robbie Robertson, Jesse Ed Davis, and Buffy Sainte-Marie. He was a Pop/Traditionalist,[100] the colors he employed as bright as those of Milton Glaser (who created Dylan's psychedelic-hair poster) or those of Édouard Vuillard and Henri Matisse. He wrote songs and poetry, and his paintings spoke as much to the urban work of Larry Rivers and Robert Rauschenberg as to the rural Kiowa-Caddo traditions in which he was raised. He was exotic in his art and dress; he was the Jean-Michel Basquiat of Santa Fe. And like musicians he revered—Jimi Hendrix, Janis Joplin, Jim Morrison—he would die young. He was T.C. (Tommy Wayne) Cannon, arguably the most significant Indian painter of his generation.

---

99   Though Cannon died in 1978, this chapter appears in the TWEN-TY-FIRST century section of *Fired On* because of the extraordinary renaissance of interest in his work, from 2017 through 2020.

100   He embraced popular art while dismissing classic Pop art, writing in a journal, "Popular art differs from "pop" art, the way the pleasure of love differs from artificial insemination. The trouble with pop, is that it pays chilly, calculated homage to mass production. You might say it's capitalist realism as opposed to artful socialist realism."

He was born to poverty in Southwest Oklahoma in 1946, the son of an electrical lineman/occasional farmer and a housewife/mother. Both seemed affectionately supportive, but T.C. spoke repeatedly of an untimely death.[101] A schoolmate, Bob Harcourt, recalls, "His many friends would say, 'We don't want to hear that. You will *not* die young!' ... He was making this prediction when he was eighteen or nineteen years of age."[102] He began sketching and painting early, as creativity both consoled and consumed him. He would write:

Art ... being the fiend that it is
wraps me in a bundle
and sends me off
to the house of myself[103]

His talent was precocious. His sister, Joyce Cannon Yi, recalls that "One day" as young children, "our parents said, 'Sit down and be quiet.' We read a comic book with Roy Rogers and Trigger on the cover, and Tommy drew the whole thing.' She was amazed. "Another time he carved a hobby horse from a piece of wood. I watched him do it."

Painting focused his identities as both Native and Anglo American. His patriarchal grandfather had been Scotch-Irish and his mother Caddo. T.C. was one-quarter white. Yet his father enrolled him formally in the Kiowa tribe at age four and gave him the name Pai-doung-u-day—meaning "One Who Stands in the Sun." He would graduate as the only Native in his high-school class at Gracemont, Oklahoma, and though elected class president would suffer discrimination. Fellow

---

101   "He'd had a vision of death," his biographer, Joan Frederick told me. "His grandmother was a medicine woman, and that power to see the future is transferred genetically."

102   Joan Frederick, *T.C. Cannon: He Stood In The Sun* (Flagstaff, AZ: Northland Publishing, 1995) 36. The authoritative biography, to which this essay is indebted, and from which I am grateful for her permission to quote.

103   Ibid, 115.

students called him "Chief." Born in postwar America, he was a product of both the white and Indian worlds in which he was raised. Yet by the time he left Gracemont in 1964, for a two-year program at the Institute of American Indian Arts in Santa Fe, he identified primarily as Native.

The IAIA would open new worlds to him. It was a federally funded, Bureau of Indian Affairs school, whose goal was to teach Natives the production of art. It was focused on the contemporary, and introduced Cannon and fellow students to modern European painting. Their favorite teacher was Fritz Scholder, a quarter-Luiseño painter whose course "gave a panoramic view of the history of art from the cave paintings at Lascaux through the abstract expressionists of the 1950s," Joan Frederick writes. "The course taught the scope and history of Native American art in tandem, yet no phase was emphasized over another."[104] Cannon's schoolmate, Sherman Chaddlestone, remembers that "T.C. commented on that class specifically. He went around telling everyone, 'Hey, check this class out.'"[105]

Historically, Native art had begun with the creation of petroglyphs, pictographs, hide, and pottery decorations, but its more recent trends centered around parfleche drawings, pueblo art and work of the Kiowa Six—early 20th century, Oklahoma painters sketching in a flat, hard-edged style. Their subject matter included horses, warriors, Indian dancers and the like. By the time Cannon reached IAIA, this "traditional" Indian painting had deteriorated to sentimental renderings that his schoolmates called "Bambi art." Cannon would dismiss this work as "cartoon paintings of my people that grace mansions at a going rate of nothing."[106]

Scholder was an Abstract Expressionist who avoided Indian subjects until the identity politics of the 1960s engulfed him. T.C. and his classmates "influenced Fritz Scholder,"

---

104   Ibid, 26.

105   Ibid, 26.

106   Kramer, 39.

Chaddlestone notes. "Fritz Scholder didn't paint his first Indian until [1967]." Scholder said that he had "to deny the Indian subject because it had become such a tremendous visual cliché. Not only a visual cliché, but a psychological cliché."[107] After 1967 he would paint Natives with Francis Bacon-esque facial distortions that were a dark knockoff of Cannon's and other students' manner. Chaddlestone says, "I don't think T.C. specifically influenced Fritz as much as it was the student movement at that time that influenced Fritz."[108] Earlier, he and teachers at IAIA had encouraged that movement to move away from traditional, Studio School art to a more contemporary style. That move affected everyone. Alfred Young Man remembers that his and Cannon's contemporaries "reveled in the popularity of pop and op art, abstract expressionism, and ... how the French impressionists painted."[109] And they drowned in the new music.

People who knew Cannon do not hesitate to call him a Renaissance figure, adept at painting, literature, and music. He sang, and played guitar and harmonica; one of the first things he did at IAIA was to join a band called The Fauves.[110] Young Man recalls that Cannon "sang in the style of Bob Dylan." He became The Fauves' "front man and sang rock songs or the likes of Woody Guthrie and the blues. He sang clearly, unequivocally," and in his painting, "he wove rich fragments of poetry and lyrics onto his canvases with a sense of humor and

---

107   Lowery Stokes Sims, ed., *Fritz Scholder: Indian Not Indian*, (National Museum of the American Indian, Munich, Berlin, London, New York: Prestel Publishing, 2008), 130.

108   Frederick, 32.

109   Alfred Young Man, "Institute of American Indian Arts 1962-1972: Where It All Began," in *Celebrating Difference: Fifty Years of Contemporary Native Arts at IAIA, 1962-2012*, ed. Ryan S. Flahive (Santa Fe, NM: Sunstone Press, 2012, 63.

110   The Fauves (wild beasts) were an experimental group of European painters that included early-twentieth century artists such as Andre Derain, Henri Matisse, George Braque, and historically van Gogh. Their style, as IAIA alumna, America Meredith writes, "was aimed at liberating color from realistic depiction." (Kramer, 65—cited below.)

satire ... Cannon once wrote that his paintings were nothing but 'songs that I have lived through.'"[111]

Like Dylan, Cannon was a product of small-town America and an artist whose ethnic heritage set him apart.[112] And like Dylan (who paints and sculpts), he was interested in the synthesis of folk and Pop. Cannon made several portraits of the singer-songwriter, and his canvases bear the titles or lyrics of his songs: "It's Alright Ma, I'm Only Sighin'," "All the Pretty Horses," and "Mona Lisa Must've Had the Hiway Blues," to name three. Cannon's ex-wife, Barbara Warren Cannon Ross, remembers, "Dylan was *it*. T.C. had all [Bob] Dylan's albums. We'd play music all the time."[113] Frederick writes that during this period "Social issues attracted T.C.'s attention ... Bob Dylan and Woody Guthrie were perhaps his musical role models, men who used music to share their ideologies with the world ... he sang and recorded his own versions of Dylan's classic songs, appreciating the pathos and passion for life Dylan translated into musical terms."[114]

Cannon owned over 400 albums, "ranging from opera to jazz, blues, Cajun, classical, country, big band, rock, folk, and reggae."[115] His friend, George Oswalt, remembers that "when I first met him, he was heavily into blues music ... Then T.C. went through his country-and-western phase ... there were a lot of people like Willie Nelson and Waylon Jennings who were kind of the anti-establishment country and western singers. There was kind of a 'new wave,' like T.C. was 'new wave Indian' and they were new wave country-and-western."[116]

New-wave Indian shouted synthesis. Genetically, Cannon

---

111   Karen Kramer, ed. *T.C. Cannon: At the Edge of America* (Salem, MA: Peabody Essex Museum, 2018), 152.

112   Dylan grew up in Hibbing, Minnesota. He was Jewish, and antisemitism was prevalent there.

113   Frederick, 65.

114   Ibid, 111.

115   Frederick, 111.

116   Ibid, 111.

may have been one-quarter Anglo, but culturally he was half-Indian, half-white. A 1971 painting, *Soldier*, expresses this reality. The work is "one man divided," his former teacher, Bill Wallo, says. It shows a figure split down the middle, "the left side Indian, the right side Blue Coat soldier." It was, "almost Op Art in concept, including the red, white, and blue color scheme used."[117] It was patriotic the way Dylan's song, "With God on Our Side" was patriotic. Split down the middle.

Cannon "was a country-and-western painter of sorts," Oswalt says. Dylan had had his country-and-western phase, but what may have influenced Cannon more strongly was Dylan's folk-rock period. That had been highly synthesized. Folk in Dylan's work led to fine-art ballads, blues led to hard rock, country led to country rock. And in Cannon's visual imagery, traditional Native styles combined with modernism led to New Wave Indian—a mixture of folk and the new.

A painting done while Cannon was at IAIA suggests this. It is titled *Mama and Papa Have the Going Home Shiprock Blues* and shows a seated Navajo couple, perhaps waiting for a bus. Except for shades worn by the woman, the figures are clothed in quasi-modern dress. Behind them are the letters DINEH, referencing "Diné," or "Navajo." At the image's bottom are two unfinished canvases, showing the couple in similar poses. Except that sunglasses are now worn by the man. Peter Schjeldahl of *The New Yorker*, in his 2019 review of a show in which it appeared, would call it an "amazing painting—a masterpiece, really."[118] And Chuck Dailey, former director of IAIA, says *Shiprock Blues* was "the *Les Demoiselles d'Avignon* of the contemporary Indian art movement, or 'Pop' Indian art ... *Shiprock Blues* is the breakthrough which led to the modern Indian art movement, 'super' Indian images, and the first 'Pop' Indian painting incorporating words and multiple images." It is "the single most important painting in

117   Ibid, 81.

118   Peter Schjeldahl, "Ablaze," (*The New Yorker*, April 15, 2019) 80-81.

the Institute of American Indian Arts permanent collection and has been photographed and studied by more researchers, IAIA students, and interested parties than any other painting in the entire collection."[119]

Later Cannon wrote a Dylanesque song with the painting's name. Its first verse went,

> I been out there
> where the v.c. stay
> write home most every day
> It don't seem to ease my pain at all
> 'cause I long for the sand
> and the piñon trees
> sheep manure up to my knees
> and in the evening my greasy jo-babe squaw
> oh mama, papa's got the blues again
> oh mama, papa's got the shiprock blues again
> and he's had them since you don't know when."[120]

By then Cannon was home from Vietnam, a service ordeal that partially he brought upon himself. In 1966 he had been studying at San Francisco Art Institute, but became disenchanted with school. Impulsively he enlisted in the Army. He told a friend, "I guess I did it because of emotion." His intimates thought he'd joined because it was the "'honorable thing to do,'" or that "'it was the Kiowa way to be a warrior."[121] The Kiowas, as Southern Plains Indians, had a tradition of fiercely defending territory. His friend, Kirby Feathers, says that "I really got mad at T.C. ... I told him, 'You're stupid for joining and you shouldn't have done that.' He said, 'I'm a Kiowa' ... His tribe, the Kiowas, and mine, the Poncas, our whole societal structure is based on warriors."[122] That

---

119   Frederick, 30.
120   Ibid, 30-31.
121   Ibid, 39.
122   Ibid, 40.

tradition was prevalent among Natives. Forty-two thousand would serve in the Vietnam war. Though Cannon later would be inducted into the Kiowas' Black Legging Warriors Society, a high honor, his experience in Vietnam was bitter.

He served in the 101st Airborne Division, and after possible combat as a helicopter gunner, was stationed at the Bien Hoa Air Base, near Saigon. He would become the personal secretary of the division's commanding general. This did not shield him from danger.

As Frederick writes, "T.C. became friends with the [then] personal secretary of the commanding general for the 101st Airborne. One night as they were casually sitting and talking in his office. T.C. heard a noise and looked around. Within seconds, he turned back toward his friend, and saw that the young man's face had been blown off. This event shattered T.C., not only because the young man was his friend, but also because it dramatically reminded him that there was absolutely no safe place in Vietnam, no place secure from death and tragedy."[123]

He would write to Harcourt, "Yesterday morning [the general's] steno was killed while sitting in his office, so I'm taking his place. He was a real good friend of mine ... I hope I don't meet the same fate as my predecessor."[124]

He had his guitar and sketch books at Bien Hoa, but had little time for art. In January of 1968, on the Tet holiday, the North Vietnamese launched an offensive. His air base was overrun by Vietnamese special forces troops. "We have been awake and more or less under siege here for about thirty hours," Cannon wrote to Harcourt. "There is still some small arms fighting going on down the road. These are hard-core Viet Cong who would rather die than surrender."[125] Feathers remembers that "T.C. was in the compound with the commanding staff of the 101st Airborne, but snipers had reached

---

123   Ibid, 45.
124   Ibid, 46-47.
125   Ibid, 46.

the perimeter and had made it into the compound ... Part of T.C.'s unit, the 101st, reclaimed the embassy, floor by floor. They landed on top of the U.S. Embassy and went down floor to floor and took it back. There were a lot of officers killed inside when the enemy breached into the generals' area. Of course, the commanding generals split, but T.C. was left there. He helped defend the commanding general and he won the Vietnamese Cross of Gallantry."[126]

He was awarded two bronze stars for valor by the U.S. Army. He wrote to Harcourt, "We fought for a day and a half right outside the headquarters here. We killed about six hundred of them ... we haven't been getting much sleep because of the VC mortar and rocket attacks." His combat experience radicalized him: "I am fed up with this gung-ho caste-like way of life. I mean a man is a man is a man (as Gertrude Stein might put it), and I see no formal way of saying, 'Well, young man, You have earned the GENOCIDE AWARD OF 1968 for killing the most people in the shortest time with as little effort as possible toward our goal of total annihilation of the sectarians that dwell in our neighborhood. What a myth. What a piss-poor situation that generates my shotgun nerves ... Someday I'll probably be assassinated by a Republic Indian."[127]

Cannon admired the Vietnamese, particularly the Montagnards, whom he saw as the country's native tribe. Feathers said, "T.C. always admired and felt sorry for them like I did. They were persecuted and discriminated against by the Vietnamese, although they were the true inhabitants of Vietnam."[128] As Cannon wrote to Harcourt, "I was at war with humanity and in love with people."[129]

His service in Vietnam shattered, then focused him. "I think that Vietnam was a rite of passage for T.C.," Oswalt says, "he

---

126   Ibid, 47.

127   Ibid, 48-49.

128   Ibid, 48.

129   Ibid, 51.

became more of an Indian because he went to war."[130] His guitar teacher and friend Mike Lord says, "I think Vietnam really tore T.C. in two … He did things that soldiers are supposed to do, but I think it had a profound effect on him, because part of him did not want to be doing those things … it haunted him … it was probably part of his reclusiveness and his becoming more of an introvert … [Vietnam] probably had as large an effect on him as a human being as anything that he did … He said, 'I'm in this beautiful place killing these beautiful people. It's just like what was done to my people.'"[131]

Cannon returned stateside in 1968, and left the army in August of 1969. By the early seventies his rejuvenated sense of identity would surface in art. He drafted the ink-on-paper sketch, *T.C. and Skeleton*, in 1971, which shows a shirtless Cannon naked but for fatigue trousers, holding a beer and his chest spattered with blood. His arm is around a helmeted skeleton, dressed in bloody fatigues, with its bony hand on T.C.'s shoulder. The identity theme is better focused in 1971's *On Drinkin' Beer in Vietnam in 1967*, also ink on paper. Here T.C. and an Indian friend, in fatigues with Airborne patches, their hair unrealistically long and punctuated by eagle feathers, stand at an in-country bar, a mushroom cloud forming in the window behind. Though the men pose as if for a photographer, their expressions are grim, as the war continues behind them. The marker-and-ink sketch, *John Wayne's Bullet* (1973), is less traditionally antiwar, but speaks to the movies' depiction of plains conflicts. It shows a Native blown back, having been shot in the chest, yet transfixed by the blood spouting from his wound. "I suspect this realistic nuance is from his first-hand observation of violence during his military service," says IAIA alumnus, Frank Buffalo Hyde.[132] *Two Guns Arkira* (1974-77), depicts an older Indian, seated in an arm chair and dressed in a combination of traditional and

---

130   Ibid, 40.

131   Ibid, 56. And conversation with the author, July 2, 2019.

132   Kramer, 150.

contemporary clothing, who glares as he holds crossed re-
volvers on his lap. This is a painting, Schjeldahl writes, that
"blazes with special promise ... The picture's uniformly intense hues—including, at my guess, purple, red-orange, burnt
orange, lilac, terre verte, sienna, cerulean, golden yellow, vi-
olet, black, and white—generate a visual cadenza, violently
serene."[133]

Cannon would have himself photographed, in combination
Native and contemporary dress, holding a war lance and rifle
while seated before a wall holding his battle decorations ...
as well as pictures of Bob Dylan and Sitting Bull. He seemed
to be redefining his essence into synthesis. Yet he wrote, in an
unpublished preface to his literary endeavors, "I am just like
you and countless millions—threading the needles that patch
our individual universes into our totally selfish puzzles ... I,
myself, work on many levels and each is built to give feedback
to the totality of myself ... To be able to forgive gracefully is
the treasure of that for which I work."[134]

In August of 1969, he moved with his new bride, Barbara
Warren—a Ponca woman from Oklahoma—back to Santa
Fe. Though he attended school there, "He didn't go to many
[music] shows," Barbara recalls, "but he would always go to
the singing things with the folk singers. He knew a lot of people, and they would say, 'T.C. Cannon's here. Come on up!' so
they'd play."[135] He would sing in the coffee houses, jamming
even with the folk trio, Peter Paul and Mary, when they traveled through.

He had his first one-man show, titled "American Before
Columbus," that fall at the Larkins Gallery in Santa Fe. Lord
remembers that "When we were going to hang that first show
of his, there were two or three small paintings on top of the
car, and we put the big ones inside ... We drove over and were
trying to find some of the paintings, and they weren't there.

---

133   Schjeldahl, 80.
134   Frederick, *[vii]*
135   Ibid, 62.

260

Then we realized we had left them on the roof of the car! I said, 'Let's go back and look for them.' T.C. said, 'Nah. They weren't that good anyway."[136] The show proved a raucous affair, virtually selling out.

Cannon did not stay in Santa Fe, but returned to Oklahoma to finish his education. He and Barbara had decided the scene T.C. had enjoyed during the sixties in Santa Fe was finished, and that they should enroll in Oklahoma's Central State University at Edmund, for its state-fee potential. And for its art program. Cannon studied there on the G.I. Bill, and got more fiercely into music. Wallo recalls that "he seemed to have a twenty-four-hour day, working diligently at all hours, and sometimes showing up at our door at two o'clock in the morning, ready to party ... when things quieted down, he would pull out his guitar and beautifully perform music of all kinds without pretension."

Wallo had special insight into the divisions in Cannon's personality—before and after Vietnam: "I always saw two sides of T.C. One side was that of the reticent Indian/cowboy. He could sing like the incarnation of Woody Guthrie and Bob Dylan ... He also had a Will Rogers style of wit. The label on his guitar case said it all: 'Get Drunk and Be Somebody!' Indeed, he drank, but we never saw him drunk. His other side was that of an amazingly serious and sober veteran, aged far beyond his years, and incredibly dedicated to study. In fact, he was the most bittersweet, haunted, and mystifying person I have ever known ... His silence engulfed you and you could almost taste it. It was a profound weight."[137]

His marriage to Warner did not last. She admits that it was she who ended it: "It might have been a bad mistake on my part, but I think it was a good move for T.C., because I think I would have held him back. When he would have said, 'I've got to go to New York or France,' I would say, 'Oooooh no, I don't want to leave Oklahoma and my roots.'" We were only

---

136   Ibid, 63-64.
137   Kramer, 166-167.

twenty-one then ... I couldn't let loose enough to be a part of the art world."[138]

The art world came to Cannon in the form of two career-changing invitations. The first was from the Southern Plains Indian Museum, in Andarko, Oklahoma, for a solo exhibition that, according to Frederick, "was the force that catapulted him to international fame."[139] The show's curator, Rosemary Ellison, wrote for its brochure: "It is Cannon's philosophical approach to modern Indian art which places him in the vanguard of contemporary Indian Painting today."[140] Frederick adds that "T.C.'s first major exhibit would be the last in which he was considered 'up and coming.' From this point on, his work was hung in the finest museums and galleries of the world."[141]

His second, career-changing break came at the invitation of his former teacher, Fritz Scholder. Since Scholder had appropriated the Cannon painting, *Indian Man* (1967), reproducing it as 1969's *Indian with Beer Can*, but with Bacon-esque features and a Coors in front of him, the painters' relationship had cooled. But when Scholder was invited by the Smithsonian's National Collection of Fine Arts[142] to lead a two-person, Washington exhibit, and to choose an associate, Scholder suggested Cannon. Their show, "Two American Painters," Frederick writes, "proved to be the karmic event that propelled T.C. into the fast lane of international art and enabled him to accomplish his goals in the short years he had left."[143] Between 1972 and 1973 the "Two American Painters" exhibit toured Europe, introducing Cannon's work to viewers in Berlin, London, Belgrade, Skopeje, Istanbul, and Madrid. By the time this exhibit returned to the States, T.C. was again

---

138   Frederick, 74.

139   Ibid, 74.

140   Ibid, 74.

141   Ibid, 74.

142   Today, the Smithsonian American Art Museum.

143   Ibid, 77.

primed to paint, write, and sing.

A key benefit of "Two American Painters" was that it caught the attention of New York City dealer, Joaquin (Jean) Aberbach. Jean had a Madison Avenue gallery and, with his brother, Julian, was a music publisher who owned Hill & Range songs—an enterprise controlling the rights to music of major rock and country artists, including Elvis Presley. This must have intrigued Cannon. Jean bought all of T.C.'s available paintings and offered to represent and support him with monthly stipends so he might continue to produce. T.C. accepted the deal. "Cannon was no longer poor," Dan L. Monroe writes, "He had achieved national recognition and brisk sales of his work before reaching the age of thirty."[144]

It was 1972, and as Wallo says, "T.C. had been gone for two years, doing relatively nothing [artistically], and then this 'culture' machine took him from anonymity to international recognition virtually overnight. It was a manic experience for him."[145] Divorced, young, "romantically handsome,"[146] and celebrated while still in school, he partied hard. "Basically a shy and sincere man ... He experienced life to the fullest, enjoying all the things that made him happy: music, writing, literature, money, fame, women, and his native culture."[147] That happiness was tinged by darkness, however. "I think he was lonely," Wallo says. "Some nights he would get drunk and come to my house with his guitar and sit and talk with me and sing songs. He'd talk about what a sad, hard case he was, and nobody understood who he was."[148] Feathers says, "T.C. never got real wild," but "After Vietnam T.C. contemplated suicide a lot ... T.C. was a very moody person, but very talented, and like all talented people, he had various quirks." Oswalt says, "He wrote, he painted, he drank. He would start

---

144   Kramer, 20.
145   Ibid, 78.
146   Schjeldahl, 81.
147   Frederick, 86.
148   Ibid, 86.

drinking early and go into the wee hours. Then he would wake up and go chase women ... let's just say that women found him attractive. He had many."

A Cannon poem went,

> the women i've loved,
> for sport or hunger are
> not treated as toys in my
> memory. they were, and will remain golden prima
> donnas in gauze.
> i remember each breast and
> how it was shaped on each
> chest, and smells of sweaty
> gardens. I'll never forsake
> their openness and grandeur.
> soon I will be too old and dead
> to get it up.
> shit!![149]

His obsession with love as antidote to mortality continued. His death preoccupation may have been survivor's guilt, or remorse for the killing he did in Vietnam ("he was primarily learning how to accept and forgive himself"[150]), or possibly a late-adolescent mourning for his youth. His hero, Dylan, was not a veteran, but had suffered emotionally; four of the songs on Dylan's first album (recorded when he was 19) concerned death, and later classics like "The Lonesome Death of Hattie Carroll" and "Knockin' on Heaven's Door" were about it. Dylan had abused drugs to the threshold of death, and had nearly killed himself in a motorcycle accident. Like Dylan, Cannon read deeply in Beat Generation literature,[151]

---

149   Kramer, 200.

150   Wallo in Kramer, 167.

151   "He wrote poetry and prose, and was especially influenced by the work of poets E.E. Cummings, Arthur Rimbaud, and Allen Ginsberg. He was a prolific and wide-ranging reader and thinker who ingested the work of major philosophers and writers, including Jean Paul Sartre, Friedrich Nietzsche,

and identified with its culture. "T.C. was basically a beat-artist type," Oswalt says, but "it was country-and-western beat. That was his whole attitude of what an artist was: to live intensely. Maybe his premonition of dying early helped foster that, too, or maybe he helped foster that premonition."

The principal Beats alive were William Burroughs, Gary Snyder and Allen Ginsberg. Neal Cassady had overdosed on drugs in 1966, Jack Kerouac had drunk himself to death in 1969, and Beat chaos reigned. As Ginsberg wrote in *Howl*, "I saw the best minds of my generation destroyed by madness, starving hysterical naked, dragging themselves through the negro streets at dawn looking for an angry fix ...."[152] And for Cannon, in addition to Beat and rock 'n' roll deaths, there was that of Vincent van Gogh.

Vincent had presentiments of early death years before he shot himself and died at age thirty-seven ... his last words being "The sadness will last forever." He had been alcoholic, epileptic, seriously depressed and manic. Cannon may not have been any of these, but while in basic training he eagerly had read van Gogh's letters to his brother, Theo. Later T.C. included images of and visual references to the artist in various paintings. His self-portrait, *Collector #2* (1973), includes a van Gogh print on the wall, as does Collector #5 (1978). His portraits of native people show them seated in three-quarter profile, as van Gogh had posed his subjects. Karen Kramer writes, "Van Gogh's bright, opulent palette and the shifting relationship between background and foreground connect the two artists ... Whereas van Gogh's *La Berceuse* floral wallpaper symbolizes gratitude and maternal fruitfulness, Cannon's wallpaper of circles represents the dots warriors see during a Sun Dance ceremony, a purification ritual of prayer and renewal."[153]

Samuel Beckett, and Albert Camus." Dan L. Monroe, in Kramer, 21.

152   Allen Ginsberg, *Howl and Other Poems*: (San Francisco, CA, City Lights Press, 1956) 1.

153   Kramer, 46.

Color was everything to Cannon. His former teacher, Fritz Scholder, had taught students that colors only came alive when placed beside one another, and said the most important elements in his [and others'] work was "Color and a strong image. Color is what makes painting different than any other medium and the challenge for any visual artist is to produce a strong and new visual experience for the viewer. Third in importance would be subject matter...." [154] He believed his art was valued because, "Young Indians dig it ... because they are a swinging group who aren't all hung up in identity crises." [155]

The hip scene for Native and other Southwestern artists was on Santa Fe's Canyon Road, and T.C. returned there in 1973. Frederick writes, "In Santa Fe T.C. spent a lot of time doing the things he enjoyed most—backpacking, riding horses, reading, playing music, going out [cowboy] dancing, composing songs, writing, and painting. He developed a routine in which he painted late in the afternoons, went out to eat, came home and read, listened to music, or wrote poetry, staying up until dawn. He slept until noon, then began the cycle again." [156] He lived in a ground-floor apartment (with five cats) and wrote, in e.e.-cummings-lower-case, that

> the beauty of living a solitary existence is that you never have anyone to blame. the disciplines of the late-afternoon studio and early-morning writing table are my only points of reference for days on end ... i have no choice but to sit, listen, and obey the ghost muse." [157]

He'd begun a novel (about Native culture's assimilation with white) as well as a play; he performed at coffee houses, wrote songs and poetry, drove an orange 1959 pickup with a pair of 101st Airborne Screaming Eagles on the doors,

---

154   John P. Lukavic, *Super Indian: Fritz Scholder 1967-1980* (Munich, London, New York: Delmonico Books, Denver Art Museum, 2015) 29.

155   Ibid, 29,

156   Frederick, 133.

157   Ibid, 139.

and painted. Like the singer-songwriters' work of that era (Dylan's to Billy Joe Shaver's), his paintings married folk-traditions and subject matter with ultra-modern techniques. His 72 inch x 52 inch oil, *Self-Portrait in the Studio* (1975) is case in point.

This may be his most revealing work. It shows him dressed in a patterned cowboy shirt, overlong bluejeans, tan boots, a white ten-gallon hat and aviator glasses. His hair curls to his shoulders and a bandanna blows in a nonexistent wind. He holds a half-dozen brushes as if they were arrows, and stares without expression. His costume is rigid as a suit of armor. A striped "chief's blanket"[158] is in the foreground, but behind is a picture window through which is visible a daunting New Mexico landscape. To Cannon's right hang two paintings or prints: one of an African mask, the other of a Matisse-like nude.

"I remember him talking about Matisse," Oswalt says. *Self-Portrait* "has a very Matisse-like decorativeness." Fellow student Marvin Embree adds, "I sent him that poster of that mask. I was real surprised to see that up on his wall ... I know T.C. was very superstitious about things like that ... He felt there were a lot of things that had a lot of power, and you shouldn't mess with them or be around it."[159]

The most powerful aspect of the painting is the landscape behind Cannon's figure. It shows a twilight-blue sky broken by clouds above dark mountains, and partially lighted scrub meadows above dark-purple foothills and a stone-speckled yard. A golden river twists through the foothills. Cannon poses before the immensity of this landscape as if it were eternal.

A poem, titled "Self-Portrait in Studio," accompanies the painting. It reads:

wondering
whether to leave or stay a bit longer.

---

158   Ibid, 90.
159   Ibid, 91.

should i stay the night
and paint the purple area out of that corner
or maybe add some political ague to that dancer's face?
wasn't that a great river i saw this morning?
i wish i knew someone important or holy
to share it with ...
shit, i hope that my spirit is stronger than that
decaying purple corner over there. if elizabeth was here
i wouldn't be so afraid of it all.
if i had been considerate, elizabeth would be here
and i wouldn't be so afraid and criminal-like ...
all the lies were worth this moment
the darkness worth the light
the comedy worth this solemnity
enough of this poetic parody
i must turn my attention to the critical moment
at hand. i'm glad i see rivers free ...
where are all the rivers at this time of night?

The Elizabeth he references probably was not his last girlfriend, Elizabeth Dear, but more likely the Elizabeth he painted in 1974's *Collector #3*. "Elizabeth R." in his poem of the same name. Dear tells Frederick, "*Collector #3* is indeed Elizabeth, but it is not me. T.C. dated a woman in Oklahoma for a short period of time named Elizabeth who came out and visited in Santa Fe a few times ... The 'Oklahoma' Elizabeth was not in T.C.'s life for long, but she held a special place for him."[160]

By all accounts, the relationship was tempestuous. Chaddlestone says that Elizabeth R. "was the 'collector' of broken hearts."[161] Embree adds, "She was the love of his life one day and then an outcast the next ... He painted that picture [*Collector #3*] after they broke up."[162] Lord adds, "He told me afterward that she was the one he really wished he hadn't

160   Ibid, 67.
161   Ibid, 67.
162   Ibid, 67.

driven off ... All I remember was that she was a white gal ... I don't think she was an artist, just a person. She's very shadowy."[163]

In the painting, she's portrayed as Native. Semi-nude but wearing a purple skirt, concho belt, and concho-decorated boots, she lies on a red and black rug holding a Valentine-shaped heart. Her dark hair falls below her shoulders, her uncovered breasts are prominent and her eyes are closed. A poem, "Collector #3 / Nothing Cold as Ashes," (the lyric from a Loretta Lynn / Conway Twitty song) accompanies the canvas:

> there is a prison in the painter's heart wherein he keeps
> all of the memories of every beautiful woman he's ever known.
> it is, of course, preposterous, selfish and silly to
> feed and build a romantic penal architecture in the
> rooms of the heart, at least, that is what the porticos
> of the new revolution tell me.
> they have not, it is quite certain, ever seen or held
> elizabeth, the beautiful partisan!

Much has been made of the painting and of Elizabeth. Melanie Benson Taylor writes, "That Cannon chose to present her as Indian suggests another level of symbology; wherein the unattainable lover is embodied by an Indigenous seductress who doesn't just hold, but seemingly weighs the artist's heart in the palm of her hand ... There is a cruelty implied in the way this composite woman holds his heart forward, simultaneously a trophy and an offering; yet her eyes are closed, foiling the portal of connection or intimacy."[164]

Cannon wrote in a second poem titled "Collector #3," with "Elizabeth R." crossed out,

---

163   Ibid, 67.
164   Kramer, 181.

the world is at odds with itself
about situations like this
there is a lady in a room of no windows
there is a lady in a room purged of love
I am at odds with priests and worlds ..."[165]

Love haunted Cannon. As Schjeldahl writes in *The New Yorker*, he was "tormented, he reportedly said, by 'the inability to fall out of love.'"[166]

Music was the all-purpose salve. Dylan's *Self-Portrait* had dropped in 1970 (did *Self-Portrait in the Studio* reference it?), and *Blood on the Tracks* would not appear until January, 1975. *Collector #3* was painted before that album's release. *Planet Waves* was released in January, 1974, before Cannon painted *Collector #3*. He would have been familiar with the LP. Dylan sketched its cover art, and its songs were drenched in Dylan angst. They largely referenced domestic strife. Dylan's marriage was breaking up; and though a work like "Wedding Song," contains the lines "I love you more than life itself," it recognizes that the singer cannot recapture the Eden he'd known "before the flood," and that nothing in romance lasts. The song "Going, Going, Gone," may be a suicide note and "Dirge" indisputably concerns death. The album's classic is "Forever Young," Dylan's ode to his children's youthfulness. Cannon had a goddaughter, but otherwise could not relate.

By the mid-1970s, T.C. was busy writing lyrics, playing at Santa Fe's Three Cities of Spain coffee house, and painting. He had met Dear by then, "at a show at the Wheelwright [Museum of the Indian], in Santa Fe," she remembers. "I was working for the Museum of New Mexico, as the head of programs in the education department."[167] Her impressions of

---

165   Ibid, 189.

166   Schjeldahl, 81.

167   Later, she would curate for, and direct the C. M. Russell Museum, in Great Falls MT.

T.C. were that he was "Quiet, but with a great sense of humor. We just laughed. He was reserved if he didn't know you, almost introverted. That alternated with being extroverted." Cannon was slight, "about five-foot-nine, definitely not a six-footer." But he had "an incredible spirit. He was powerful, in a way I can't put into words." Despite his military honors, "he was in no way macho. He had many women friends. He liked women."[168]

His life was a mix of painting, writing, and partying. Dear, who would date him for two years, says that Cannon "stayed up all night," mostly working, but sometimes partying. "He liked to dance country-western."[169] As she told Frederick, "I saw T.C. drink often, usually every day: Coors beer out of a can. He had a large capacity for drinking beer, but he did not get drunk."[170] Other friends corroborate this capacity. Shaddlestone says, "T.C. wasn't an outdoorsman, he was more of a lounge person. We used to party real hard, but T.C. never got *too* loose. He always seemed to be in control ... We used to party all night, sit up drinking beer ... He would bring his guitar out and start singing."[171] However Cannon in his poetry seems to fret over his use of alcohol and drugs ("there were only rumors of cocaine," Lord says, "but we smoked a lot of pot and drank a lot of beer.") "An Account of My Day Today ... Non-Fiction" sketches a hangover wakeup call followed by a liquid brunch *"in the plaza bar,"* with *"those peaceful mid-morning drinking partners,"*[172] and in "Querido Microwave Mama" he writes,

> it's kinda late here in my little house ... the country music station plays on and on, I'm stoned, semi-drunk, perplexed ... i am deliriously happy to be alone tonight and the music

---

168   Conversation with Author, June 27, 2019.

169   Ibid.

170   Frederick, 171.

171   Ibid, 96.

172   Ibid, 154.

makes me forget about everyone on the face of the earth, and then i get the blues, and then i get the blues."[173]

To the world he was successful, famous, and admired by friends and lovers. At home he was driven toward sex, drink, and the production of art, in the face of his lingering preoccupation with death.

"He constantly talked about [death]," Embree says, "and he said that he would die early because all the other great artists of that particular era like van Gogh and Lautrec all died in their thirties. He felt like he would, too. He might even kill himself."[174] Oswalt adds, "T.C. was pretty preoccupied with suicide and death. In fact, the first time I met him, that was our conversation: suicide."[175]

Cannon's health troubled him. "Early in 1978," Frederick writes, "T.C. began to experience physical problems that suggested heart trouble. He had pain in his chest, as though a heavy load was pinning him down, so he sought medical advice."[176] His physician diagnosed an anxiety disorder caused by stress. Cannon, a heavy smoker, was burning the candle too brightly. He wrote in a letter/poem, six weeks before his death, that,

> labor pains at the easel almost made a catastrophe of winter, paint paint paint paint ... evenings reserved for the bar and later poetry and music ... i buy books by the dozens, the women come in singular units ... soft bodies ... in the morning i tell them that i am a priest gone astray, they ask and demand nothing more. So glad the spring is here. working on my third book of poems ... attempting biofeedback therapy to combat my nervous anxiety, it works....[177]

---

173   Ibid, 153.
174   Ibid, 165.
175   Ibid, 165.
176   Ibid, 159.
177   Ibid, 162.

Aberbach had a major New York show planned for Cannon in October, 1978, and T.C. labored at new work. He wrote of his previous commitments, that *"toiling over commissions and requests for more ART almost moved me into heaven or that other place. the opera here demands much ... new york demands little and so my direct emotion goes toward that show in October."*[178] He had made art for the Santa Fe Opera Guild, and one of his last paintings, *A Remembered Muse (Tosca)*, shows two Natives in period dress listening to that opera on an antique phonograph.[179] Dear says, "Aberbach was closely involved with the Santa Fe Opera ... because of this, T.C. was excited about having his works used by the opera. And again, opera was one more art form that he was interested in."[180] He wrote "In the Wonderful World of Opera," a poem, that,

> i have been without a viking helmet all my life ...
> in the wonderful world of opera
> i am a stagehand in corduroys and leather hat
> with a sheaf of literature well-read between acts
> and semi-smile when the stage is dark ...
> i alone am the only refugee
> the only partisan
> the last soldier to remain alive.
> my heroine still sings in the forest east
> of here.[181]

His major focus, the previous year, had been the completion of his largest and most ambitious work, a 96 inch x 264 inch mural for the United Indians of All Tribes Foundation in Seattle, titled *Epochs in Plains History: Mother Earth, Father Sun, the Children Themselves* (1976-77). Cannon described it as an "8 x 20 foot canvas" concerning:

---

178   Ibid, 163.

179   "We'd listened to *Tosca* as kids," Joyce Cannon Yi told me.

180   Frederick, 163.

181   Ibid, 155.

the religious and social epochs in Plains history, with emphasis on the great tribes of the Southern Plains, namely the Kiowa, Comanche, Cheyenne, and Arapaho. Starting from the left edge, the painting is dark, partially lit by a hundred-mile prairie fire and an ancient moon under which traipses a small clan of the old people. They are lost in darkness and superstition, but their land before them is lit by a holy light ... emanating from the large figure of Mother Earth throwing out gifts of buffalo and medicine. The right side of the panel contains three major figures, the first being a sun dancer, the second a Kiowa peyote man, and the third, a gourd dancer that dances off the panel's right edge.[182]

Cannon has painted himself, or his doppelganger, as the gourd dancer, in a near-replication of the costume he wore in *Self-Portrait*. That is, as an Indian in a cowboy's clothing.

Dear photographed Cannon at work on this,[183] and says, "The last thing that he told me he wanted to do, which he didn't get to do, was to see the mural hanging in Seattle ... it's pretty incredible and is his last masterpiece. It may be his major work. There's nothing else like it."[184]

The mural speaks to themes he was exploring in his unfinished novel. Frederick reports the book "centered on a transition (turn-of-the-century) Indian man's experiences in trying to assimilate into the white culture that conquered the Plains Indian way of life. "T.C. felt this pivotal period profoundly, and his intent was to illuminate the hardships and pain, the enormous changes in their daily living, and the emotional and spiritual upheaval they experienced during that time. The main character encountered problems similar to the ones T.C.'s own father probably experienced as an Indian

---

182   Ibid, 156-157.

183   "I watched him paint often," she told this author. "He was a fast painter. He would do sketches, and he would rub things out and do them over. He was a big fan of Hundertwasser's work. That flatness."

184   Frederick, 159 and conversation with the author, June 27, 2019.

growing up in the 1920s and 1930s in Oklahoma."[185] Wallo adds, "T.C. mentioned at the time [before he died] that he was writing a novel that seemed to serve as a personal review of his life ... T.C. kept saying that he needed to work in other media and that he needed to stop painting for a while. The novel was on a broad 'epic' level, much like his epic mural from the same time period ... He said that the novel dealt with the final assimilation of the Indian/Native American into Anglo values and culture ... I had the feeling that he was well over half-finished."[186]

"Unfortunately," Frederick notes, "the whereabouts of this manuscript is still unknown. It was never found among T.C.'s things after his death. It is possible, but not likely, that T.C. destroyed it himself in a fit of critical dissatisfaction...."[187]

In 1975, Cannon not only had a summer residency teaching at Dartmouth, but as Davig Rettig writes, met "the Japanese-born master woodcutter Maeda and master printer Uchikawa ... Planning and collaboration evolved over the next year and five of Cannon's paintings were selected for translation to the woodcut process."[188] T.C. had been busy with that, and his exhaustion with painting was evident in talk of firing his agent and making a go professionally as a poet/novelist/songwriter. He'd become intrigued by the mystical side of Judaism, identified with Jews' history of persecution and reclamation of their native land, and wore the star of David. "T.C. was very enamored of Jewish people," Lord says. His agent's family was Jewish, and he was attracted to Jewish women. "He became very conscious of oppressed people, and pretty much, I think, a champion of them."[189] Dear adds that, "He considered himself a religious person and was deeply interested and involved in his traditional Indian beliefs, along with several other religions, including Judaism ...

---

185   Frederick, 154.

186   Ibid, 155.

187   Ibid, 155.

188   Kramer, 136.

189   Ibid, 135,137.

he once gave Jean Aberbach a note he had written and asked him to take it with him on a trip to the Middle East and place it in the Wailing Wall in Jerusalem, which Jean did. He felt that this message from a non-Jewish artist and Indian from the Southwest might do some good in the world."[190]

Dylan, during this period, visited the Wailing Wall but within a few years would embrace fundamentalist Christianity. Cannon would not go that far. The most devout lines he wrote were to Harcourt from Vietnam. They were composed in resignation:

> Soon it will be over for me ... and then I will only have to push all the harder to make a condition for myself and others ... to paint and paint and paint ... Yes, how thoughtful of God to provide a life-stream such as art. A most important life-stream.[191]

On the evening of May 7, 1978, Cannon met a friend, the actress, Irene Handren,[192] at Santa Fe's La Posada Inn, a favorite hangout. Friends had been concerned about him. Dear says, "T.C. talked to me several times about his own dying, which upset me tremendously ... He said that he had had a vision of his own death which he believed, and, therefore, he knew that he was not going to be in this life much longer."[193] Oswalt had seen him at a party. "I noticed when I shook T.C.'s hand that it was very fragile ... I just remember thinking that he really felt fragile ... he just seemed pale and fragile. He never was a real muscleman, but ..."[194]

Little is known about Handren's and Cannon's activities that night. Hendren told Joyce that Cannon offered her a ride,

---

190   Ibid, 147.

191   Ibid, 55.

192   Later, Irene Handren-Seals would appear in various Hollywood pictures, including *Powwow Highway* (1989), *Into His Arms* (1999), and *Lakota Woman: Siege at Wounded Knee* (1994).

193   Frederick, 168.

194   Ibid, 170.

because she was too tipsy to drive. What *is* certain is that they left La Posada before closing and drove out the Old Las Vegas Highway. "For no apparent reason," Frederick writes, "the pickup veered off the straight road and plunged into some trees and an embankment." Cannon's new gray-and-maroon truck "rolled over several times while skidding and came to rest upside down, with the cab smashed flat to the hood." Handren was unconscious and Cannon dead, his handsome face macerated.

Lord says that Handren told a filmmaker that she had had too much to drink, and Cannon was driving her home. En route he'd said, "There's a song I want you to hear," and reached toward the glovebox for a tape of Bob Wills. "This is the music my father listened to."[195]

"That's when he ran off the road."[196]

Frederick's chapter, "Into the Mystic," elaborates: "Miss Handren reported the she was unconscious for some time, but upon regaining consciousness, found she was unable to extricate herself from the wreckage because her legs were pinned. She called out repeatedly during the night, but no one heard or came until daybreak, when a passing motorist saw the wreck from the road and stopped to help." The police arrived and found Handren seated on the ground. Inside the truck, Cannon was unresponsive.

"Many things about T.C.'s death remain a mystery," Frederick argues. "Rumors spread concerning the cause of the accident, whether or not it was alcohol-related, while all of T.C.'s friends confirmed that T.C. was never one to drive intoxicated." Had he given his keys to Handren and asked her to drive? "Miss Handren stated in the accident report that T.C. was the driver of the pickup; however the right side of the vehicle had the most damage, and T.C.'s family was unable to have an open casket, because the right side of T.C.'s face was destroyed ... Miss Handren survived the crash with

195   Joyce Cannon Yi, to the author, in conversation.
196   Lord. Conversation with the author, July 2, 2019.

broken ribs and cuts."[197]

Cannon's father, Walter Cannon, was devastated by the loss and seemed suspicious of Handren's story. "T.C.'s death was the worst thing that ever happened to me ... The girl who was with him in the accident never mentioned who was driving. She always said, 'When it happened ...' in the paper. She said, 'I took my eyes off the road for just a second or two, and the next thing I knew we were in the woods.' When she came to see me, she said, 'He must have had a heart attack.'"[198]

Dear believes Cannon was the truck's driver: "I talked to Irene. Yes, he was driving. Something happened, he blacked out. He had some kind of condition. It wasn't alcohol. I never saw him drive impaired. He was a very careful driver, too careful sometimes."[199]

Returning from a trip the night of the accident, she had driven past La Posada. "He and I used to hang out there. I saw his truck and thought about going in. Then, 'No, he's doing something else.'"[200] She lived only a mile from where he died, and felt that night "That he was around, and there was something going on that I couldn't put my finger on ... it was one of those feelings you don't want to pursue[201] ... The next morning I was giving a talk at the museum when I heard the news. I couldn't believe it." She went to T.C.'s house, which already had been burglarized of art and tapes. "It had to have been someone who knew him." A friend handed her one of T.C.'s kittens, saying "Here's your new cat."[202] The next day she visited the accident site and discovered in the grass, "notes

---

197 Ibid, 174.

198 Ibid, 173.

199 Conversation with the author, June 27, 2019.

200 Ibid.

201 Frederick, 172.

202 "My cat's name was Georgia, named after O'Keeffe, as I thought she should have an 'artistic' name. She came with me to Montana and lived to be eighteen years old. I returned her to NM to be buried with her best friend, Jasper, my dog who also came to MT from NM." E-mail to the author, June 28, 2019.

that he had written, about buying a piece of land." He'd outlined the cost of buying ten acres of land, near Lamy, and how proceeds from sale of the woodcuts would pay for it. Dear found these notes haunting. "What he was thinking was there lying on the ground."[203]

Cannon was dead at thirty-one years of age, much as he had predicted. Years before, in a poem to the Wallos, he'd written,

> all I know is that you ... my friends
> will be far away when I die ...
> none will see my final grimace of pain
> and smile of diamond clenched teeth bones
> on that final bed of sand and cactus
> out there where it gets lonely in the
> early summer rain.[204]

His fear in Vietnam that "I hope I don't meet the same fate as my predecessor," in having his face blown off, was largely actuated.

Bob Dylan, in 1978, was on a hugely successful world tour. Within a year, he would embrace Christianity and, for preaching his faith on stage, would endure years of shrinking album and concert sales, before two dark releases in 1997 and 2001, various gallery shows of his art, a well-received memoir and a Nobel Prize for Literature in 2016 brought him back to prominence. It's difficult to predict what heights Cannon might have reached had he lived. Dear says, "Trends change. The recent exhibits[205] have done a lot to get his art work into

---

203   Conversation with the author, June 27, 2019.

204   Ibid, 164.

205   Notably the traveling exhibit, "T.C. Cannon: At the Edge of America," curated by Karen Kramer of the Peabody Museum, in Salem MA. It opened at the Peabody in March, 2018, then traveled to the Gilcrease Museum in Tulsa in July, 2018, then to the Smithsonian's National Museum of the American Indian in New York City, in May, 2019. At the latter, a tape of Cannon's rendition of "Mama and Papa Got the Shiprock Blues" played, over speakers above his vintage 1939, 000-18 Martin guitar. "He traded a

the public eye. I think he'll be recognized as a major Native American artist. And if people can see another dimension to his work, what he was thinking, saying, understanding." She pauses. "He was playing with different cultures, mindsets, and environments. He made them dance with each other."[206]

She told Frederick in 1995 that T.C.'s artistic longevity will extend "Not because he's an Indian who was a painter or a painter of Indians, but because he was a painter working in a style that no one else was, a style that he developed ... However, I hope that he will not be remembered solely as an Indian painter but for being the fine artist which he was."[207]

Kramer says, "One of Cannon's greatest legacies is that his work commands such a presence that it goes beyond the borders of Native American art. Certainly he acknowledges his Native heritage, but he wanted to be understood as an artist writ large—he wanted to be understood as an American artist *and* a Native artist."[208]

Though Dear feels "T.C. didn't aspire to be famous. He wanted to paint,"[209] his ex-wife, Barbara (former Commissioner of Indian Affairs for Oklahoma) speaks of Cannon's larger successes and ambitions: "I think he was perceptive in the time and age that he was in ... He put feelings that and he knew that other people felt on canvas and portrayed them ... If you met him or can appreciate his work, you can feel it, that inner part of him that was so unbelievably complex ... He'll make the big collections, and he's going to be a 'Remington' in the museums. That's where I think he'll end up, and he'd love it—right up there with the Remingtons."[210]

Embree adds, "The only thing I remember T.C. saying

painting for it," Lord says.

206   Conversation with the author, June 27, 2019.

207   Frederick, 185-186.

208   Gussie Fauntleroy, "T.C. Cannon [1946-1978]" *Western Art & Architecture*, August/September, 2018, 98.

209   Conversation with the author, June 27, 2019.

210   Frederick, 185, 187.

about a purpose in his life was that he wanted to have his place in the history books. That was his purpose for painting. He wanted to be known along with the other greats whose works were in the [history] books. It would be nice to open an American art history book and see his works in it."[211]

Cannon was buried in the family plot at Andarko. His memorial was "basically a military funeral," Oswalt remembers. In 1988, he was inducted into the American Indian Hall of Fame, also at Andarko. "A bronze bust of his likeness stands beside the Indians' most famous and revered heroes, part of a long line of brilliant war strategists, poets, and mystical leaders."[212] Aberbach postponed Cannon's New York show until December 10, 1979, and opened it as the T.C. Cannon Memorial Exhibition. Frederick writes, "Collectors from all over the world attended, as did T.C.'s parents and his girlfriend, Elizabeth Dear. It was an emotional evening for all but definitely a successful event."[213]

Dear recalls that "The opening of T.C.'s exhibit fell on my birthday, and I always thought that somehow T.C. may have arranged that from wherever he was."[214] The show subsequently toured, appearing in various U.S. museums. Perhaps the most fitting one Dear organized at the Museum of New Mexico in Santa Fe.

Lord remembers, "It must have been 1981 or 1982 ... She had a boom box playing Bob Dylan music—probably *Highway 61 Revisited*—and right next door to the exhibit area was the great big auditorium, and in the auditorium were the Santa Fe Symphony people who were practicing for something. They complained about the loud tape and could they please turn it off. The manager of the place kicked the orchestra out. She shut down their rehearsal and said, 'You go away, and you can come back after the show is over,' and that was

---

211   Ibid, 185.

212   Frederick, 181.

213   Ibid, 176.

214   Ibid, 177.

that. There were all these angry, scowling musicians stomping through the exhibition because that was the only way out, you know, carrying their instruments, and they all went away!"[215]

Asked why she chose Dylan to accompany Cannon at the retrospective, Dear laughs and says: "It just seemed appropriate."[216]

2020

The author is grateful for permission to quote from
Cannon's poetry, songs, letters, and other writings.
All quotes are used by permission of Joyce Cannon Yi
and the estate of T.C. Cannon.

---

215   Ibid, 178. And conversation with the author, July 2, 2019.
216   Conversation with the author, June 27, 2019.

EPILOGUE: CATHRYN REITLER, A.D. MADDOX, AND PARKS REECE— #METOO, THE ART BIZ, BUG-GUT PAINTING, AND MOUNTAIN-WEST TROUT

At the Green Door Gallery, upstairs at Elk River Books and the Wheatgrass Saloon, a group of extraordinary paintings met the visitor. They were the work of Cathryn Reitler, an artist from the small town of Glasgow, Montana, and were portraits made from paint, fabric, and assorted media. They were part of an exhibit of paintings and sculpture that included pieces from three other women, Tandy Riddle, Angie Froke, and Jane Deschner. The show was titled "#MeToo: A Visual Dialogue."

Its occasion was a Livingston Art Walk, one of several during summer festivities, when the city's fourteen-or-so galleries offered new work and hors d'oeuvres for strolling viewers. At Green Door, what confronted them were Reitler's[217] life-size portraits of four partially nude women engaged in nontraditional jobs—as a firefighter, a commercial fisherman, a railroad engineer, and a police officer. The women were seen "as their male coworkers might have seen them," Reitler said—naked and sexualized. She had painted these nudes on the uniforms they wore, had sewn those uniforms onto

---

217   Her married name is McIntyre.

canvasses, then embroidered quotes from interviews onto them.

The series was titled "Female Chauvinists." And a wall card read,

> I am sharing artworks that investigate femininity within the context of rural Eastern Montana culture. I have a fascination with role (female vs. male) and with 'objects' ... I believe our clothes and the objects in our lives carry the residue of their nature, of their use; the imprint of the person who 'possessed' them." Her works were "of two parts: the painting itself and the object which the image is painted (or drawn) upon.

The result was stunning.

Reitler stood surrounded by women who appeared energized by the exhibit. Later she would tell Gwendolyne Honrud, of *The Glasgow Courier*, "The most gratifying element of this particular show was in shaping work that I have not shared within the state of Montana and in meeting the many women at the opening with whom the work resonated." Reitler, to the male gaze, was an attractive yet slight brunette in her mid-thirties, who had grown up in Saskatchewan and Las Vegas, and who had an air of self-assurance as formidable as the paintings she'd produced. She would tell me that the inspiration for the series came from her "sexualization as an artist"—specifically while working at the Miles City Bucking Horse Sale, a spring festival in rural Montana, "where this tricked-out cowboy told me he'd buy something if I'd paint myself naked."

The mixed-media series first had been shown at the College of Southern Nevada in 2013, long before the #MeToo movement gathered force.[218] "In these works," Reitler wrote, "I was interested in the experiences of women who are

---

218   It did so in October, 1917, after movie-mogul Harvey Weinstein was accused by numerous women of workplace-related sexual harassment and assault.

surrounded by men in their workplace; who are perhaps sex-ualized, or perhaps de-sexualized; but whose striking physical appearance and gender have at some point been a factor in their interactions at work. I sought to paint the women as they might be imagined in the male eyes, stripped of their work uniforms."

Native Americans, in western art, had been stripped of their uniforms at least since the semi-nudes of Titian Peale and George Catlin, and the artists Paul Kane and Emanuel Leutze had nearly fetishized them. There was sanctity in their nakedness (a holdover from Romanticism's noble-savage par-adigm), and European figures such as John Gast's semi-nude in *American Progress* (1872) and the topless Indian maiden in Victor Nehlig's *Pocohontas and John Smith* (1870) tipped their hats to neoclassicism's idolization of the female form. Nudity of women in barroom art had been prevalent during the 19th century, and later photographs of prostitutes, or "soiled doves," were popular. But nudity in contemporary western art was rare.[219]

What separated Reitler's paintings from modern counter-parts was their narrative format, dependent upon interviews Reitler had done with her subjects. On the nude of a police officer (posed in little but her gun belt), Reitler had sewn these words: "I was working fire security in Augusta and had to ride along with this guy who was driving to and from the fireline ... this guy who I'd never seen before says, 'Can I kiss you? You don't have to but can I kiss you?' No flirting, noth-ing. I hesitated and he said, 'If you don't want to you can just get out.' Working with guys, I expect a certain professional-ism. I don't expect random shit like that ... I told him no, and I didn't get out of the truck."

On the nude of the commercial fisherman, posed in shades

---

219   The occasional nude of T.C. Cannon, and the semi-nude sculptures of Montana artist, Dennis Harrington, seemed an exception. But Living-ston-based painter, Edd Enders, noted that "Nudes are the hardest of all art to sell."

and a life vest, she had sewn, "There was a guy I worked with in NY, who was 19 and who was working his first fisheries job. I had been in the field for 6 years and was used to the male ego. Nonetheless this guy was always saying something rude. One day he commented, 'It irritates me how broads get paid so much for so much less work.' By the time I left the job, three women had filed against him but he was still working there."

Quotes from the railroad engineer expressed similar grievances, and the portrait of the firefighter had these remarks: What I've noticed when we train and I pass a guy is that it's mentally crippling to a guy to be beaten by a girl. I had to train my mind not to give up, that just because I was a girl, it didn't mean that I couldn't do what the guys did. I've never felt ashamed to be a girl ... Anytime I'm off duty and I tell someone I'm a firefighter and they don't believe me, I get frustrated. They can't believe that I'm actually pulling hose and that pisses me off that I have to try to convince them. So I don't tell people I'm a firefighter anymore ... Everyday I'm a woman first and a firefighter second. I find myself slipping into a female role at the station, and I end up cooking and cleaning.

Other pieces by Reitler were embroidered on lingerie, and a small work, suggestive of a homily, held more directly her thoughts: Mary Mary quite contrary, how does your [garden] grow? I live in a flat, you fucking twat, so how the fuck should I know? ... Little Miss Muffet, sat on a tuffet, her clothes all tattered and torn. It wasn't a spider that sat down beside her, but little boy blue and his porn ... *Why is that men can be bastards and women must wear pearls and smile?* ... Jack and Jill went up the hill to have a little fun. Silly Jill forgot to take her pill, and now they have a son ... *The closer women come to power, the more physical self-consciousness and sacrifice are asked of them. Only thirty years ago our mothers burned their bras and picketed* Playboy *and now we are getting implants and wearing the bunny logo as supposed symbols of*

286

female liberation. Ideas about beauty have evolved since the industrial revolution side by side with ideas about money.

Reitler was not shy about getting paid for her work, and the necessity to make a living was evident on her website. The majority of pieces displayed were in traditional western forms: wildlife paintings, commissioned portraits, pictures of barbed wire, ranch trucks, rodeo buckles and license plates, but each done in her distinctive style. "It pays the bills," she said. Did she feel burdened by making commercial art? "I once did," she said. "But I have so much joy in the creative process. It's compelling to work with these ranch artifacts, these personal heirlooms. They tell a family story for my clients. I coax the conversation."

———➤

A Livingston-based artist who was equally as open about getting paid for her work (and who had suffered sexual harassment from potential clients, initializing her first names to degender herself) was the painter, A.D. Maddox, whose gallery a block from Green Door featured enormous paintings of brown, rainbow, and cutthroat trout.

"People ask me why I started painting trout," Maddox said laughing, "and I say, 'money!' I'm not doing this for a little hobby." Her comment seemed disingenuous, as the images were high art. And oddly personal. She indicated a yellow-and-gold portrait, *Strawberry Cutty III*. "I think what touches me about that piece is that it looks like a gold nugget. The vertical trout and all these lemon yellows. It just makes me really happy."

To enter Maddox's gallery was to descend into a spring-creek pool where enormous fish eyed you quizzically. The oils on Belgian linen ranged from 24 to 72 inches in width, and were saturated with reds, greens and yellows so bright you reached for your Polaroids. The trout were presented in vivid closeups, their expressions nearly human, each distinct from the other. Maddox's brushwork was precise, her images like nothing you had ever seen. They reminded you of your small-ness, your fragility, and susceptibility to harm. Here one was not top of any food chain. They were the Mountain West incarnate, and thrust me back to 1990s Livingston.

The most influential piece of Montana art, over the past thirty years, had been the movie version of Norman Maclean's 1976 novella *A River Runs through It*—the shooting of which I had witnessed. Robert Redford's 1992 film had earned just $43.5 million but had sanctified fly fishing as a near-religious activity and drew countless would-be celebrants to the state. Filmed in and around Livingston, it featured Brad Pitt as a bad-boy reporter whose only state of grace was in fishing and whose shadow casting would be memorialized by the film's poster, and imprinted on the angler's heart.

"I loved that movie because of its aesthetics," Maddox said. "And young Brad Pitt ... Come on, man. Shut the front door! I've definitely been inspired by Redford's movies. The winter of 1992 was when I moved to Jackson Hole."

The summer before that, director Redford had shot a scene for *River* adjacent to Maddox's B Street gallery, had altered shop signs, and filled Callender Street with dirt to run wagons across. "This movie is going to change everything," he told locals. "Get ready." It did, and Montanans hadn't.

In November of 2018, Maddox relocated to Livingston (her family keeps a vacation house nearby), the major reason being its art scene, which had exploded during the 1990s and 2000s. She had bought a 1902 commercial building which she'd refurbished. "It's a gold mine here for artists," she told me. "Grab these old buildings, renovate them, turn them into galleries and get the movement going. This is the place to do it, because Bozeman's gone, man. It's gone!"

She referred not only to nearby Bozeman's population (up from 24,830 in 1992 to 50,000 in 2019) but also to the prevalence of its galleries, of which there were more than a dozen. Livingston had fourteen, but its population growth was less pronounced: up from 6,701 in 1990, to 7,529 in

2019.[220] Montana's population in those years had grown from 822,436 to 1.07 million. And largely because of a movie.

If Westerners' fears, historically, were of the other—European and Chinese immigrants, Honyocking homesteaders, Indians and African Americans—today they were of the relocating affluent. Family ranches were being divided into twenty-acre ranchettes, housing prices were exploding, and rents were so high that working people could not afford them. Perhaps Remington's and his fellow Easterners' dream of a West populated by the Anglo-Saxon moneyed had come true. That dream was called gentrification. Perhaps it was America's destiny–manifested.

Maddox was a tough-talking, motorcycle-riding, fifty-year-old beauty in jeans and a Ducati T-shirt, her blond hair up, and with a visible undercoat of vulnerability. That undercoat seemed the base upon which her personality was sketched. She had grown up around wealth in Tennessee and Arkansas, and her Nashville grandfather, "Black Dan Maddox," had earned his first million, she said, "when he was forty." Black Dan had invested in oil wells, real estate, and auto finance, was on the board of directors of Gulf and Western, and at his death left $100 million to a charitable foundation, short-shrifting his children for their perceived ingratitude.[221]

Nevertheless, A.D. said, "We were raised really, really well. In fact, spoiled rotten. I was Cinderella!" Ignored financially by Black Dan, her father made his wealth in commercial real estate. "Dad was big on us working really hard. To this day, I don't take money from him unless he gives me a gift ...

---

220   Eight-hundred-and-twenty-eight new people require substantial housing. It was found or built for them.

221   In a 1997 letter to an advisor, he wrote, "Considering the problems I have had with my children, and the minimal appreciation I have had for putting them all on a basis to where they can live on their investments alone without working, it does not compare with the personal satisfaction of the results I have produced by putting my money in carefully selected charitable supports." Stephanie Strom, "After Donor Dies, Battle Erupts over Fund's Future and Venue," (*The New York Times*, February 16, 2005).

like for my birthday, he might buy me a set of tires for my car." Her mother, raised on a farm, planted artistic seeds in her children. "My parents are the reason I'm here today," Maddox said. "They would not allow my brother and me to watch much TV, they pushed us to go outside and play, and be creative, and build forts and paint and do sports." Maddox was a top-seeded gymnast in Arkansas, and later a triathlete.

The inheritance she may have gained from her father and grandfather was not just their considerable talent for business[222] but their love of the outdoors. "GranDan was the world's greatest hunter," she said. "He won the Weatherby Award[223] in 1967." A.D. remembers that as a child, "it was different going to the grandparents' house, than to be at our house." It was opulent, and filled with Black Dan's trophies. "The railings were made of elephant tusks. My brother and I would remove the tongues from the lion rug, and what eyeballs we could pop out. We would mix them in a bag and play this game of sticking tongues in the jaguar, chasing around the house with the zebra tail, which was a whip ... so dead animals to me were absolutely nothing." The familial atmosphere there was stiff, with her grandparents' servants and breakable antiques. "It was tense. It wasn't as playful as

---

222   A.D.'s business acumen is evident not only in the marketing of her paintings, but in her licensing of her images for merchandising: "Everything I paint will go to merchandise. It always does. For Patagonia, StealthCraft boats, Croakies, Montana Fly Company, Fincognito, American Dakota, and Buff USA." Her images appear on T-shirts, belts, lanyards, retainers, hoodies, hats, webbings, dog collars, leashes, rugs, women's scarves, and boxer shorts. "We stopped doing the iPhone cases, but I *will* work shoes. We're waiting for Nike and Teva."

223   "If it is accepted that the Weatherby Hunting and Conservation Award is the world's most prestigious and desired hunting award then it follows that the accomplishments required to win it are among the most difficult." *Weatherby Award homepage: What It Takes to Win the Weatherby Hunting and Conservation Award.* In addition, "No one can win without a significant number of sheep, goats, chamois, the big five, spiral horned antelope, pygmy antelope, and most of the North American species. Collecting the Marco Polo, Mountain Nyala, Polar Bear, Markhor and other very difficult species weigh heavily in the judging." Ibid.

being at the other grandparents' house, where you could spill a drink on the floor, or you could go freely to the kitchen and fix your own meal. Not a cent in GranDan's will went to any of us."[224]

Pressed on this, Maddox said, "GranDan had done the same thing with Dad that Dad did with us. There's a cutoff period where you don't get anything, and you're living with cockroaches if you don't have any money. You've got to work your way out of the soup to do really well and make it on your own—before there's a little bit of a cushion that comes in. And then of course you have to be smart with your cushion."

Maddox's earnings had gone toward purchasing this gallery ("I said to Dad, 'you're not buying my building'—so I buy this one and he tells his friends, 'I could have bought it for her'—he's such a turkey!"), and she lived in a windowless apartment at its rear. It was a loft-like existence, bunkerish, but surrounded by her paintings and crafts-pieces, she felt comfortable. Several early portraits—of glamorous, disco-queen women and vaguely Bacon-esque cowboys—differed greatly in style from her newer work.

"Those are my *Chicks*," she said of the women. "That was the early nineties and I was really into super models with the glam. I was trying to find my way and get into something that was beautiful. That's why the *Chicks* started coming about. When I moved to Colorado I was doing the cowboys and the Indians and the horses and the rodeo pieces on clothing. Then when I moved back to Jackson Hole, it was buffalo, elk, deer, pronghorn, the moose, the grizzly bear, you name it."

---

224   Maddox told me that her grandparents died on a duck hunting trip, "in 1997, in the Louisiana bayou. They were crossing early in the morning, with the fog, and an oil ship ran right over them. One of those cruisers that was going out to the Gulf. Just toppled them. The guides were killed, two brothers that were in their early twenties. It was real tragic. We think Mimi and GranDan were killed instantly, because they were in the boat sitting down. In a yacht-type sitting area. The impact of it was instant death. I was shocked. Utter shock. I was twenty-seven. It was an unbelievable accident."

Maddox had acquired a taste for partying, and the retreat to Jackson provided a much-needed reprieve. "Mom and Dad used to take us kids to Jackson Hole. So I always had a soft spot for it. When I was twelve, I wrote, 'this is the magical land where God lives and it's so beautiful, and I have to live here one day.' When I moved back I was twenty-seven. After I had wrecked and railroaded my life good enough, it was time to turn it around."

Though painting trout was her "successful action" financially, doing so seemed to center her emotionally—more so than painting fur bearers. The West was in her psyche. An anxious teenager, she had been shipped to a San Antonio boarding school, just before her parents divorced. "That's pretty much what set me off. I was in rebellion then. And I was afraid, lost. I hated being away at boarding school. So I got kicked out for drinking, and started going off the deep end."

She attended college at Auburn and then the University of Colorado at Boulder, traveled, lived in Atlanta and briefly Jackson Hole, then moved to Denver. There she clubbed mightily, and behind the signature, Amelia (her first name), created the *Chicks* and *Cocaine* series—executed beautifully, despite the impediment of night revelries. Then, "I had this really creative idea that I was going to have to separate old art from the new [western] art. Cause I was going in the galleries. I had announced to my friends that I was going to be a world-renowned artist. So I said, 'I can't have my *Cocaine* paintings or the *Chicks* competing with that.' I decided to sign my paintings 'A.D. Maddox,'[225] so no one would know I was a girl. I'd observed that most of the ones who were really making it in western art were the guys. So I went in as a dude." She shrugs. "I've been quite a few people to get where I'm at."

In Jackson she painted wildlife canvasses, wildlife furniture, and wildlife clothing. "I was painting on the back panels

---

225   Her full name is Amelia Drane Maddox.

of denim jackets, and on jeans. I did a T-shirt for Jackson Hole called 'Jurackson Hole.' That was when *Jurassic Park* was big. It had a dinosaur with the Tetons in the back." She guffawed. "Working with dinosaur establishments! It was hilarious!"

In Jackson, she was diagnosed with attention deficit disorder. "The psych told me, 'We can get you on Ritalin.' I thought, wow this is doctor-prescribed speed and I can take as much as I want. So I became this wiry looking addict-artist, painting fifteen-hour days. It wasn't healthy. I was getting really sick. Ritalin went to Adderall, and that went to Prozac."

She kicked psych-meds fifteen years ago. The withdrawal had been difficult. "All my problems that I was doing the drugs for just came rushing in on me. I had so much shit going on in my head … like trying to reconnect with life and cope with everything that was in my universe. It was hard for me to be around myself. So I just needed time." She exercised vigorously, competing in triathalons, and anchored her sobriety with a move home to Nashville. "I needed to be around my family," she said. "I was there for eight years. Slowly but surely I sorted out my demons."

Before that, in Jackson, the most difficult drug to quit had been Adderall. "Because it was speed," she said. Off it, her life slowed intolerably. "I didn't want to paint. I was *scared* to paint. So I bought a Ducati and started driving this motorcycle, always over a hundred." Road speed gave her the rush drugs had provided … and helped tame her restlessness.

It spurred her creativity, as well. "When I bought that Ducati I did a series of Bug Gut art." She tied a wet canvas to the handlebars of her bike, rode fast on a buggy evening, and harvested insects. The Bug art was fishing-directed, as the insects she collected were part of a hatch. In fact, she called the series, *Smash the Hatch*. But it was eccentric. In a 2007 YouTube video, titled *A.D. Maddox—World's first Ducati-riding, Catholic schoolgirl uniform-wearing, bug-splattering artist*, she told the camera, "See, I'm an artist. And I do what I do. I love being creative. I found myself out on my bike riding, and

I thought, 'What if I strapped a canvas to my bike to collect these bugs?' … Because they were all over my leather jackets when I'd come back from riding. I don't feel bad about killing bugs. If they get pissed off at me in their next life, they can come back and bite me. I'll plow them again … and cash another check." Dismounting her red Ducati, she saw the bug painting and laughed. "The last thing that went to their head was their ass!"

She said of the video, "The crazy artist—I did that well. I was really in a bad place. When he shoved that camera in my face at the [Bug Gut opening] I had eaten like five brownies. So I was on speed! But I was being a little shithead."

The landscape artist Greg McHuron had been something of a father figure to Maddox, and had taught her much about color. "I think he was a little bit younger than my dad, but he was one of these old-school Jackson artists who literally could stand in front of the flippin' Grand Tetons and paint them perfectly. He was a plein air artist and he understood everything about light and how to capture the Tetons. Because the Tetons are that rose granite, right? So when the cobalt blue from the sky hits them, blue goes to red, what do we get? Purple. I thought, *shut the front door*, are you kidding me? I'd load up in his van and we'd go ride around Grand Teton National Park. There were so many things I was looking at, and he would explain the whys."

Earlier that afternoon I'd interrupted her work on a medium-sized portrait of a mustang's head. Its face was black with blue highlights that Maddox was laboring to temper. "I'm going through this transition where I'm trying to get out of the LaLa land of colors, and more into realism. Doing more value painting, lights and darks … the space where I am creatively, I feel that's something I just want to do for the challenge of it—to create really good art. What I've noticed is, my work has been getting brighter and brighter and brighter. I feel like I'm missing the depth of the piece by not getting all the different values of the dark. I want to get my pieces a little more moody. A little bit more drama. Instead of painting happy little trout, let's make them look really, really mean! Moody as hell! Bite your hand off! So I want to get into a little more drama with the darks." She stepped back. "Sometimes you go into the darks, right?"

Hers was, in part, a marketing move. "It's harder to sell the blown out, bright golds," she said, "which I love painting. If I expand into horses, and I really nail it, I've got some Texas magazine doing an article,[226] and I roll out into the horse industry. This is going to roll into," she whispers, "a really expensive painting!"

Again, this bowed to her heritage in, and love for, business. I offered that most creative people didn't have a problem with artists being compensated. "Hell, if I was totally into money," she said, "I'd be dating one of these multi-millionaires who chase me with airplanes!" She mock finger-phoned: "'Hey, I'm in Florida. Want to get dinner?'" She snorted. "I know deep down that the only way to continue to grow in this career is to expand. I need to be challenged, I need to reach out and venture to new places." She glanced behind her. "But never will I abandon the trout. That's my successful action. The horses are bringing me back to what I painted *before* trout. The mustangs are wild and of the West." And they would be good sellers. "I hate to sound like I'm all about money, but ask Lucas or Spielberg if they're going to do a B-list movie. It ain't going to happen."

———➤

Days later, a gathering was held south of Livingston in Paradise Valley, that rural enclave of artists, billionaires, and hardscrabble ranchers who shared its extraordinary beauty. The party was thrown by the fine-art photographer and musician

226   Her paintings have made the covers of dozens of magazines, domestic and foreign. Covers include ones for *Gray's Sporting Journal, L.L. Bean, On the Water, Complete Fly Fisher, The Fisherman, Montana Trout, Angler's Digest, Catch Magazine,* and *On the Fly.*

Audrey Hall and her husband Todd Harris, a computational biologist. The occasion was a recital by the Nashville singer-songwriter, Lilly Hiatt. Maddox arrived in jeans and a camouflage jacket, having spent the day hanging with the Idaho artist Scott Christensen. "He told me my frames are wrong," she said, "and that I should change them and that I should be charging $50,000 a painting. We're going to paint together tomorrow."

Christensen's canvasses were landscapes, widely shown and expansive. The beauty this evening in Paradise Valley, with its still-green fields, lines of dark trees, and the gray Absarokas, was notable enough for him to have painted. A storm blew in and Maddox poked her phone's camera at the lightning. All around, artists, musicians, and actors milled—as well as potential clients. A.D. mixed readily, her energy and humor easing her way toward their affections. She jiggled to Hiatt's music as Lilly sang from a high-ceilinged living room with the refrain, "There's just so much you don't know about me."[227]

"A lot of truth in that song," A.D. muttered. Then turning toward the storm-tossed mountains, her face calming, said, "I'm in heaven."

The Maddox gallery, which had opened formally on June 28, already seemed a triumph. "I sold eleven paintings," she would say in the building's living space. "The recent buyers were coast to coast. I had guys come in, one from Chicago, one from Indianapolis ... a lot of people who follow me on Instagram came in and bought ... one from North Carolina, others from St. Louis, California, Seattle, Colorado." These were for paintings that sold from between $3,000 and $12,000. "Then there was one I sold to Los Robles Vineyard. North of Santa Barbara. This guy wants to do wine labels. I said I would do a

---

227   Lilly Hiatt, "So Much You Don't Know," (*Trinity Lane*, New West Records, New West Independent Music Publishing (BMI), 2017.

trade out for wine instead of for cash. Because I have to serve it for the openings."

As if on cue, the front door opened and four customers stepped in. They were fans of Maddox, and cooed and flattered in her presence. She was welcoming, describing in detail each oil. It was obvious from her visitors' demeanor that they would not buy any multi-thousand-dollar paintings, but she handled them graciously. "It's a kick in the pants," she said, "to go to the easel and paint something with your heart and soul, and then have people come in and buy your work. It takes my breath away. Somebody's so touched by a piece they want to have this original."

Her colleagues were in her corner. The wildlife painter John Banovich told me, "Every once in a great while you meet someone whose identity is purely rooted in the place where passion and talent converge ... yet on a platform of scholarly knowledge about a single subject. A.D. was born to fish and born to paint. It's her *raison d'etre*." Of her technique, Banovich added, "Water is the most difficult element any artist can attempt. Because nearly all of its form and color is defined by what's around it. It reflects light, color and hue but it wears a translucent mask. And water is in constant motion, even when it's still. A.D. understands this thing called water both inside and out and has found a way to capture it with a simple brush and paint ... her recreations share its color and excitement so we feel like we are seeing it for the very first time. Few artists are bold enough to include water, fish, and movement in nearly every one of their works. She does this better than anyone out there."

A fitting tribute. And one that was satisfying to her. Several evenings previous, at an open air concert in Pine Creek, A.D. had complained of being "excessively happy," and here I allowed that my initial impression of her had been one of vulnerability, gentleness, *and* artistic strength.

"I have this story," she said. "I've come from a self-created hell to get myself up to a place where, yeah, there's strength and gentleness, and a lot of gratitude. Which I didn't have early in my days ... but now I can see. I didn't know how to paint what I was looking at. Now I see all the variations of the color, and know that I can execute the painting and everything will transition ... I can actually see more in life than what I could see prior." She looked up. "Also, that same energy that got me into trouble is what drives me to paint ... the easel is where the magic started, the easel is where the magic will die."

She touched her cheek. "Being on the easel for me is spiritual. It's almost like I leave this universe and escape through a high, high frequency of aesthetics. It's a Zen-like happy place, where I'm creating my own universe and my own world ... I disappear and go away. There is something magical about that state, the concentration ... and I could segue that magic to the concentration that I've seen and I've experienced when casting a line out there. To fish and wait for that trout to rise ... the spiritual aspect of fly fishing is that it really pulls a person into present time ... if you're going out fishing, you're not in circuitry any more. You're in present time, experiencing all the elements: the wind, the guide, the fish, the what have you."

I noted, too obviously, that she'd had quite a journey.

"It's been this progression of getting better," she admitted. "I'm turning into this beautiful butterfly. But I've come from the depths of hell ... there's worse hells, I know there's people who go through some really rough blows in life." She exhaled. "Not everyone has this Cinderella ride."

On Friday evening, Livingston's Main Street was crowded with Art Walk revelers and the artists they adored. Painters predominated, but in ways the city had morphed from its roots as a literary and film-based organism to a musical one: singer-songwriter John Mayer was a part-time resident and the former Sony producer, Joanne Gardner, with her husband, musician John Lowell, organized a yearly street concert that over five summers had featured Vince Gill, Rodney Crowell (with Mayer on guitar), Bill Payne, John Cleary, Tracy Nelson, and Marcia Ball. Artistically, the painter Russell Chatham—who had fathered a school of western landscape art—had left for California (he would die there in 2019), but Livingston still held Edd Enders, whose neo-Expressionist canvasses were striking, Linda Barnsley, whose plein air oils would hang in exhibition at Green Door, Janie Camp with her gorgeous Montana landscapes, Robert Osborn, whose overlarge photographs of cowboys and beaten-down Indians crowded his gallery, Amber Jean, whose reliquary sculptures and paintings hung in several galleries, photographer Audrey Hall, the celebrated John Banovich, whose 10 feet x 10 feet foot canvasses of African wildlife sold internationally, Malou Flato, whose Impressionistic land, water, flower, and forest paintings were Livingston and Austin favorites … and at the far end of Main Street, Parks Reece, who had re-imagined the painting of trout, reinvigorating the wildlife genre.

Reece's 1904, tin-ceilinged gallery was a hodgepodge of stuffed animals, wrought-iron benches, lithographs, and paintings of fur bearers *and* signature trout—humorous renditions of which crowded the walls. In one, a cowboy rode a rainbow as if it were a bronc; in another, two brookies smoked cigarettes *After the Spawn*, and in *Adam and Eve Tour Yellowstone*, a naked couple rode out of paradise in a trout's open mouth. The fish were painted realistically, but the compositions' backgrounds were wondrously abstract. They were an odd amalgam of humor and skill.

"What I am up against is a *serious* art world," Reece said. "William Hjortsberg wrote a review of my art. He said, 'The art world today is a sepulcher. You go in and see the newly sanctioned masterpiece—but in the hands of Parks Reece, fine art becomes fun once again, and God bless him for that.' What I have going against me, to be taken seriously as an artist, is *humor and animals*. Those are red flags. 'Oh, that's not serious,' critics say."

Yet his art was wildly popular. The *Winston-Salem Journal* had written, "Think of what would happen if you crossed a fine wildlife painter with Gary Larson of 'Far Side' cartoon fame, and you get a hint of what Parks Reece is like." The *Los Angeles Times* wrote, "take a walk on the wild side with alchemical artist Parks Reece ... he gleefully dances on a razor's edge ... tweaking our notions of reality with wit and beguiling us with mystery." And WBUR, Boston's NPR station, called Reece, "the Royal Jester of modern western art ... an unsentimental, exquisitely modern painter of the West." Even China's Yan Zhuping, curator of 188ART, a Shanghai gallery that, with the Yellowstone Asia Initiative, had taken Reece to China five times, weighed in: "We are touched by his superb artistic techniques. Moreover we find the historical responsibility of a mature artist. His mind is across the boundaries of nations, and reaches the deepest heart of every audience."

Raised in Wilkesboro, North Carolina, Reece spoke with soft mountain inflections. At sixty-five he was fit, his angular face topped with brown hair turning gray. He sat on a wrought-iron trout bench, at the rear of his gallery, greeting patrons and discussing his art.

Though it was largely of fish and other animals, he seemed ambivalent about the genre of wildlife painting. "I get tired very quickly of the regal elk posing and bugling. I do that stuff, but I juxtapose them in impossible or strange worlds. I like to see ideas ... I like to see art that comes from the place where dreams originate."

His mother had been an artist "and a clairvoyant," Reece said, seeing ghosts and predicting people's deaths from dreams. She was a finger painter, having been tutored by Ruth Faison Shaw, who invented the craft. His mother introduced Reese to painting when he "was three or four." Shaw was a friend, and Reece said that she and his mother approached art from an odd direction: "It was not painting a pretty picture, it was something that was coming from the unconscious. Ruth Shaw told me—and when a five-year-old hears this, it makes an impression—'Son, what's going down on that paper, through your hand, is coming from the place where dreams originate.' I never tried cognitively to imagine what that was. But I arrived at a place where I thought I was doing it. I couldn't explain to you the technique, but I evolved to where I believed that I was doing that. And I still do."

His father worked "at a little factory that my grandfather owned." It built stone grist and mobile saw mills. "I know that during the time when I grew up, if it said 'Stone Ground' on a package of whole wheat flour, our factory made the mill. They sold all over the world, because they were the only guys who made stone grist mills."

Reece was an adventurous child, at home in the woods and solitary. His father traveled for work and his mother was an invalid suffering from brittle diabetes. "She was in hospitals a lot, and I was alone a lot. But I lived in the middle of the woods. I grew up with guns in my hands, hunting. My grandfathers were legendary hunters and shots. And I just ran around the woods all the time. I loved it."

His mother's condition demanded attention. "She would wake up and have these insulin shocks. And when my father was traveling, I'd have to get up in the middle of the night, as a child, and run in there and save her life. Put sugar down her throat, or orange juice ... and I'm pretty sure I got post traumatic stress syndrome. I made straight As through the fourth grade, but then I just didn't concentrate anymore."

He was a star high-school footballer though, playing "every second of every game" on offense and defense. "What that did was acquaint me with violence," he said. "I don't like violence, but I know how to hurt people and I can. I just used to take people *out*." He was offered an athletic scholarship to Appalachian State University, but didn't accept it. "I was finished." Though he still painted, his mother's condition distracted him. "She didn't take care of herself. The diabetes was so bad that she couldn't control it that well. She hated it, and it made her depressed. My father, I guess he was having some affairs, and she did too. They split up when I was a sophomore. She married an English infantry guy, a Rolls Royce salesman. She moved to L.A."

Reece shifted. "She died on his watch, of insulin shock. I'd spent my childhood preventing that! She died of the same thing that I used to go in and put sugar down her throat to fix. She went into a coma and never came back. He wasn't around. She was forty-six. I was nineteen."

Reece sat back distractedly. He'd told me that he had been studying art at East Carolina University. Soon he would transfer to the San Francisco Art Institute. Of his mother's death he said, "I hated it. I went sort of crazy. I'm sure I must have been depressed."

Had it affected his art? "Probably, because it affected my whole being. I couldn't really talk to people very much. I'm sure I had what could have been diagnosed as depression. Sometimes I couldn't even hardly function. I was somewhat reclusive. I couldn't hardly carry on a conversation. It was all related. I'd always done wild things, dangerous things. I did *more*. I climbed out on the Golden Gate Bridge," a beacon for suicidal jumpers. "I almost died every time I went past one of those upright girders. I wasn't thinking about suicide, I was just doing dangerous things."

His art turned toward abstract expressionism—a form that provided a mature journey to the dream-space his mother had introduced him to. But the San Francisco Art Institute proved a disappointment. "It was highly prestigious and sort of hard to get into. But it was more, 'Oh, just paint what you feel.'" It also was theory based. Tom Wolfe's *The Painted Word* had appeared, a book arguing that the conceptual art of the 1950s through the 1970s depended upon critical theory for its understandability. "Without a theory to go with it, I can't see a painting," Wolfe wrote. Reece said, "That's what the Art Institute was all about. I couldn't buy it."

He was successful there, showing at San Francisco galleries

and graduating with a Bachelor of Fine Arts. "But I was fairly disgusted … the art world really didn't hold it for me, the way it was set up. I loved the painting, but I didn't really like the theories … just do some bullshit and try to talk your way into walking up the ladder with that." By 1977, he was working as a bicycle messenger and attempting to join the Merchant Marine, when "an older lady, a Brahmin from back on the East Coast that had a working ranch in Wyoming said, 'Come on out and work for me.' She had an etching press and I helped her with that, and painted murals for her. I worked on the ranch as well. I did that for a couple of seasons. That was in Big Horn, Wyoming."

It was his first experience of the mountain West, and it transformed him. "I had been doing abstract expressionism, and there's a real visual language there. But I wanted more people to get it. I wanted to make it so that it wasn't obtuse. I'd been around art, and had enough shows to realize that you only got a small percentage of the population to even come into a gallery. They felt threatened and pissed off. 'My third grader could do that.' And I was thinking of my family— other than my mother, who was dead by then and had loved everything that I would do—and I wanted to bring them in … my grandfather particularly, who thought it was frivolous to do art. I loved abstract expressionism, but I wanted to take it a step further and make it something that more the average person, or at least an intellectual or a reader, could understand. So I started poking fun at the art world. And parodying art, though not overtly."

He followed a girlfriend to Bozeman, and then to Gardiner, the northern entrance to Yellowstone Park. "I just lived around wherever I could—on people's floors and couches for a while. Instead of trying to earn money, and work shitty jobs, I tried to live on *nothing*. So I went out and caught fish and hunted, and lived off that. I didn't have a car, so when I got my first job in Livingston, I hitchhiked fifty-five miles from Gardiner to Livingston and back every day.

The job was at the Danforth Gallery, a nonprofit that paid Reece minimum wage through CETA. "First I was education director, and then director. I had a BFA from San Francisco Art Institute, and there wasn't anybody around here who had anything like that." He kept a studio above the gallery, and slept there off and on. But the art life required risk, so he persisted in hitchhiking.

"One night, [the novelist] Richard Brautigan came to an opening and I said, 'You know, I've got to walk all the way up to the edge of town to start hitchhiking.' And he said, 'Shoot, we'll give you a ride.' I'd had fun with him that night, drinking and talking, and he said, 'I don't advise hitchhiking. The last hitchhiker I saw was standing in Big Sur, buck naked, with an axe.' I said, 'Well, I'm going to be clothed, with no axe.' He said, 'Still, it's not anything you ought to be doing.' I said, 'Well, I kind of have to now.' And sure enough, a truck driver picked me up and down toward Gardiner, he rolled three times, totaling his pickup and almost killing me. His little dog was in my lap and it flew out and got crushed dead. I locked myself up as we were rolling, and kept his wife and me in the truck. It ripped the door off. That would have been certain death. It did kill the dog. I was a little pissed off at the guy for wrecking me. Somebody stopped on the road and said, 'Are you alright?' Everybody was bleeding and I said, 'Yeah, can I have a ride into town?' I was going to a dance. I could barely walk that night. I could not walk the next day. I had purple and black and green bruises all over me."

The Danforth in its previous incarnation had been The Antlers Bar, and patrons stopped in occasionally, saw the art and muttered, "What the hell?" Reece said, "It was a different culture then. In 1980, Livingston was still old sheepherders and ranch hands, and retired railroad workers who were a little bit on the edge of society. They often didn't have families. They'd walk up and down Main Street, which was bar row, and go into every one and drink and talk and visit. They'd give the bartender their Social Security check and say, 'Tell me when it's all gone.' One day at the Danforth a drunk strolled in and took a piss in the corner. I said, 'What are you doing?" He said, "Well, that's where the toilet used to be."

During Reece's tenure the Danforth received national attention. In 1980, *People* magazine featured a Russell Chatham show. "I found myself in the magazine," Reece said. "I was young and looked good, and was helping him carry up a painting. Russell had a studio above the gallery."

To its board's consternation, Reece had moved away from fashionable abstract expressionism and had begun his unusual paintings. "I would do murals. I did one in Sheridan, Wyoming, in the Professional Building. It was an optical illusion of a giant train, about ten feet high, in a stairwell. Right in your face. And there was a little rabbit right in the tracks. I was just trying to create an exciting illusion." This was in addition to his smaller, humorous oils. "The people who hired me said, 'We thought you were going to do [art] like you usually do.' I said, 'Thanks a lot, I like this.' I wanted more people to get it."

His paintings contained images with titles such as *Call of the Wild*, showing a moose using the telephone; *Fishing the Rockies*, with a trout impaled on an elk's horn; *Re-introducing the Wolf in Yellowstone,* where a cowboy shakes hands with a wolf, and *Chocolate Mousse*, where a raccoon and a pileated woodpecker nosh on a stationary ungulate. The wildlife images were realistic, if a trifle cartoonish, the titles pun-driven. But the backgrounds were resplendent with color, abstract the way finger painting could be abstract, even surrealistic.

"The *New York Times* gave me a little write up, recently," Parks said. "It called me 'the Montana Surrealist.'"

I asked what the reaction of locals had been to those early paintings. "People liked the humor, and the beauty and skill involved. Some people just liked the humor."

He was four years at the Danforth. For his final show, he chose to exhibit his own work. "I painted all small things. It was all humor. Mel Ziegler, who had just started Banana Republic, came in. He bought three paintings and said, 'I want you to do work for me. Send my art director your portfolio.' I didn't have a frigging portfolio. So I scrounged something together. It was stupid, it wasn't professional or anything. The art director sent it back. I should have called Mel. I had his personal number. But I never did.

"Then [*Outside* columnist] Tim Cahill bought a painting and wrote an article about me. I had just gotten back from Mexico. I had caught the most-wanted criminal in the province where I was staying. Because he robbed me. I chased him down in my underwear. Tim wrote about my art, but he put that in there, too."

The legend of Reece as a feral, barely controllable artist intensified. "Rules are made to be broken," he said. "I believe in the rules of visual language. If I didn't have command of the basic principles of color and design I couldn't do what I do. So I believe in that much ... then it's wide open." He took chances in his art, and took chances in life. He drank to excess, and took risks. "Adrenaline junkie," he said. "That would be me. That's why I catch rattlesnakes."

This was nothing new. He had caught snakes by hand when he was a boy in North Carolina, but the south-facing cliffs behind his Montana house offered new opportunities. He caught them, used their skins for craft objects, and played pranks with them. "Part of it again was thrill seeking, adventure, and doing something that scares you. My father was a renowned snake catcher. When I was six years old, he caught a seven-foot indigo and wrapped it around me. He handed me the head. He said, 'Don't let go of that head. Go on in and say hello to your mother and her bridge club.' They were up off their tables and headed for windows and doors. That's when I got interested in snakes. I've never lost my fear of them. I'm very respectful around them. A rattlesnake especially can fuck you up."

Again, snakes seemed an addendum to his art, if only as

performance props. A Chinese restaurant in Livingston had asked Parks for a snake. "One night the Depot was having some fancy reception, and I had just caught a rattler. I had it in a pillow case, there was some big function, with everybody dressed up and all the high-toned folks, so I went ooh! I was on my way to the Chinese. As I got in the Depot I kicked that snake and it rattled, *Krrrrrr*. I walked around the Depot and people went, *Arghh*! *Arghh*! After I got sufficient jumping going on, I took it over to the Chinese place. It was packed full of people. I walked toward the kitchen and kicked it again, and it went *Krrrrr*, and diners jumped. I gave the snake to the Chinese and they were *so* happy. They killed it and said, 'You come back, we eat." I was really looking forward to that, but when I got back, all they'd done was cut its head off, I think—I'm not even sure they cut its head off. They hacked it into pieces, guts, skin, everything. And boiled it, with some onions and vegetables. I couldn't eat it!"

Contingent upon such pranks was Reece's physical bluster, a brand of machismo that he downplayed with humor. Machismo seemed at odds with his artistic sensitivity. "It's because I grew up in sort of a hillbilly, male society. I had to walk that walk. But I don't think I put a whole lot of effort into trying to act macho." He'd been a rascal, socially, but in 1982 he met Robin Ogata, a Japanese-American woman with whom he would have a son, Myers. His and Robin's was a twenty-one-year relationship, that after nine became a marriage. The marriage ended fourteen years ago.

"It was sad, like a death. We were madly in love. I'd been a little wild—drinking a lot. And after twenty-one years, she wanted to see outside the pasture." Reece shook his head. "At the time I didn't want it to end, but once it did I was kind of glad." He looked toward the front of his gallery. "It was just painful."

The log house on Cokedale Road now was occupied solely by himself, and was a testament to his passions and creativity. At its front yard, visitors were met by a sculpture of a naked man wrestling a python, numerous animal skulls and horns, a wrought iron bench with a trout sculpted into it, more horns and skulls, and in his living room, an 8 feet x 5 feet chandelier made from antlers Reece had collected. Guitars, wildlife artifacts, magazines, books and junk crowded the space. Reece built the house with the help of friends, and Ogata's influence could be seen in the bedrooms' paper walls and in other Japanese fixtures.

Reece's interest in things Asian had been heightened by his five trips to China. His visits there began with an assignment in 2014 by the Yellowstone Asia Initiative, "which was trying to capitalize on the Chinese coming to Yellowstone Park. The Chinese love nothing more than the American West. It's captured their imagination. Twenty years ago, only a few could afford to come here. Now as they manufacture all our goods for us, they're minting millionaires all the time. These guys came to me and said, 'We'd like for you to design a mural for us. To commemorate the Chinese coming through here," as sort of a diplomatic thing. They came to me and I said, 'How about this?' I named the idea right then and there, and they said, 'You're on. It's you.' I got it." The result was a 48 feet x 17 feet mural in Livingston's Miles Park—the work of Reece, artists from China, and other artists. It showed a grizzly bear and a panda, capped by one of Reece's jumping trout. A Chinese businessman saw the mural, came to Reece's gallery, and signed him to a two-year contract to visit Shanghai. His last show there was in the second-highest building in the world. Despite Reece's popularity in China, his and two other artists' visits were not without practical jokes.

"The Chinese are terrified of snakes," Reece said. "While we're there, they tour our group around in buses, with all the good Chinese artists. On one trip I pulled a rubber snake out on a bus, and they went 'Ahhh!' and went running off— one of them even fell down trying to get off the bus—and I thought, 'Darn, I shouldn't have done that.' I showed them it was rubber and they laughed until tears came out of their eyes. Nobody every does anything like that in China."

Whether his marriage to Ogata or his visits to Asia had

influenced his basic creativity was an open question. In recent years, he'd taught a class in finger painting, and had revisited the medium. The results were swirling abstracts of vivid intensity.

He'd told Cahill, "There's a sensation I get when I'm painting ... it's like things happen of their own volition. Stuff zips down out of the ether ... There's a euphoria ... It's kind of a flow. I think people who do meditation might feel it. I mean, I can paint, and, if it is going well, six hours can go by. Seems like six minutes."

That remark was comparable to the state A.D. Maddox had described. Maybe it revolved around trout. "You know, Robert Redford bought one of my paintings," Reece said. "So did Tom Skerritt, who played Brad Pitt's father in *River.*" He donned a contemplative look. "I have a lot more fame than fortune. I'm sort of a wild man, and I attract attention. The art speaks for itself. And I just don't have the patience for the after-hours work of self-promotion. I'm just lucky to stand out. When you fall into that vein, you're constantly thinking, 'Oh, I'll go to a dinner party and ... it's constant self-promotion. And I just never ... I've never been there on that page."

————

Cathryn Reitler certainly wasn't, and as I drove northeast toward Glasgow, the likelihood of artists thriving in this region's vastness seemed less and less likely. Judith Basin to Lewistown was Charlie Russell country, the cantilevered ranchland punctuated by low mountain ranges—the Big Snowys, the Little Belts, and the Little Rockies—and near Zortman the Missouri River itself. Yet in this landscape art galleries existed ... at Lewistown, Malta, and even Glasgow, a railroad and ranch town on the Hi-Line, with a population of 3,319. A few bars and motels there serviced tourists visiting Fort Peck Lake and its dam on the Missouri. That dam had been constructed during the 1930s, and with the Great Northern Railroad, dry goods stores, and ranches, historically had been the city's chief employer. Glasgow Air Force base had taken over, from 1958 to 1976, but had long since closed. *The Washington Post*, in 2018, identified Glasgow as "the middle of nowhere" in the lower forty-eight. "Of all towns with more than 1,000 residents, Glasgow ... is farthest—about 4.5 hours in any direction—from any metropolitan area of more than 75,000 people."

I checked into the Rundle Suites Hotel and took a walk around town. In its nearly deserted avenues, there was nevertheless a hip coffee shop, an upscale deli, and Eugene's, a highly rated pizza parlor. "The best pizza in Montana," Cathryn had told me. One wouldn't rate Glasgow as gentrified, yet it possessed the Wheatgrass Arts & Gallery, Sean R. Heavey Photography, the Pioneer Museum, the Children's Museum of Northeast Montana—its collection mostly taxidermy—and the Montana Bar where snapshot photography was the art, and tall tales the vernacular. I stopped there for a Diet Coke.

Glasgow's periphery held big ranches, the largest of which, at approximately 30,000 acres (including land leased from the government), was the McIntyre spread, the heir to which, Mitch McIntyre, Cathryn had married. He was a thirty-year-old metalwork artist who had been a ranch hand, a professional bull rider, a classic-car restorer, and all-purpose cowboy. He and Cathryn had a new son, Charley Blue McIntyre—the name perhaps inspired by that of Teddy Blue Abbott, a legendary Texan cowboy. Wearing short hair and a bushy goatee, Mitch collected me at the Rundle in a growling, four-person ATV. "You okay with this?" he said. Then turned the side-by-side toward his ranch's acreage. A rocking, rolling ride ensued as Mitch described the fields' cultivation, the damage flooding from the Milk River did each year, and how one spring he'd spent seventy-nine days calving, sleeping in his truck between deliveries. Mitch was agitated; his father recently had retired, the family had sold its cattle and leased the ranch to outsiders. Mitch had toiled on that land, beside his father, his entire life.

"I'm not going to work for somebody else," he said,

emphatically. "I don't know what I'm going to do."

Cathryn met us at their house's drive, which held an old pickup, a rail dragster, and the rusted chassis of a Model T. "Sorry to keep you waiting," she said. "My little fellow has been having a rough afternoon." She wore jeans and a colorful shirt and despite having given birth four months previous, looked much as I recalled. She offered her hand, then led me to the studio she shared with Mitch.

Both house and studio were opposite the McIntyre Ranch; its acreage was visible through a portico that led to the workspace they'd created from what must have been a garage. Everywhere was art. There were metal sculptures by Mitch, inventively conceived, as well as a pristine 1958 Ford Ranchero that he and his father had restored and a 1954 Chevrolet Handyman wagon that Cathryn's father had rebuilt. On Cathryn's side were the "Female Chauvinists" pieces from her Livingston show, mixed-media work commissioned by locals, pieces she'd made with Mitch, and a nearly Surrealistic painting, called *What Was Left Behind*, that I recalled from Livingston but had not paid sufficient attention to. It contained images of animal skulls and an abandoned livestock shed, beside pieces of salvaged floor linoleum, flattened tin cans and swatches of fabric. She had told me earlier that its presence in the studio meant much to her.

"I did it for a group show in Las Vegas," she said. "We were supposed to create pieces that would investigate mortality. I always incorporate objects that have a personal history of their own. In this case, the surface itself is made from paneling." She pointed. "You can see the patterns showing through, of the bird ... and it was paneling that I pulled off my parents' house[228] down the street. The reason that I'm drawn to that sort of imagery is because it typifies this area. It's a very good representation of the culture that I feel is still present. My husband knocked down a shed on my parents' property and

---

228   Cathryn's parents moved from Las Vegas, where she graduated from high school and college, to Glasgow in November, 2018.

linoleum started showing up as he was pushing things over. It's linoleum flooring that's pretty recognizable for the era. Just like the paneling itself."

I asked what she'd planned when she arranged these objects. "A lot of what I thought about for the piece was abandoned homes, abandoned homesteads, and farmsteads. In those abandoned buildings, you see these surfaces a lot. There are often doilies and cans, and all those things that are left behind. And of course there are the bones of the animals themselves that are usually at those places—or nearby. I have a fascination with the delicacy of the bones. And the beauty of the bone itself In the piece itself. When I look at this piece, it feels like a self-portrait. Because there are so many of the things that I love that have gone into it. Almost all of the fabric pieces that I make, I intentionally try to incorporate something that has been sewn or handmade by another woman. Because I feel myself to be part of that female lineage."

And the images of skulls? "They're all from Mitch's father's collection—there's a horse's skull, a bear's, there's a lion skull, a cattle skull, this one is a fox's ... I could draw skulls for days. It's the delicacy of the bones, I love the lines of the bones, that these things occur in nature. And for the materials themselves. I have—like a crow, I guess—this affinity for objects themselves. And these particular objects speak to me, they speak to my experience of this place."

That experience had been, and perhaps was, emotionally ambivalent ... an ambivalence she'd expressed in the thesis she'd written for her Master of Fine Arts degree. On an Andre Agassi scholarship, she had earned a Bachelor of Fine Arts from the University of Las Vegas in 2006, and a Master's from the University of Montana in 2011. Since then she'd exhibited her work in Seattle, Troy, New York, Las Vegas, of course Livingston, and as her website stated, "in many other locations across the country." She taught art in her studio and for Glasgow's schools—the latter in an as-needed capacity. "Our high school could not recruit an art teacher," she told

312

me. "They were looking at a year with no art classes whatso-
ever. I'm kicking myself, imagining my professional sacrifices
in studio time. But I couldn't imagine there being no art in
this town."

She had forwarded to me her master's thesis, and as she'd
said the previous summer, it focused on the interaction between her work in art and the isolation of life in rural Montana. Her first marriage had been challenging, and though
it had given her a son, Rivers, now eight, it had ended after
nearly as many years.

For her thesis,[229] titled *Inbetween*, Cathryn had used changes
in her life to explain and defend art submitted to fulfill her
requirements. In its preface she quoted Robert Rauschenberg
that "I work in the gap between art and life." She wrote, "Little did I know that my experiences in graduate school, and
the translation of those experiences into artworks, would be
defined by 'gaps': the physical gap of 450 miles, separating me
from my [then] husband, the intellectual gap representing the
types of conversation I found myself engaging in, the illusive
gaps between the different 'roles' I have always used to define
myself. In the past three years I developed an awareness of my
social situation, during which I have found (and continue to
find) myself mentally shifting from one foot to the other; always aware of what can or cannot be said, questioning which
act is appropriate in which particular situation. The past two
(of the last three) years have been spent investigating that
space of in-between, the area of middle ground; a place of
slight and constant disquiet, both tangible and illusive. The
collaged surfaces, embroidered text, drawn elk and carefully
rendered forms attempt to describe my understanding of 'In-
between.'"

She'd been at the University of Montana in Missoula, separated from her husband by the distance of nearly the entire
state. And when she returned to Glasgow she became acutely
aware of the female role she was expected to play: not that of

---

229   Quoted by permission of the artist.

an artist but that of cook, housemaid, and compliant lover.

She wrote, "Thoroughly entrenched in sappy newly-wed love, during the first year of marriage I slipped into the role of 'woman, homemaker': removing all items which referenced Jack's[230] previous state of bachelorhood, washing floors, bathtubs and underwear with determined zeal, cooking and baking unrelentingly, and insisting every evening after work that Jack enact the role 'man, provider': kick up his heels and relax." This was not her Canadian family's behavior: "the women I had grown up surrounded by were strong, forthright, no-nonsense business-owners who placed a dedication to their profession alongside allegiance to family, and who had uncompromisingly followed their dreams and ambitions. Their marriages were complementary partnerships in which roles of husband and wife, father and mother, manager and secretary had no basis in gender."

She continued: "The role I [currently] had been enacting reflected a rustic ideology that [even] I had been thoroughly schooled in: that of boy/girl games on the playground, man/woman 'games' expressed in pages of young-ladies magazines; the realm of young-in-love bliss featured in fashion photos taken in the middle of a 'hayfield, and of country-western songs describing the romance to be achieved by riding alongside one's 'cowboy' in the muddy pickup truck. All elements of a package designed to sell one particular ideology: that of the fulfillment to be found in 'getting a man.' Of course, once having achieved the illusive man, the task shifts to 'keeping a man,' (through, one might assume, proper wifely conduct). From the vantage point of a year, and the distance of 450 miles, I reexamined the woman I had become and undeniably still was: every trip home still found me cleaning corners and cooking dinner."

It wasn't her husband's fault. "Not only did I fall in love with a man and his place, but also with a social/commercial ideology with foundations firmly planted in an era one might

---

230   Name changed to protect privacy.

assume long gone. It was as if in receiving wedding linens from the women of Jack's town, I also received subtly conveyed principles bound amongst the fabric fibers, dictating: 'Femininity belongs to the home, in the home...a world to be invented and managed by women.'

Her first elk hunt changed her perspective, and resulted in several works of northeastern Montana art—ones more intellectual than the wildlife pieces she would do for ranchers. That hunt had been traumatic: Jack had mistakenly shot two elk, rather than one—a cow and one of her two calves. The blood from the gunshot wounds, and how the surviving calf plaintively regarded its mother, disturbed Cathryn. The elk in no way looked like the romantic portraits she'd seen in popular art or in photographs she'd studied at the Rocky Mountain Elk Foundation: those images "bore little resemblance to the elk [I] remembered from Jack's first elk hunt. [His] elk had been fleeing, in a blind panic, from the hunters that pursued them ... both the hunters and the animals were half crazed with lust: the hunters for the kill, the bull elk for cows."

Cathryn knew that the depiction of elk, deer, moose, and antelope was a tradition in western American art. "In the living room of almost every house," in Glasgow, "one would find the mounted 'Trophy' head of a game animal positioned to appear either in the act of 'bugling' or gazing in triumphant glory towards some distant foe. And adorning at least one wall in every professional practice in the area was an overpriced, elaborately framed commercial wildlife print," as well as "vividly colored reproductions of wild game, used on clothing, bumper stickers, lawn ornaments, fridge magnets, and window decals. All of which dripped with the romantic nuance that the hunters in the area were most fond of: animals portrayed in majestic splendor, bathed alternately in golden sunshine or soft, wet dew."

In a series of paintings with the titles *Agony/Ecstasy*, *Meet/Meat*, *It's a Bitch Being a Cow*, *The Candor of an*

Inescapable Assignation, and *Bound in a State of Transition,* she subverted traditional wildlife art and brought her conceptual aesthetic to it. Blood coated the elks' horns, their expressions were frantic, and she found that the animals' instinctual behavior oddly paralleled that of western male hunters: "These parallels were based on the observation that many elk 'social structures' and habits are similar to social practices unwittingly observed in small 'human' social circles; specifically, in rural locations. For example, when a male elk is not 'in the rut' (meaning, when the male is not interested in finding a mate) most bulls are 'bosom buddies...and stay in male bands' (Ballard, 2007[231]). Likewise as I have observed in Glasgow, most men are comfortable in other male social groups, especially once these men have reached 'social' maturity and have settled down with a wife. Just as bull elk returns to familiar locations of congregation, I've observed my husband's weekly 'Meeting with the guys at [a local] shop for Thirsty Thursdays.'"

An incident of questionable behavior at Thirsty Thursday had bothered her, and had inspired an exemplary painting, *With (dis)Regard for the Orthodoxy of Gender:* "My husband asked me to prepare and bring a meal to the guys weekly 'Thirsty Thursday' get together. I cooked and hauled the requested 'Indian Tacos' to the shop (furnished with old couches, banged up coffee tables, and a beer fridge). After putting the food out I told the guys the food was ready. I was completely unacknowledged—a slip of etiquette that I chose to overlook. The food cooled for another few minutes and then I mentioned, in a slightly louder voice, that the food was ready to be eaten.

"After the second request the owner of the shop came over to me with a grin on his face. Smiling broadly he spoke in a conspiratorial tone. 'You know hun, I think they heard ya the

---

231   J. Ballard, *Elk Hunting Montana: Finding Success on the Best Public Lands.* (Guilford, CT: The Lyons Press, 2007). Rocky Mountain Elk Foundation.

first time. Why don't you just quiet down, and they'll come and get it when they're good and ready.'

"Everything about his expression and tone engendered trust and camaraderie, but I felt as if I had just been slapped. His words made it clear that I was allowed in their domain only because of what I'd brought, that I was still a woman in a man's cave and that I was subject to their 'rules.'"

This experience, and others, helped Cathryn to formulate her thesis's organizing statement: that in rural Montana, and perhaps elsewhere, "Getting married is the Best/ Worst thing a woman can do." And, "Through the research, I became aware that by moving to rural Montana, my creative spirit; my 'female power,' had been threatened. I had been tricked and lied to by the commercial entity which romanticized 'marriage to a cowboy.' And had I chosen not to pursue my degree in studio arts, the 'feminine impulses and gifts of psyche' would have been killed off."[232]

Seated now at her dining table, her infant son asleep beneath a living-room tipi and her husband sharing *Star Wars* books with her eight-year-old, this seemed an odd sentiment. We had been speaking of "the male gaze" as she'd described it in her "Female Chauvinists" series, and I asked if she could imagine painting a male gaze that was positive.

"Oh, absolutely. Within the context of my marriage. I have so many negative feminist ideals and feelings that this man really widened my perspective on ... by giving me a positive male influence. He's a man who has not demeaned me, who has not ... and this has been a really wonderful thing for me, having a baby with him ... he is just as comfortable staying home and feeding ..." She turned toward the living room. "It's like the dynamic you see in a city. Except that here it's *really* rare. For me to be trotting off to school, and he's right here with the baby doing the dad thing. And his being the type of man he is has made it possible for me to just kind of step back a bit from those righteous feelings of indignation that I had at

---

232   Emphasis the author's.

the time of my thesis. And to appreciate the romanticism that is part of western culture. Especially country-western culture. The love songs ... so if I were to make a piece that had to do with a positive male gaze upon me, it would be a reflection of what I've learned as a result of this relationship."

Would her next piece suggest how she's grown in relation to the male gaze—and to herself? "I can honestly say that painting a self-portrait for this series was one I was comfortable with, up to a point. But as I already have trouble with that sort of attention, I don't really want to encourage it artistically. By doing a nude self-portrait. Maybe someday. It's not something I'm really comfortable with yet, though. Because I've felt it as an influence in my career that hasn't always been a positive one. To me that is demeaning of my work. Because I want to be considered for my work first, and for my appearance second. Maybe it's because of my own discomfort with that duality. It's easier to portray someone else who's struggling. Because essentially I'm dealing with the same issues, within my career, as the women I'm portraying. So it's easier to examine it from a distance."

Who was the new model? "The woman whom I would like to pose for the piece is from a ranching family, and she is beautiful. I'm thirty-six, so she's got to be in her early thirties. Traditionally the ranch is a male inheritance, you've got to have the son to run the ranch. Well, her brother wasn't really interested in running the ranch. And she ended up stepping up. She does all of the physical things that the man on the ranch would do. Now she's building the herd with her own cattle, and she's marrying and her husband has his cattle. So she's taken the reins. She's getting married in about a month, so she's bartended at a couple of different bars. For a while there she dated my current brother-in-law. Small town culture being what it is. And you see a lot about people's lives from social media. Maybe those insights led me to investigate her more deeply for this work. She posts pictures of when she's farming ... looking out the window of the equipment she's farming on. Pictures of herself in the feed truck with her dogs.

Photos that show she's doing a lot of the heavy work of running the ranch. She's rolling up her sleeves and getting the job done. I know that she had siblings that could have stepped in, but she's her dad's right hand man, so to speak.

"So in that sense I'm really interested in her. Especially because, when I originally started the series, one of the goals I had for the work was, I did want to play devil's advocate and put myself *in* the male gaze. Or try to imagine myself in the male gaze. And one of the things I thought about, through that gaze, is what an ideal woman according to this demographic, in this region, would be. And this woman fits it. She's got blue eyes and pretty blonde hair and a beautiful body. And a gorgeous smile, and is bubbly. She's also got an edge to her. There's so many women ... people throw around the term, pretty freely, of the idea of tribe. 'They're in my tribe,' you know. You hear it all the time. But there's a breed of woman in this area that identify with my work really readily. Like when I first had this series, I invited a group of women to see the work. Before it left the area. And they were very similar to this young lady. Have you ever read *Breaking Clean*? By Judy Blunt? The type of ranch women that she describes, they would have tea together, and they'd put their pretty gloves on. Most of the time they had really work-worn hands under their pretty gloves. So this woman is the modern connotation of what Blunt wrote about in the seventies."

What ideas did she have for settings for the portrait? "I really like the idea of involving the hay bales, because for me that feels like hay would be a beautiful thing to paint. Baling, and the process of baling, the amount of money that goes into buying feed and all of that and the process is something I really began to understand intimately through Mitch. There are all these steps involved. Maybe I'll have her fork hay, maybe have her move a square bale, which I know from experience is exhausting. Something very physical. And I want to involve the landscape more than I have in the past. Because I wasn't comfortable in painting landscape earlier. And I've become comfortable with it ... having something to contextualize it as being from this region."

Did she know the expression, "A roll in the hay"?

"Yes. That's a really good reference. I didn't think of it." She laughed. "I do want to sexualize her, to a certain extent. That's an aspect of the work. But not sexualize her in a demeaning way. In a respectful way. The work is intended to show how a male would see a beautiful woman like her."

Would she use fabric on the canvas? "Yes, I'll have her give me her old clothes. Which is what I've done with each of the works. I like that there's a biological component to them. She's worn this. It's covered her skin. And I'd want some old gloves from her, some old shirts, some old jeans. And I'll probably use ... I've always been drawn to fabrics that have some sort of printed material that has to do with the content of the piece that I'm working toward. Also stitches." She tapped the table top. "Our conversation has made me realize that this is still a current series. So I think it would be important to bring the series to current."

How had she posed other women in the series? "All of the women who modeled for me, in the previous work, were painted from photos I took of them in the nude. And usually on a physical location. The patrol woman, she and I went out this road to a little secluded spot. And she got out and I took the pictures of her. We talked about position and all of that. And then the gal who worked for the railroad, that was the best. We drove for an hour, traveling east, to try to find an engine that wasn't occupied, so that we could get her nude on it. I introduced her to American Honey[233] at the same time. We were doing a good old booze cruise, which is what they do around here. Anyway, we couldn't find a train. The next day she calls me and says, 'There's a train! It's downtown!' I said, 'Are you kidding me?' So we parked the truck by the railroad. And I still have the most vivid image of her running through this waist-high grass, bare as the day she was born.

---

233   A Wild Turkey liqueur.

With zebra-print slippers. And then hopping on the side of a train. It was within a visual distance of the Montana Bar. We were right downtown."

"They would have talked about that for six months," I said.

"At least."

———————

Mitch was behind the wheel of a red 1970 Ford pickup named Ferdinand, a pinup-girl calendar ("Every bar has one,' Cathryn said) above its ignition and its tailpipe roaring as we traversed pasture one of the McIntyre Ranch. Mitch had been describing his history in rodeoing and how neither his mother nor his father had wanted him to ride bulls—"I spent too much money on those teeth to have you lose them," his mother, Netty McIntyre, had said ... and after one ride, during which he'd gotten hung up and tossed, she—a nurse practitioner—had closed his cuts and his father, Ted McIntyre, had set his dislocated shoulder, saying, "You still want to ride bulls?" Earlier, Ted had told me a bit of the history of the ranch, of how his great-grandfather, a businessman in the 1940s, with a bar downtown where taxi dancers and no doubt prostitutes worked, began buying forty-acre tracts that homesteaders had abandoned, and worked other deals until 7,000 acres of McIntyre land had been accumulated, and 23,000 to 24,000 acres of government land had been leased. It was a fabulous piece of property. As we jostled up a jeep road across the corrugated, high desert landscape, I couldn't help but imagine how Cathryn might paint it.

"The ranch has been a source of deep inspiration to me artistically," she said. "The experiences with the cattle were revelatory ... but the landscape itself, in particular the land 'out south' has always been what inspired me most deeply."

Her early childhood was spent on a farm in Saskatchewan, but her father, Bruce Reitler, was a California potter, and her mother, Cynthia Reitler, once the family moved to

Las Vegas, became a union representative. Cathryn would tell me by email that "My dad and mom moved to Canada after graduating from college in California, to take over the family farm (which had been abandoned for thirty years, the original homestead dating to 1911). They wanted to raise their children in the prairie instead of the city. He and my mom farmed but his talent for pottery became the primary income. He continued to farm all my childhood, but the pottery was the real livelihood. He had a studio in the yard, built the year I was born. My sister and I grew up in that studio, playing with clay; my early aptitude for drawing and painting was always encouraged by them, and further blossomed as a result of the early and constant exposure to the Saskatchewan creative community. My dad was part of the Saskatchewan Art Council and other guilds; had pottery in over ten galleries and sold work at six art shows every year. We grew up surrounded by the same group of artisans: my earliest memories are of admiring the talent of these people, whose kids were my age. They hired us to watch their booths when we weren't helping my parents sell pots. So many memories I have of those shows; helping pack, unpack, price, display work. Talking to customers, watching my dad demonstrate throwing pots. I remember vividly the skill of an artist whose drawings made me absolutely yearn to develop that skill myself. I stared for hours at his work."

The women of her youth that Cathryn remembers clearly were ones she'd known in Saskatchewan who had been artists in sewing and quilting. She'd written for her thesis, "As a child I was fascinated by the quilting process, especially by the large rack holding the quilt until each delicate stitch had been placed. Candace, the quilter and business-owner, was not so different from my father's mother, who was an entrepreneur as well. I grew up surrounded by the vestiges of my grandmother's sewing business; some of the earliest memories I have are of afternoons spent in her sewing closet playing in the button tin, of listening to the whir of her machine, and of taking naps beneath the polyester and rayon folds of the crazy quilts she sewed."

Cathryn had taken me to meet Ted and Netty, who lived a short way from the younger McIntyre's house. "They were my first patrons," Cathryn said. "They bought several of my works." Ted was a gentleman rancher, in pressed jeans, a good shirt, and an immaculate haircut … Netty a dark-haired ranch-woman in jeans and a loose blouse. Their walls were chock-ablock with original art, which included pieces by Cathryn, Charlie Russell, Frederic Remington, and Will James. Many of the images were of bucking broncos, and in a glass case was a collection of perhaps fifty sets of antique spurs. "Those were made in New Jersey by August Buermann,[234]" Ted said. He told me a bit more of the ranch's history, and said that in his newly begun retirement he planned to travel. "One of the things I might do," he said, "is drive around to see a few of the places where Charlie Russell lived."

A River Runs through It had reached Glasgow in 1992, but there had been scant trout fishing nearby and no observable gentrification. For money Cathryn made "commissioned" art. With her talent for marrying clients' wishes to her own, the results proved satisfying. But showing her fine art in north-eastern Montana was a challenge. "I was scared to exhibit the 'Female Chauvinists' series," she said. "In ways, my art is more valid here because the situation is difficult. This insular community makes it more interesting—almost like a diamond in the rough."

She continued. "There's very little professional conversation here. I'm isolated artistically. There are few other artists. And no conceptual one. The town clings so hard to the past."

I asked for her thoughts on contemporary western art. "Currently," she said, "it's enchanted with the romantic

---

234   August Buermann (1842-1915) immigrated to the US from Germany in 1864, joined the Union army and fought in the Civil War. Afterward, he settled in Newark, NJ (a large manufacturing town) and began designing and making his own spurs in 1866. He produced as many as 441 spur styles and 496 bit patterns.

narratives of days long past. So many artists paint in the imagery and style of 'what once was,' because 'what now is' lacks the grit, the color, the realness of what was. Many of the most noteworthy contemporary western artists[235] are doing something bold and strong with their palate or brush technique but I think that very few of them invest much thought to the conceptual end of their work. I am as guilty as any in playing this game. And have painted plenty of noble elk and handsome buffalo. But the notable western American artists of the past weren't painting meticulously designed scenes, utilizing photography and the assets of our digital age. The artists of the current age have all of the tools, but many of them lack the real-life experiences to contribute a sense of reality. They paint beautifully, but many do not seek depth beyond beauty. A large part of me wonders if that's enough: pictures that give us glimpses of a romantic reality filled with beautifully pastured horses and rainbow-soaked buffalo. Maybe that's all that is desired by collectors in big cities on the east coast. I think our art—western American art—is still figuring out what it 'looks like now,' since the imagery that's inspired it for so long no longer exists as it once did."

The imagery of this landscape appeared unchanged. The McIntyre ranch seemed without boundaries. Jostling in the ranch truck, I asked whether it got lonely here. "No," Cathryn said, "there's something special in the isolation. And in wanting that to define my career. It's a rare opportunity."

We drove through the widening prairie as Ferdinand sputtered against the grade. The sun began to set, and the light across the scrub, prairie grass and rock formations took on an ochre tint. Suddenly we lurched higher, leveled off and stopped. Mitch cut the engine. "Here you can see almost to Fort Peck Dam," he said. "Anyhow, it's our land." It was land that no house had sullied, where dinosaur bones popped through the topsoil, and only bison, the McIntyre's cattle,

---

235   Carol Hogan, Harry Koyama, Kevin Redstar, Allen Knowshisgun, Tobias Sauer, and Erin Thormodsgard are ones she admires.

and Indians had ever called home. "You can see tipi rings all through there," Mitch said.

The broken prairie was magnificent. Meriwether Lewis—camped nearby in 1805—wrote: "The country we passed today ... is one of the most beautiful plains we have yet seen, it rises gradually from the [Missouri] river bottom ... then becoming level as a bowling green ... as far as the eye can reach."

"It's called Lookout Hill," Cathryn said. "Mitch proposed to me here, in a blizzard in December. It's one of the most recognizable and significant geographic locations in pasture one."

The landscape was vast as any that Bierstadt had painted, its sky colorful as any Russell had conjured, and tender as any Chatham oil. I had no idea what proximity to it meant in terms of western American art, but this land—as wild as when fur trappers saw it—offered this young couple much with which to work.

Cathryn said, "I like to think that the ranching came to an end so that Mitch, the property itself, and our little corner of the world, might evolve into something else." She crossed her arms, looked south. "One of my favorite daydreams is of creating an artist residency here, utilizing the space and the landscape for the inspiration of others."

I took in my new friends, this staggering vista, and what possibly might be a future. The wind picked up and we turned back toward town.

2020

ACKNOWLEDGMENTS

The author would like to extend his thanks to the artists and scholars cited herein (particularly Joan Frederick, Joyce Cannon Yi, Peter Hiller, Kenneth Lister, Christine Podmaniczky, John Taliaferro, Debby Bull, Elizabeth Drew, Mike Lord, Mike Beck, Jim Jarvis, Dan Bergan, E. Jean Carroll, Pat Miller, and Felicia Wivchar); to the museums and galleries (Smithsonian to the Metropolitan) showing so much western American art; to the friends and editors (Ken McCullough, Belinda Winslow, Sandy Rock, Nancy Milligan, Lauren Coleman, Seabring Davis, Carter Walker, Christine Rogel, Corinne Garcia) who supported this project; to the magazines (*Western Art & Architecture* and *Big Sky Journal*, especially) who published much of it, and to Allen Jones at Bangtail Press who designed and edited this book. It would neither have been written nor made without these people's help.

Back Cover Details

T.C. Cannon "Anadarko Princess Waiting for a Bus" Used by permission of Joyce Cannon Yi and the estate of T.C.Cannon	Tom Murphy "Snow Pillows" Used by permission of the artist	Xenia Cage "Portrait of Blue Bolt"
Cathryn Reitler "With (dis)regard for the Orthodoxy of Gender: Fighting Fires" 2013 Used by permission of the artist	Tom Russell "Crow Indian" Acrylic Used by permission of the artist	A.D. Maddox "Mustang Series 4" Oil on Canvas 2020 Used by permission of the artist
Charles M. Russell "A Bad Hoss" 1904 Lithograph Public Domain	Russell Chatham "Paradise Valley in August" Used by permission of the estate of Russell Chatham	Paul Kane "Chualpays jouant à l'alcoloh" Ca. 1851-1856 Oil on Canvas Public Domain
Jo Mora "Decorative Map of Yosemite Valley" 1931 Public Domain in the United States of America	Grant Wood "Appraisal" 1932 Oil on Composition Board Public Domain in the United States of America	George Catlin "Stu-mick-o-súcks, Buffalo Bull's Back Fat, Head Chief, Blood Tribe" 1832 Public Domain

ABOUT THE AUTHOR

Toby Thompson is the author of five previous books, including *Positively Main Street: Bob Dylan's Minnesota, Riding the Rough String: Reflections on the American West,* and *Metroliner: Passages, Washington to New York.* He has written for publications as diverse as *Vanity Fair, Esquire, Rolling Stone, Men's Journal, Playboy, Outside, Gray's Sporting Journal, Western Art & Architecture, Big Sky Journal,* and *The New York Times.* He teaches in the Creative Writing program at Penn State, and lives in Cabin John, Maryland, and Livingston, Montana.

Photo by Rob Story

CPSIA information can be obtained
at www.ICGtesting.com
Printed in the USA
FSHW011522280820
73330FS